Lamentations

T&T CLARK STUDY GUIDES TO THE OLD TESTAMENT

Lamentations

Series Editor
Adrian Curtis, University of Manchester, UK
Published in association with the Society for Old Testament Study

Lamentations

An Introduction and Study Guide

BY
JILL MIDDLEMAS

t&tclark
LONDON • NEW YORK • OXFORD • NEW DELHI • SYDNEY

T&T CLARK
Bloomsbury Publishing Plc
50 Bedford Square, London, WC1B 3DP, UK
1385 Broadway, New York, NY 10018, USA

BLOOMSBURY, T&T CLARK and the T&T Clark logo are
trademarks of Bloomsbury Publishing Plc

First published in Great Britain 2021

A catalogue record for this book is available from the British Library.

Library of Congress Control Number: 2020947742

ISBN:	HB:	978-0-5676-9692-2
	PB:	978-0-5676-9691-5
	ePDF:	978-0-5676-9694-6
	eBook:	978-0-5676-9693-9

Typeset by Integra Software Solution Pvt. Ltd.

To find out more about our authors and books visit www.bloomsbury.com
and sign up for our newsletters

CONTENTS

PREFACE

As I finished my revisions on the biblical book of Lamentations, the corona/SARS-2 virus was spreading and wreaking havoc in communities large and small, and individuals dedicated to justice and human rights supported the Black Lives Matter movement in ceaseless protest throughout the United States of America and the world. There is something cathartic about reading and listening to a variety of different articulations of experiences of suffering, their calls for attention and justice along with the wide variety of reactions, reflections and responses made by individuals and local communities.

Because my father is a retired MD, I kept thinking particularly about the heroes on the front lines in the hospitals – the nurses, EMTs, hospital staff at the front desks, on the phones, in the cafeterias and in charge of maintenance, moving patients and cleaning as well as the doctors and third-year medical students in training. These people are heroes who dedicate their lives, their time and their emotional, physical and spiritual energies to tackle an enemy they cannot see and in spite of the lack of necessary equipment to protect themselves and their patients. This book is partly dedicated to them in honour and respect of their service, commitment and care.

It is also dedicated to two I have recently lost and want to remember, to our former neighbour, good friend in Oxford, and also the godfather of our daughter, Ian Bird, who fought against but, to our great sorrow, lost his battle with cancer on 18 January 2018. And to our beloved Whizz who died shortly after Christmas in 2019 also from cancer and who left us much too soon.

Like the cacophony of images that circle and swirl in Lamentations, tragedy crashes around and hits individuals, families and communities in waves. The present guide seeks to honour different, yet compatible, ways of reacting to, mourning over and expressing disaster, loss, grief and injustice that I hope will bring recognition to, but also the acceptance of, pain, suffering and calls for change. What may be overshadowed by the depth and breadth of this introduction is that lamentation is not only the expression of sorrow, but also the call for, even insistence on, change and justice. To that end, I am reminded of Billie Holiday's haunting text in her song "Strange Fruit" that lies firmly in the tradition of the biblical Lamentations and resonates with its powerful message – Southern trees bear a strange fruit / Blood on the leaves and blood at the root / Black bodies swinging in the southern breeze / Strange fruit hanging from the poplar trees. In the end, I hope that the different academic responses to Lamentations surveyed here inspire new readers to appreciate not only the haunting beauty of its ancient and timeless poetry, but also its tragic testimonies and persistent calls for righteousness.

Jill Middlemas
Copenhagen 2020

INTRODUCTION

"So lonely sits the city that was once full of people" begins the compact biblical book of Lamentations with a sense of abject loss and abandonment that reverberates in hauntingly grief-filled poems over war and its aftermath. In only 154 lines, the five poems of Lamentations include a dizzying array of emotions, reactions, and exclamations that attest to the brutality of war and the fruitlessness of human tragedy. In its combination of prayer, protest, emotional outbursts of confusion, shock, and horror and searing pain as well as abject and depressive silence and reflection, the biblical Lamentations resonates with the poetry of fallen cities that stem from ancient times and the third millennium BCE up to today. Survivors who reel in the aftermath of a great and sweeping disaster grasp at the ability to convey their wounded reactions to loss, pain and victimization.

As the English title suggests, Lamentations is a collection of laments that include sorrowful reflection, vociferous complaint and persistent protest as well as astonished dismay, calls for revenge and agonized silence. The poetry captures individual and communal reactions to and reflections on a series of tragic circumstances experienced in the near or distant past that continue in the present. From a wide variety of angles and in various degrees of detail, the five poems of Lamentations present sustained grief and horrified reactions to what is traditionally understood to be the fall of the city of Jerusalem in the sixth century BCE. Nevertheless, the devastating toll of an unnamed disaster on a city's infrastructure and, more significantly from the perspective of the lamenter, on its human inhabitants, could well be dated and is certainly relevant to any catastrophic event in Jewish and human history. In Lamentations, the survivors and mourners of assault, violence and disaster finally have their say.

THE BOOK OF HOW

In the Hebrew Old Testament, Lamentations is known by its first word, 'ĕkah, which is an exclamatory particle meaning 'Ah!', 'How!', or 'Alas!' (Lam. 1:1; cf. 2:1; 4:1). The Hebrew title effectively calls the collection 'The Book of How'. The opening 'ĕkah captures at the forefront a sense of horrified astonishment, "How lonely sits the city!" (1:1), as well as aching questions about tragic collapse: How has such a thing occurred and how even to convey such an unspeakable tragedy (Seidman 1994: 282)? Elsewhere, the term 'ĕkah tends to appear in laments over the dead (as in Isa. 1:21; Jer. 48:17). Generally speaking, it is equivalent to 'ĕk found in the grief-stricken exclamatory lament over the deaths of King Saul and his son Jonathan attributed to David, who mournfully exclaims, "How the mighty have fallen!" (2 Sam. 1:19, 25, 27).[1]

---

[1] Biblical quotations and citations are from the NRSV, Anglicized Edition, unless otherwise stated.

The naming of a biblical book after its first word is not uncommon in Jewish tradition as reflected in the Tanak. For example, the first book in the Bible, Genesis, is referred to by the word with which the chapter begins, *bᵊrēʾšîth*, meaning 'in the beginning', and the second book is then known as *šᵊmôth*, meaning 'Names of' instead of Exodus and so forth. In keeping with this tradition, Jews refer to the book as *Eicha*. The English title 'Lamentations' actually stems from Jewish and Christian traditions rather than from any word that is found within the poems themselves.

In Jewish tradition, the book was called *Qînôth*, a Hebrew word meaning 'funeral eulogies or dirges'. The title *Qînôth* appears in the Talmud in a list of the order of the books in the third section of Jewish Bibles known as the Hagiographa or Writings (*b. Baba Batra* 14b) and in a list of works attributed to various authors, "Jeremiah wrote the book which bears his name, the Book of Kings, and Lamentations" (*b. Baba Batra* 15a). Although a *qînah* (singular of *qînôth*) represents technical language for a funeral song as exemplified in David's lament over the deaths of Saul and Jonathan (2 Sam. 1:17) and the murder of Abner (2 Sam. 3:33), later Jewish tradition understood and used the term more broadly. In late biblical Hebrew the *qînah* or 'funeral dirge' came to be used as a general reference to lamentation which is the sense that best corresponds with Jewish and Christian terminology today (Berlin 2002: 23). Notably, the titles of the book in the Greek (*threnoi*) and Latin (*lamentationae*) translations in antiquity also reflect the broader sense of 'lament'.

The post-biblical reference to funeral songs or *qînôth* apparently reflects the tradition that Jeremiah eulogized the death of Josiah as recounted in 2 Chronicles with laments that became associated with the collection known as Lamentations (2 Chron. 35:25). The tradition of Jeremianic composition is made explicit in the Old Greek translation of the Bible called the Septuagint (LXX). The LXX contains an added heading that explicitly links the book of Lamentations with the prophet Jeremiah: "And it came to pass after Israel had gone into captivity, and Jerusalem was laid waste, that Jeremiah sat weeping and composed this lament over Jerusalem and said ...." The heading in LXX Lamentations corresponds to other textual witnesses from antiquity, including the Latin Vulgate, the Syriac translation called the Peshitta, the Jewish translations and expansions of the Bible in Aramaic called the Targums, and the Babylonian Talmud, with which we have already dealt. In antiquity, then, the book is called 'The Lamentations of Jeremiah' with the title 'the prophet' or 'the prophet and High Priest' sometimes added after his name.

In many respects, the different titles for the book correspond thematically to the contents of the poems. At the same time, in his commentary Johan Renkema has made the important observation that *qînôth* is actually not an adequate or appropriate title for the book when it is understood in the strict sense of a funeral song (Renkema 1998: 33). He points out that the actual word 'dirge' is missing entirely from the collection, all the elements of a funeral eulogy are not present, and the poems include other types of communication to God including supplication, protest and petition. Referring to the book as 'Lamentations', then, captures a sense of the different kinds of grief and expressions thereof found in the poems, while the funeral dirge points to the type of speech used in some of them. In this way, it is important to hold the lament and the dirge in mind when reading or hearing the poems. At the same time, neither lamentation nor dirge captures the entirety of the poetic rhetoric of the biblical Lamentations which suggests that a variety of liturgical expressions were called upon to give people the ability to voice their reactions to and memories of a great catastrophe, that was, in effect, beyond comprehension and the words to convey it.

The different titles, 'êkah, qînôth and Lamentations, correspond to the language of mourning used in funeral services. However, the occasion is a great national catastrophe, so Ulrich Berges is correct to emphasize that the poems represent national mourning rather than that of a private individual (Berges 2002: 30). The poems of Lamentations were recited or prayed as part of worship services by people suffering in the aftermath of or in communal recollections long after disaster. In the ancient world as in ancient Israel, public fasts were called to commemorate political or natural disasters that affected the nation (Gunkel and Begrich 1933: 177–89). Rituals for national and public mourning were held after serious catastrophic events and followed loss in battle, a drought, other national disasters, and forced removal, exile and relocation (Ferris 1992: 78–84, 105–8).

The national disaster most often associated with the book of Lamentations is the Neo-Babylonian subjugation, defeat, and destruction of Jerusalem in a series of incursions that took place in the sixth century BCE, at the time traditionally referred to as "the Exile" (on concerns about the use of this title, see Middlemas 2007: 1–27). The themes and vocabulary of national grief also appear in a series of psalms that are frequently linked to the events and the time period that accompanied the fall of Jerusalem, including Psalms 44, 74, 79, 89, 102, 106 and sometimes also Isaiah 63:7-64:11 and Nehemiah 9 (various assessments are found in Janssen 1956: 19–20; Klein 1978; Williamson 1990; Middlemas 2005: 144–70 and 2007: 35–51). On occasion, the prophets also drew on the language of mourning to raise a qînah over the Northern Kingdom of Israel or another nation as a means to figuratively convey the surety of its downfall, as in a prophecy found in the book of Amos, "Hear this word that I take up over you in lamentation, O house of Israel" (Amos 5:1, see also Jer. 9:10; Ezek. 19:1; 27:32; 32:16). The book of Lamentations contains a significant amount of grief work captured in what appear to be eyewitness accounts, which suggests that the poems were written after a great disaster rather than in anticipation of one.

Consistent with the tradition of mourning in the ancient world, the poems of Lamentations vividly capture the exclamation of national grief at the unexpected and unbelievable fall of Jerusalem to enemy invaders and the devastation wrought therein. However, its mournful tone and general applicability to many disasters commend it for liturgical use. Indeed, in Jewish tradition, the book is recited annually on Tishah B'Av, the Ninth of Ab (the fifth month in the Jewish calendar, so July or August), to commemorate the fall of the two temples in Jerusalem (in 587 BCE and 70 CE) and other tragedies down through the centuries. In Christian tradition, certain texts form part of the Holy Week services and are used in Tenebrae and Good Friday services.

PLACEMENT IN THE CANON

Traditional association with the prophet Jeremiah meant that already in the Greek Septuagint, the book of Lamentations followed that of Jeremiah, to which the Letter of Baruch, a work that purportedly stemmed from the scribe of the prophet (see Jer. 45), was sometimes also appended. The placement of Lamentations among the prophetic literature and after Jeremiah on traditional grounds is also found in the Latin Vulgate, the Syriac translation of the Bible called the Peshitta, and in many Christian Bibles in their various translations today, but the traditional ascription was known already in the early Common Era by the Church Fathers and possibly also by the Jewish historian Josephus.

In Jewish Bibles the book of Lamentations appears in the third section known as the Hagiographa or Writings (*kᵉṯuḇîm*), where it is included among a series of five (little) scrolls used for liturgical purposes called simply the Scrolls (*mᵉgillôṯ*). These biblical books are read on festival days in the Jewish calendar and include the Song of Songs for Passover, Ruth for the Feast of Weeks, Lamentations for the Ninth of Ab, Ecclesiastes for the Feast of Booths and Esther for Purim. The order of the five scrolls varies according to tradition so that they are found either in order of their appearance in the Jewish festival calendar, that is, the Song of Songs, Ruth, Lamentations, Ecclesiastes and Esther or according to a chronological order based on traditional ascriptions of authorship – Ruth by Samuel, the Song of Songs and Ecclesiastes by Solomon, Lamentations by Jeremiah, and Esther by Mordecai. According to the Babylonian Talmud, "The order of the Writings is Ruth, the Book of Psalms, Job, Prophets, Ecclesiastes, Song of Songs, Lamentations, Daniel and the Scroll of Esther, Ezra and Chronicles" (*b. Baba Batra* 14b).

TRADITION OF AUTHORSHIP

The poems of Lamentations have long been associated with the authorship of the prophet Jeremiah. An importance was ascribed in antiquity to the association of collections of material with authoritative figures. For example, King David is traditionally considered the author of the Psalms, wisdom material has been associated with King Solomon and the book of Lamentations was ascribed to the prophet Jeremiah. Already in the Septuagint, the oldest translation that we have, the collection known as Lamentations was attributed to the authorship of the prophet in a prefaced heading, "When Israel had gone into captivity and Jerusalem had been laid waste, Jeremiah sat weeping and sang this lament over Jerusalem and said …" The association of Lamentations with Jeremiah is ancient and also found in the Targums – that is, the Aramaic translations of the Old Testament – with varying degrees of expansion, the Latin Vulgate, the Peshitta and the Babylonian Talmud (*b. Baba Batra* 14b–15a). In fact, a general consensus of Jeremianic authorship emerged from sources in antiquity, including the ancient versions, the Rabbis and the Church Fathers, and continued up through the Middle Ages until the Enlightenment period. The first divergent opinion was expressed by the German Orientalist, Hermann von der Hardt in 1712 (Rudolph 1962: 196–9).

Within the Bible Jeremianic authorship can be traced back to the reference to his grieving the death of King Josiah in Chronicles, "Jeremiah also uttered a lament for

Josiah ... they are recorded in the Laments" (2 Chron. 35:25). The capitalization of the term 'Laments' in the NRSV reflects the tradition followed by the biblical translators that the laments or more accurately 'the dirges or funeral eulogies' raised by Jeremiah were recorded and collected in the biblical Lamentations. Interpreters bolster hints of Jeremianic authorship by noting correspondences between the prophet's personal concerns found in the so-called Confessions of Jeremiah (Jer. 11:18-12:6; 15:10-11, 15-21; 17:14-18; 18:18-23; 20:7-13, 14-18) and some of the vocabulary, phraseology and sentiments found in Lamentations. Worthy of mention also is that readers have long characterized Jeremiah as the weeping prophet and his name even forms the basis for a shorthand reference for complaint in English, 'the Jeremiad', which also speaks to associations between the prophet and Lamentations.

Although internal biblical details likely provided the original source of traditions in antiquity linking the prophet Jeremiah with the biblical Lamentations, it is unlikely that the collection actually represents the laments designated in the Chronicles reference. Notably, Lamentations contains no mention of or allusion to Josiah, and the terminology of the funeral dirge in Chronicles (from the verb *qyn* and the noun plural *qînôth*) is not found in Lamentations. In addition, commentators draw attention to subtle differences between the thought of the prophet and statements in the poems. One prominent example is Jeremiah's harsh critique of the king (Jer. 37:17-20; cf. 22:13-30), the nobility (5:4-9) and the priesthood (2:26-8; 20:1-5) and more positive attitudes towards the same found scattered in Lamentations (Lam. 1:6; 2:2, 6, 9; 4:7, 16, 20; 5:12). Another important factor is that the prophet Jeremiah is not named in Lamentations. It is difficult to explain the loss of his name over the course of time had it been original to the text. In general, it is more likely for a name to be added over time than erased. The placement of Lamentations in the Hebrew Bible and Jewish Tanak among the five liturgical scrolls that appear in the Writings rather than with the book of the prophet as reflected in Christian tradition speaks against Jeremianic authorship.

Interpreters have also drawn attention to differences in the vocabulary and phraseology between the two books. For example, the title 'Adonai', 'my Lord', is found fourteen times in the first three chapters of Lamentations in speech to and about God. In contrast, when Adonai is found in the book of Jeremiah, it is always found accompanying the proper name of God, Yahweh, and never used alone in place of the deity's name as in Lamentations. Another linguistic difference is that the relative pronoun *š* ('who, that') sometimes replaces the more common *'ăšer* in Lamentations (Lam. 2:15, 16; 4:9; 5:18), but not in Jeremiah. Finally, in a thorough analysis of language use, Max Löhr showed at the cusp of the nineteenth century that Lamentations shares more vocabulary overlap with Ezekiel, Deutero- or Second Isaiah (Isaiah 40-55), and the Psalms than with the book of Jeremiah (Löhr 1894 and 1904). The linguistic data suggests a different author than the book named after Jeremiah.

Although Jeremianic authorship is unlikely, a number of scholars in more recent years have moved away from a historical debate by linking the two collections on the basis of *figurative* representation. There are a number of speaking voices in Lamentations, including the city of Jerusalem figured as a woman in mourning, a dispassionate eyewitness reporter in chapters 1, 2 and 4, a suffering individual in chapter 3, and sporadic communal voices in chapters 3, 4 and 5. The various speakers represent implied authors manifested within the textual world who personalize the events related, but do not represent actual, historical figures in any real sense (Berlin 2002: 30–2). When seen in this way, it is useful to regard Jeremiah as the figurative representative of the voice in dialogue with the personified city in chapters 1 and 2 or as the individual sufferer in chapter 3 (see Lee 2002). In understanding the perspective of the different speaking voices it can be helpful to associate them with biblical exemplars, and Jeremiah is one such paradigmatic figure. In general, the association of representative figures with the various personae in Lamentations illuminates the speaking voices and helps us to better understand traditional interpretations of authorship and canonical placement in religious tradition.

A BRIEF OVERVIEW OF LAMENTATIONS

Images of suffering and destruction swirl chaotically in the poems of Lamentations with almost no sense of order. The traditional titles of the book, *Qînôth* or Lamentations, are plural referents which suggest that it is a collection of different psalm-like responses to a tragedy that have been gathered together, much akin to the book of Psalms. Consistent with most of the psalms in the Psalter, the poems of Lamentations are thought to represent examples of liturgy used in the cult rather than in private, personal reflection. Each one of the five poems of Lamentations focuses on a different aspect of the catastrophe mourned and together they offer a fuller picture of the events and circumstances that are associated with the invasion and destruction of a beloved city and the human consequences thereof. The "story" of Lamentations is conveyed through the perspectives of different speakers who detail their experiences, fears and even hopes in personal accounts.

Chapter 1	Chapter 2	Chapter 3	Chapter 4	Chapter 5
Verses 1-11, 17 Eyewitness Reporter	Verses 1-19 Eyewitness Reporter	Verses 1-21 and 48-66 The *geber* (Hebrew for 'strong man', 'war hero' or 'a superior')	Verses 1-16 Eyewitness Reporter	Verses 1-22 Communal Voice 'we'
Verses 9c, 11c Interruptions by Jerusalem, the personified city	Verse 11 Possible interruption by Jerusalem, the personified city	Verses 22-39 A Sage conveys a Wisdom Interlude	Verses 17-22 Communal Voice 'we'	
Verses 12-22 Personified Jerusalem = Daughter Zion	Verses 20-2 Personified Jerusalem = Daughter Zion	Verses 40-7 Communal Voice 'we'		

As a whole, the biblical Lamentations is characterized by an overwhelming sense of loss captured by what appear to be snapshots of a chaotic interplay of images like those experienced by individuals who suffer from post-traumatic stress disorder (PTSD) or who are in the process of grief. In this way, the biblical Lamentations invites each reader to become an interpreter. The wide diversity of and ambiguity in thematic expression related to systemic collapse, personal loss, and expressions of grief and protest can thus be made sense of in different ways and the following provides a rough outline based on a thematic organization.

Chapter 1	Chapter 2	Chapter 3	Chapter 4	Chapter 5
A City Suffers & the Agents of War		An Individual Sufferer & Divine Causality	Human Suffering & Subjugation	
Lament over Destruction and the "Death" of Jerusalem	Lament over the Brutality of the Divine Warrior and Human Enemies	Lament over Captivity and Orientation to God in Prayer and Confession	Lament over the Reversal of Fortunes of the Ruling Classes and Ordinary Citizens	Lament over Subjugation to a Foreign Authority and Lingering Questions about Divine Restoration

For comparison, Jeffrey Tigay and Alan Cooper's outline of the dominant themes of the five chapters echoes the chart I have drawn, but is articulated somewhat differently (Tigay and Cooper 1972). In their reckoning, the first chapter focuses on the personified city of Jerusalem as lonely, defiled, abused and abandoned by former allies and inhabitants in exile. God's role in the disaster and references to destruction in parts of the city appear prominently in the second chapter. The poet's own suffering and recognition of sin or incomprehension at God's anger combined with hope resting on God's compassion are themes in the third chapter. The suffering of the city's inhabitants permeates the fourth chapter. Finally, the distress of those who remained after destruction comes to the fore in the fifth chapter.

What remains undisputed among interpreters is that the first poem concentrates on the city of Jerusalem. It is a lament over Zion, the destruction of its infrastructure, the invasion of the temple figured as a rape and the death of the city personified as a woman. In the second poem, the devastating effects of the siege, battle and destruction of the city fade into the background and the poet focuses instead on the human invaders and the devastation they wrought at the behest of the deity who is named most frequently Adonai (2:1, 2, 5, 7, 18), perhaps to protect the identity of Yahweh from the depictions of violent destruction, figured on occasion akin to physical abuse. The third chapter turns away from the portrayal of the city and its destruction towards an individual sufferer who reflects on his or her own personal pain and becomes contented through reflections on the goodness, mercy, love and determination of the deity. The poem concludes with language in which the awareness of the lamenter orients towards the deity and exhibits a structure that pushes beyond the expression of grief to contrition, confession and thanksgiving. The tentative optimistic turn towards a core belief in divine purposes for restoration and salvation in the third chapter crashes into a renewed sense of ongoing calamity and actual human tragedy in the last two chapters. The fourth poem turns to the human casualties of war, with little or no consideration for the destruction of physical structures like the temple, the king's palace and the city walls as in the first two chapters. Survivors lift their voices in the final chapter to reflect on protracted suffering and exploitation by a foreign, presumably imperial, authority. Lamentations concludes mournfully with the community raising their concerns, their despair, their fears and their doubts to an absent God.

ATTEMPTS TO SYNCHRONIZE LAMENTATIONS

Given the rather disparate nature of the material, it remains a challenge to organize it in any consistent way. Nevertheless, certain themes repeat in the poems and there have been various attempts to trace synchronicity in and through them. One of the first attempts has been made by Johan Renkema, who sought to trace themes according to corresponding lines of the poems (Renkema 1988: 38–40). A consideration of the beginning verses of the chapters provides a convenient entry to his view. In the first poem, the city is described as a widow (1:1b) and traditionally, widows cannot wear jewellery, which links to the second chapter that opens with the depiction of the deity taking away the jewel (= NRSV 'splendour') of Israel (2:1b) which in turn resonates with the darkness that accompanies the day of divine judgement in the third chapter (3:2) as well as the dimming of the gold (4:1a) and the destruction of the temple (4:1b) in the fourth. The disgrace (1:1) and destruction (2:1; 4:1) of Zion as well as the individual of chapter 3 (3:1) are included within the statement of the humiliation of the community referred to in the concluding lament in the fifth chapter (5:1). Renkema links continuity, then, between the poems in conjunction with corresponding verses, but many commentators regard his approach as being too contrived and even at points strained. Although at times it stretches the limits of reason, his reconstruction still offers a constructive way to find unity in and through the poems.

Attempts to recognize a sense of order have also been made on the basis of observations of the structure of the poems. Chapters 1, 2 and 4, for example, can be broken down into two halves of material, according to a fact half and an interpretive half (Johnson 1987; cf. Heater 1992). The description of disaster is followed by its interpretation. In the first chapter, though, the fact half is actually interrupted on four occasions by two interpretative statements and two prayers made directly to the deity:

- "because the LORD has made her suffer for the multitude of her transgressions" (v. 5b)
- "Jerusalem sinned grievously, so she has become a mockery" (v. 8a)
- "O LORD, look at my affliction, for the enemy has triumphed!" (1:9c)
- "Look, O LORD, and see how worthless I have become". (11c).

Each interruption corresponds to a theme that will recur in the rest of the poetry in varying degrees of intensity – divine agency, human sin, the exaltation of the enemy, and the disgrace of the city and members of the community (Middlemas 2005: 184–97, cf. Hunter 1996, who finds eleven recurring themes in the first verses).

The intrusion of these themes into the surrounding material suggests their importance both within the first chapter and more broadly within the collection as a whole. Two are interpretive statements, of human sin and of disgrace and humiliation. The other two intrusions stem from the voice of a survivor who urgently interjects the words of a lament into a dirge-like account of devastating loss (1:9c, 11c). Suffering is the catalyst that motivates what is thought to be the personified city of Jerusalem, victimized by violence, to claim her truth and hold onto life in the midst of the overwhelming stench of death. Her interruption of the eyewitness account of disaster in the interpretive half gives voice to survivors who have the need to tell of their misery and their story, to draw attention to their plight, and to grasp at the possibility that the dire present can be changed to a better tomorrow (Middlemas 2012). The insertion of interpretation and lamentation within the fact half of chapter 1 signals important themes that will recur in varying degrees of intensity throughout the five poems of Lamentations: divine agency, human sin, the exaltation of the enemy and the city's disgrace.

Beyond the first half of the first chapter, the thematic emphases recur within and reverberate throughout the collection. The first response to the opening verses of the book of Lamentations is made by Jerusalem, personified as a woman, who speaks in the second half of the chapter (1:12-22). The personified city focuses attention on the intentionality and activity of Yahweh (vv. 12c-13, 14c-15, 21c-22) who treads 'the virgin daughter Judah' as in a wine press (v. 15c). Jerusalem also speaks of the actions of human enemy combatants (vv. 16c, 19a, 20c, 21) and the humiliation that comes from being an object of scorn (v. 21b) and alone (vv. 16b, 21a). In her speech, the dire present is considered to be a consequence of rebellion against God and the efficacy of human sin (vv. 14ab, 18a, 20b, 22b). To some extent, Jerusalem's claims corroborate the observations of an eyewitness whose report takes up much of the first eleven verses. The reporter then speaks of the agency of the deity and the enemy (v. 17b) as well as the disgrace and solitude of Jerusalem (v. 17a and 17c).

The concepts of divine agency, the role of the enemy, the attribution of human sin and disgrace recur in the other poems again with one or two themes being more prominent than the others. The second chapter emphasizes the agency of the deity who fights as the divine warrior against god's own people. Human enemies are also mentioned, but their role was attributed to the intentions of the deity who is in reality the focus of the entire chapter. Only one statement of human sin appears. It attributes transgression to the prophets who saw false visions for and gave incorrect advice to the people (2:14). With such a great emphasis on the agency of the deity and the role of human agents, it is only natural that the theme of disgrace also recurs time and time again, and from the first verse (vv. 1a, 2c, 6c, 7a, 15-16, 17c).

The third chapter also highlights the significance of the agency of Yahweh throughout the poem (vv. 1-13, 15-16, 22-38, 43-5, 55-66). The lament reveals that nothing good or bad could take place without divine determination. In contrast to the image of the divine warrior figured so prominently in the second chapter, the poet stresses the image of the divine saviour. Sin is mentioned only rarely (v. 39) and a truncated confession of sin appears (vv. 40-3) in a petition to God. Human enemies feature here, albeit rarely (vv. 46, 52-4), and the humiliating circumstances of the speaker reverberate throughout (see especially vv. 14, 45, 61-3). In distinction, the fourth chapter emphasizes the worthlessness and disgrace of Jerusalem and its inhabitants depicted through the portrayal of unending suffering which the poet attributes to divine agency (4:11, 16a). Human enemies feature as the ones who entered the gates of the city (v. 12), pursue the survivors (vv. 18-20), but the poem ends on a cry of revenge against one particular foreign enemy, the Edomites (vv. 21-2). Attention to sin appears only rarely, but prominently with reference to the transgressions of the leaders of the community, the prophets and the priests (v. 13), who led the people astray. The poet illustrates abject and protracted suffering by drawing an analogy to Sodom – the sin of the present generation is considered greater than that of the Sodomites whose wholesale destruction occurred swiftly (v. 6).

In distinction to the fourth chapter which focuses on the fate and suffering of the entire community from the perspective of an observer, the outlook of the fifth chapter is oriented from the point of view of the people who speak in the first-person common plural 'we'. The final poem intertwines the disgrace of the nation (5:1) with the exploitative policies, abuse and oppression of enemy rulers (vv. 2-18). The people acknowledge that they are paying the price for the sins of their ancestors or their political and social leaders (v. 7) and complain about the present state of estrangement from God figured as sin (v. 16b). At the conclusion of their lament, they affirm the reign of God (v. 19), but question whether Yahweh will exercise divine agency and lordship over them again (vv. 20-2).

In spite of attempts to discern a sense of order in and through the poems, it remains the case that statements, concepts and images appear disjointed. On top of the fragmentary nature of the material, the organizing topics that I have isolated – divine agency, the role of the enemies, sin and contrition, and the disgrace or worthlessness of the survivors and the city of Jerusalem in its present state of collapse – are still interspersed with other topics that highlight additional conceptual links in and through the poems. Not insignificantly portraits of human tragedy and the suffering of the innocent suffuse the poems (Moore 1983). In conjunction with his analysis of the first poem, then, Robert Salters refers to non-sequiturs and disjointed features that speak less to the poet's use of stray phrases and more to the simulation, whether intentional or not, of a grief process (Salters 2000). As in a grief process and consistent with the experiences of victims of trauma and war, the jumble of images of destruction, the horror experienced by human survivors, expressions of the raw emotions of pain, anger, revenge or despair as well as cool reflection, internal soul searching, feelings of abandonment, misery, misfortune, and affliction disjointedly bubble up to the surface in random order. In this way, the swirl of images and the articulations made by various speakers express the depth of loss and grief work that takes place in memories formulated after a catastrophe.

On the whole, then, the book of Lamentations represents a heart-wrenching series of musings, accounts and recollections of tragedy and human pain that resonate with survivors of persecution and affliction throughout time and so also today (Cohen 1982).

The deep question of 'how?' reverberates throughout the poems and through the centuries in experiences of the persecution and distress of the Jewish people who have been objectified in various ideologies, of other minorities or ethnic and religious groups that have been singled out as different or dangerous, and of various individuals who live through the violence of discrimination, exploitation, physical and sexual abuse, and torture. The themes of Lamentations and the voices that capture the rage, depression and suffering of survivors echo in the abused, downtrodden and persecuted today, while also giving voice to the burning question that victims of all ages have over the presence and indeed absence of God. In this sense, Lamentations is a timely composition that bursts forth from the bonds of scripture and its cultural embeddedness to speak to and challenge our own time. Kathleen O'Connor captures this sense well in her thoughts about the book which to her "functions as a witness to pain, a testimony of survival, and an artistic transformation of dehumanizing suffering into exquisite literature … [that] In the process … raises profound questions about the justice of God" (O'Connor 2001: 1024). The inclusion of Lamentations in the biblical canon attests to how grief, pain and even the aftershocks of PTSD find recognition and acceptance in the community which argues for the greater awareness, indeed appreciation of human sorrow and suffering in today's societies.

OUTLINE OF THE GUIDE

At Oxford University, I taught a faculty course on Old Testament Gobbets. The odd term 'gobbets' refers to short pieces of biblical texts that can be one or two verses or even part of a verse. Students are given the task to approach the gobbet as a piece of evidence and use it to show their knowledge of the fields of comparative ancient near eastern and biblical studies, archaeology, literary-historical concerns as well as theology. With respect to a gobbet, this means that students consider a verse first as a means to answer questions related to literary matters by considering the type and genre of the composition as well as evidence of its authorship and transmission. Importantly, they discuss issues related to whether there is evidence of a single author or of a composition updated by a final editor. Only once the composition question has been settled (or argued) can the student turn to matters related to provenance. A discussion of the historical and cultural context(s) of scripture is related to the transmission of a text, particularly if it represents a composite of an original work expanded at a later time and for a different audience by an editor. The final stage of a gobbet answer is the consideration, then, of what the text meant in its own time and within the framework of the theological topics found in the Bible. In this case, 'theology' refers to a word about or the understanding of God, the divine and human relationship, and speech to God.

By thinking critically about biblical literature as an artefact and the contributions it makes to various discussions, students become aware of how it came to be a unified whole and the different authors and editors who had a hand in shaping the material before saying anything about the historical and cultural contexts to which scripture speaks and then move finally to the theological and indeed anthropological arguments to which it relates. The gobbet exercise underscores that there is a critical distance between the cultural world in which the literature of the Bible arose that needs to be observed and indeed honoured in any analysis of what it means and the theological arguments to which it contributes. I have found that setting gobbets enables the appropriation rather than the application of scripture. Instead of reading an ancient text and considering how it applies wholesale to me and my present circumstances which is application, the critical distance achieved by understanding its literary features, how it came to be written down, and how it inspired new generations of readers and writers within their religious and socio-political communities assists in appropriation. In appropriation, one attempts to understand how a verse or verses meant something within its own peculiar cultural context and the nature of its contribution to the readers of its time so that individual readers can approach it from a different social location and understand a new word for his or her time.

As this is a guide, first and foremost, to interpretations of the biblical book of Lamentations, I follow the gobbet approach as I have found it to be a constructive way to teach the critical analysis of the biblical literature. In terms of the context of Lamentations, it makes sense to establish matters related to the composition of the work before tackling questions about its historical context and theology. The written Lamentations that has been passed down in tradition in Jewish and Christian Bibles includes examples suitable for use in worship, but are not necessarily equivalent to actual pieces of liturgy. So, while the individual poems of Lamentations may have their origin in actual ceremonies, they represent artistic compositions. Moreover, as a carefully constructed literary collection, the book of Lamentations discloses an intentionality in its presentation that deserves closer scrutiny before discussions of its provenance and theology.

The final form of a biblical book – the Old Testament, and the Old and New Testaments as a single interpretive unit – conveys meaning. For example, in the Jewish Tanak, the Hebrew Bible begins with Genesis and the expulsion of Adam and Eve from the Garden of the Eden at the beginning and concludes with the account in 2 Chronicles of the Persian King Cyrus issuing a decree that the Jews can return from exile and repopulate the devastated former kingdom of Judah (2 Chron. 36:22-3). When seen in this way, the shape of the Tanak with exile at the beginning and imperial authorization to 'go up' at its end conveys the importance of return from exile to a traditional homeland. By way of contrast, Christian Old Testaments conclude with the prophetic books and with the book of Malachi, which Christians interpret as the prophecy of the coming of a Messiah, regarded as Jesus Christ. The shape of the Bible conveys meaning on a micro as well as on a macro level.

The poems of Lamentations are written reflections of laments and their artistry can be better appreciated when considered first with regards to literary questions. Secondly, and perhaps more importantly, there is general agreement that the poems stem from different authors who come from different backgrounds. Only by approaching the literary questions of the material first are we then in a better position to speak about the historical and cultural contexts from which they came and only then to which they spoke. The next step in the analysis of biblical texts turns to the consideration of a message pertinent to the time in which they arose, that is, to the time and place in which they were first read or heard, and only then finally to how to think through possible meanings relevant for today.

The present guide is organized, then, such that the next two chapters deal with matters related to literary concerns. Chapter 1 focuses on outlining and explaining the poetic artistry of the poems, while the second chapter turns to matters of composition and whether there is evidence of an editorial hand and intentional shaping. The third chapter considers the historical and cultural context to which the poems relate and to which their provenance can most probably be attributed. The fourth chapter presents an overview of readings of Lamentations that stem from the contextual interests of interpreters and include an introduction to theological discussions as well as its role in trauma studies, feminist interpretation and post-colonial analyses. This chapter also surveys the book's reception history in order to convey its resonance in biblical and post-biblical literature as well as in the fine arts. The fifth and concluding chapter contains exegetical readings of the book in order to highlight areas in which the themes of Lamentations have relevance today. The last chapter offers readings related to feminist interpretation (a text of terror), post-colonial criticism (texts of silencing and exploitation) and rhetorical criticism (a text that commends human outreach and compassion).

Let me conclude this introduction with a few comments that aim to assist in reading the guide. The first point of note is that I refrain from using personal pronouns for the deity and have replaced his or her with words like god, deity and divine, where necessary. The Archbishop of Canterbury has recently stated and my own research on biblical conceptions of and language for God has born out that the God to whom the biblical literature bears witness does not have one gender and is not an anthropoid being, although the deity can take a humanoid shape (Middlemas 2014). Using pronouns such as 'he' or 'his' for God portrays and reinforces the depiction of God as human and as male, which in the Old Testament tradition is equivalent to idolatry. I leave the language for God as open as possible to the imagination of the reader and refrain from supplying my own conception, which means on a practical level that I do not follow the use of pronouns for God as found in the NRSV quotations as indicated where applicable by []. Biblical quotations are placed in double marks "" and citations of words taken out of verses or translations of Hebrew are placed in single quotation marks ''. I have tried to cite as widely and comprehensively as possible in order to present areas for further reading, but am aware that this introduction can only touch the surface of analyses of Lamentations. To guide the reader to further areas of study, a list of references cited and consulted in each chapter appears at the end of the volume along with a more comprehensive bibliography.

THE LITERATURE OF LAMENTATIONS: POETIC ART

As its English title suggests, the biblical book of Lamentations contains the laments or complaints of a grieving people captured in the evocatively emotive language of poetry. The collection is actually composed of five individual poems that correspond in their totality to the same number of chapters. Each chapter represents a complete interpretive unit that can be meaningfully understood independently of the other poems and there is no progression of thought in and through the chapters. Instead, each poem presents different perspectives on some unnamed disaster as well as different facets of the suffering and destruction that took place akin in some respects to a montage (Morse 2003). In literary studies, the poems of Lamentations are regarded as paratactic, that is, when images, themes and concepts are found side by side, jumbled associatively, with no clear rationale (Dobbs-Allsopp 2002: 12–14). As different speakers raise their voices and even interrupt each other in order to express reactions to and conceptions of tragedy, they also convey a sense of the enormity, perhaps even the totality, of a great loss and the accompanying sorrow experienced.

As poetry, the five chapters of Lamentations invite us to explore in greater detail the artistry and characteristic features of their expression. At the same time, it is also evident that although the five poems seem to represent isolated responses to a catastrophic event, they have been gathered together to form a single collection. The unified nature of the poems begs the question of its composition history. A literary examination of the book of Lamentations as literature, then, entails attention to the nature of the poetry itself as well as an exploration of issues related to its composition history, like those of form, genre and transmission. Here, we will consider Lamentations as poetry, while we turn to form, genre, and evidence of composition and shaping in the next chapter.

LAMENTATIONS AS POETRY

The five poems that comprise the book of Lamentations represent moving poetic portrayals of defeat, distress and despair that are similar in style to a number of psalms found in the Psalter. In the Bible, poetry is the mode of expression typically used by individuals and groups to convey a depth of feeling. It is found in the stirring exclamation of victory in the Song of the Sea (Exod. 15), of significant loss in Rachel's weeping over her children (Jer. 31:15), and in declarations of and musings about love in the Song of Songs. The most concentrated use of poetry is found in the Psalter, which serves as a repository of prayers used by a congregation in public recital.

As with the psalms, the use of poetry to express the sentiments captured by the chapters in Lamentations suggests a strong connection to cultic use. As such, the individual poems seem to represent the actual prayers of people who were in mourning, angry, repentant, depressed and even fighting for survival. Notably, figurative language, the economy of expression, repetition and other characteristic features of poetry serve as an aid to memory. At the same time, poetry offers an evocatively graphic and emotive form that assists a community and its members to express depths of emotion and, in this case, the myriad reactions that accompany systemic and societal collapse. On the one hand, then, the poems of Lamentations function as catharsis in that they "may enable survivors, and their descendants, to remember and contemplate their loss – not coolly, not without emotion – but without unbearable and measureless grief" (Hillers 1992: 4–5). On the other hand, though, the nature of poetic expression that swirls images together suggests that it is timeless as well as memorable so that the poetry of Lamentations remains meaningful for and applicable to new experiences of loss, disaster and abandonment for individuals and communities (Mintz 1984: 17–48; Salters 2010: 15–16). Taken together, then, the poetic artistry of Lamentations corresponds to the needs of liturgical recital and stems less from aesthetic concerns. The poetry of Lamentations represents personal and communal cries of anguish and grief expressed with the economic use of descriptive language by people of faith in the context of worship.

The chapters of Lamentations have long been thought to represent highly skilled examples of biblical poetry. The study of biblical poetry is fraught with a great deal of uncertainty (for an accessible introduction, see Alter 1985; Schökel 1988). The actual system of accents, vowels and syllabification remains a mystery because the vocalization of Hebrew manuscripts took place at least a millennium later than the original texts were produced. From this perspective, the sound of biblical poetry will remain elusive. Another compounding difficulty is that poetry was not distinguished in the Hebrew manuscripts, which not only blurs the lines between prose and poetry, but also makes the exact determination of line breaks in poems when isolated a matter of conjecture. Although some help has come from comparative Semitic studies, especially from comparisons to poetry from the Northwest Semitic Ugaritic culture, there are a number of aspects that will remain not only unknown, but also impossible to recover (Alter 1985: 4).

What is certainly true of Lamentations is that the poems in the collection lack features found in prose compositions and epic literature which evidence narrative elements such as plot, argumentation, and the description and interaction of characters. When seen in this way, the poems in Lamentations can be profitably classified as lyric poetry, which is characterized by a lack of narrative devices as well as the dependence on the use of language to convey meaning (Dobbs-Allsopp 2002: 12–20). Although there is a lack of consensus about the formal characteristics of biblical poetry, it is possible, nevertheless, to isolate a few features that enable greater appreciation of the artistry of Lamentations (see also the discussions in Hillers 1992; Dobbs-Allsopp 2002; Berlin 2008). Since the poems of Lamentations are carefully constructed literary masterpieces, "An appreciation of [their] lyricism is the key to the structure and dynamics of the individual poems, to the way in which the sequence as a whole coheres and interacts, and even to how the poet articulates theological interests" (Dobbs-Allsopp 2002: 6). In Wilfred Watson's now-classic study of biblical Hebrew poetry, he shows how poems have external and internal structure, whereby different techniques are used to organize the entire poem or elements within it (Watson 1984). The following introduction considers matters related to the external and internal structure of the poems of Lamentations as well as internal stylistic features of the poetry itself in order to convey a sense of its distinctiveness and beauty.

EXTERNAL STRUCTURE
Alphabetic and acrostic poems

One of the most striking external structuring devices found in the book of Lamentations is the use of the alphabetic acrostic (Watson 2001: 190–5; cf. Brug 1990). The twenty-two consonants of the Hebrew alphabet from *aleph* to *taw* are used to introduce the lines of the strophes in chapters 1–4. The acrostic is a highly artificial scheme imposed on the poems that attests to its written rather than oral or aural character. Watson, for example, notes that an acrostic is "intended to appeal to the eye rather than the ear" (Watson 2001: 191). In the early part of the twentieth century, J. P. Wiles reproduced the acrostic poems and metre for English readers (Wiles 1908: 123). A few lines from the first chapter exhibit the artistry of Lamentations and the skill of the poet:

Lamentations 1

Verse 1   **A**las, lone city! Where is now thy throng?
          Where is thy majesty, thou widowed queen?
          Where, empress of the lands, thy freedom strong?
Verse 2   **B**y night thine eye with streaming sorrow flows:
          No lover loves thee now, nor shares thy grief;
          Thy friends are false, yea, all thy friends are foes.
Verse 3   **C**anst thou by flight escape thy bonds and pain?
          Or seekest thou among the heathen rest?
          Thy swift pursuer scorns the effort vain.
Verse 4a **D**eserted are thy feasts, thy ways forlorn …

The use of the acrostic actually dominates the structure of each chapter in Lamentations except for the last, where it unceremoniously disappears. Although not an acrostic, the fifth chapter is still associated with the Hebrew alphabet and interpreters consider it an alphabetic poem because its total number of verses equals twenty-two or the amount of letters in the Hebrew alphabet. Furthermore, its appearance within a collection otherwise determined by and explicitly associated with the acrostic suggests that with its twenty-two verses it should be classified as alphabetic.

Additional matters of style connect the poems on the basis of external characteristics. Three poems, chapters 1, 2 and 4, are stylistically and thematically similar. They each begin with the same Hebrew word *'êkah* ('how', 'alas') and focus on the consequences of the fall of Jerusalem from different angles. In addition, chapter 1 contains the expected sequence of letters in the Hebrew alphabet, but chapters 2, 3 and 4 reveal a reversal between two of the letters in the central verses of the poem. Instead of the more common order of *ayin* before *peh* found in chapter 1, chapters 2–4 evidence the inverted sequence *peh* before *ayin* (2:16-17; 3:46-51; 4:16-17). Extra-biblical inscriptions provide evidence that the order of the Hebrew alphabet varied (Cross 1980: 8–15), so the variance could be attributed to the instability of the alphabetic sequence. At the same time, however, the use of the alphabet and acrostic in Lamentations suggests a degree of intentionality and purpose in its composition that speaks against a random change related to the lack of a fixed alphabetic sequence at the time of composition. What appears to be the case is that the striking change in the order of the alphabet in chapters 2–4 represents an intentional choice by which the poet signalled the introduction to the collection. Arguably, the striking similarities between chapters 1 and 2 in terms of theme, acrostic use, number of lines and two speaking voices provided the reason for a visible way to distinguish the first poem from the second as a means to reinforce its priority. The distinctive order in the second chapter, then, was carried forward into the subsequent acrostic poems in chapters 3 and 4 (Renkema 1998: 47–9).

There are slight variations in the use of the acrostic and the number of lines in the individual poems. In chapters 1 and 2, the acrostic introduces a three-line strophe, (v. 1 *aleph*-x-x, v. 2 *beth*-x-x, v. 3 *gimmel*-x-x etc.) that yields sixty-six lines in total. Only very rarely is the three-line strophe extended to four lines in these chapters (1:7; 2:19). In the third chapter, where the only clear articulation of hope is found, the acrostic use is noticeably intensified. Each letter of the alphabet introduces three short lines apiece (v. 1 *aleph*, v. 2 *aleph*, v. 3 *aleph*, v. 4 *beth*, v. 5 *beth*, v. 6 *beth* and so on). On the basis of the frequency of the use of the letters of the alphabet, interpreters sometimes refer to the third poem as a triple acrostic. Although each letter of the alphabet appears more frequently, the total number of verses in the third poem still equals sixty-six lines. These features suggest that the third chapter represents the stylistic, if not also thematic, highpoint of the collection. The fourth poem follows the general pattern of chapters 1 and 2, but the acrostic introduces a strophe of two lines (v. 1 *aleph*-x, v. 2 *beth*-x, v. 3 *gimmel*-x and so on), which results in forty-four verses. The fifth chapter breaks free from the acrostic form, but remains, nevertheless, inextricably linked to the alphabet by containing twenty-two evenly balanced lines.

Acrostic poems are attested to in ancient Near Eastern (ANE) literature as well as elsewhere in the Hebrew Bible. The acrostic form is found in Akkadian, Egyptian, Ugaritic and paleo-Canaanite writing (Soll 1989; Hillers 1992: 24–5 nn, 25–7). In Ugaritic, the acrostic is not found in poetry, but rather appears in compositions that seem to be training exercises for students learning to write the alphabet. Because of the nature of their writing systems, the acrostic in Egyptian and Mesopotamian compositions were not alphabetic. In Egyptian, corresponding stanzas opened with the same word and in Akkadian the individual stanzas began with the same syllable. In the Old Testament, the acrostic is found relatively infrequently, and sometimes only partially. Examples appear in a number of Psalms (Pss. 9–10 when read as one, 25, 34, 37, 111, 112, 119 and 145), Proverbs (Prov. 31:10-31) and in the deutero-canonical book of Sirach (Sir. 51:13-20) as well as in a partial acrostic in Nahum (Nah. 1:2-8) (Watson 2001: 192–200).

Various proposals have been advanced to explain the use of the alphabet and the acrostic in Lamentations. Older arguments, generally discounted today, regarded the acrostic form as a late and stylistically inferior imposition on poems handed down in tradition and cultic use. Equally less persuasive have been arguments based on the belief that the letters of the alphabet possessed the magical ability to ward off evil or that the acrostic served a pedagogical function to aid teaching the alphabet to the young as in the Ugaritic examples. Slightly more persuasive have been arguments in favour of the use of the acrostic to aid recital in the cult, but its lack in the fifth chapter speaks against this view. Watson suggested two likely explanations. The first has to do with the attempt to convey either a sense of completeness of the survey of the topic of destruction and accompanying despair and human suffering or the finality of the execution and experience thereof. The second reason focuses on the use of the acrostic to display the skill of the poet. Both explanations have received varying degrees of support in the literature, although the idea of completeness tends to have a stronger following among interpreters.

The acrostic and alphabetic poems represent the work of significant literary and thematic skill. At the same time, the use of the alphabet that either dictates the contents of each poem (chs. 1–4) or informs its composition (ch. 5) functions as a stylistic way to convey something about the message of each chapter and the collection as a whole. The acrostic provides a framework for what is otherwise a senseless mishmash of emotion, depictions of human suffering, and disjointed statements of painful exclamation, protest, complaint, hope and hopelessness. As such, the skilful use of the acrostic and the related alphabetic form freezes the many disparate perspectives that are found in ongoing rolling testimony. A number of interpreters connect the use of the acrostic and alphabetic poems to the purposes of the poet. For example, the acrostic either serves as a means to highlight the message of each poem at the central point of the alphabet or the book itself (Johnson 1985; Heater 1992), conveys movement through the poems (Dobbs-Allsopp 2002: 18; Thomas 2013: 82), or focuses sustained attention on the importance of the third poem (Brug 1990: 286). The use of the acrostic and alphabetic stylistic devices is, thus, felt to be related to the message of each poem as well as the collection as a whole, and not simply imposed as a way to contain the chaos therein.

The acrostic has long been regarded as a feature of the writing style of the sages and thus linked to Wisdom Literature. Moreover, the message, style and language of a kernel of hopeful meditation found in the exact centre of the entire collection (Lam. 3:22-39) reinforce a connection to the Wisdom tradition (Westermann 1994: 168–93). The central verses in chapter 3 correspond particularly well to the emphasis on instruction and admonition found in examples of Wisdom books, such as Proverbs and Job. Strikingly, the male lamenter in chapter 3 is cast as a Job-like figure (Berlin 2002: 85, 92–4). In addition, the contemplation and reflection that accompany his prayer reaffirm that God is in the right and, thus, shares much in common with the worldview of Job's friends who consider that suffering comes from God (Dobbs-Allsopp 2002: 119–22). The skilful use of the acrostic poetic form and the paradigmatic figure who advocates for the correct way to respond to suffering in the central chapter reinforce a link between the poems of Lamentations and the Israelite Wisdom traditions.

The connections to the Wisdom literature as well as the choice of the acrostic, which is known to function mnemonically as an aid to memory and whose sophisticated artistry superimposes a sense of unity and order on the collected poems, suggests that Lamentations could also have been used as meditation (Assis 2007). As such, each poem enables studied reflection on trauma rather than the random portrayal of cacophonous emotional reactions to tragedy. When seen this way, the poems of Lamentations actually correspond well to recent work conducted in the field of trauma studies. Researchers have drawn attention to how the chaotic panoply of disruptive and disjointed memories of traumatic or wounding experiences is shaped and organized by individuals and communities often many years after the initial cause of the suffering for purposes of survival and reflection. Ultimately, the acrostic imposes a superficial order that creates structure for the diverse images, themes and motifs in the poems. At the same time, however, through the alphabetic poem at its conclusion the collection evidences the opening up or loosening of a tightly determinative scheme and thus avails itself of multiple interpretations as an open text (Thomas 2013).

INTERNAL STRUCTURE

Parallelism

Since the masterful study of Hebrew poetry conducted in the eighteenth century by Robert Lowth, the most widely recognized feature of biblical Hebrew poetry is its parallelism, also known by its longer name in Latin, *parallelismus membrorum*. Parallelism is the seeming equivalence of two parts of a line or verse such that the first part is restated, seconded, augmented or contradicted in the second part of the line in order to convey meaning (Alter 1985: 3–26; Watson 2001: 114–59; Berlin 2008). Parallelism is also found in other writings from the ancient world, such as in Akkadian, Aramaic, Egyptian and Ugaritic, which speaks once again to consistencies between ancient Israelite poetry and its neighbours. At the same time, however, it is worthwhile noting that there are a number of verses in Lamentations that cannot be classified as parallel in thought (Hillers 1992: xxxv) so *parallelismus membrorum* offers a useful heuristic tool with which to understand Hebrew poetry, but does not define the entirety of its system.

Analyses of Hebrew poetry indicate that there are four different kinds of parallelism: synonymous, synthetic, antithetic and climactic. The two most prominent kinds of parallelism found in Lamentations are synonymous and synthetic. Synonymous parallelism means that the sentiment in the first half of a line is repeated or mirrored through the use of different vocabulary in the second half of the line and appears in such verses as:

"The steadfast love of Yahweh never ceases,
[God's] mercies never come to an end" (3:22)
"panic and pitfall have come upon us,
devastation and destruction" (3:47)
"Those who feasted on delicacies perish in the streets;
those who were brought up in purple cling to ash heaps (4:5).

Synthetic parallelism refers to the extension or the heightening of the sentiment expressed in the first half of the line in the second half;

"Yahweh has become like an enemy,
[God] has destroyed Israel" (2:4a)
"Yahweh rejected the deity's own altar,
spurned the deity's sanctuary" (2:7)
"You have wrapped yourself with anger and pursued us,
killing without pity" (3:45)

In synthetic parallelism, the concept that appears in the first part of the line becomes more pointed in the second:

"She weeps on through the night
and her tears are on her cheek" (1:2)

Less frequently, antithetic parallelism, whereby the first half of a line is the opposite of or contradicted by the second half, is also found among the poems. Antithetic parallelism exposes reversal or disappointment as in:

"How lonely sits the city
that was once full of people!" (1:1a)
"I called to my lovers
but they deceived me" (1:19a)
"Even the jackals offer the breast and nurse their young,
but my people has become cruel, like the ostriches in the wilderness" (4:3)

Finally, there are a few examples of climactic parallelism. In climactic parallelism the second half of the line intensifies the sentiment of the first half, often repeating the same vocabulary:

"[God] has made my flesh and my skin waste away,
and broken my bones" (3:4).

Enjambment

The attention focused on parallelism in the poetry of Lamentations has been challenged in recent years by F. W. Dobbs-Allsopp who has noted the prevalence of a different pattern. In Lamentations, a number of lines do not contain an end stop, that is, they do not have the significant pause evidenced in parallel lines. Instead, one line moves more or less directly into the next one, which then echoes or mirrors its meaning in some way (Dobbs-Allsopp 2002: 18–20). The difference is disclosed through a comparison of parallel lines and enjambment lines (as cited by Dobbs-Allsopp 2002: 19). Parallel lines occur prominently in the fifth chapter with its evenly balanced lines in expressions like;

"Young men are compelled to grind,
and boys stagger under loads of wood" (5:13)
Because of this our hearts are sick,
because of these things our eyes have grown dim." (5:17)

Instead of parallel meaning, it is often the case that the sense of one part of the line is carried into the next without a notable pause in enjambment as in the following examples;

"her pursuers have all overtaken her
in the midst of her distress" (1:3c)
"Yahweh destroyed without mercy
all the dwellings of Jacob" (2:2a)
"my priests and elders
perished in the city" (1:19b)

In these examples, the reader or hearer must continue to find out the sense of the line and is not given the same information again in different language.

Over two-thirds of the couplets in the poems feature enjambment and its use is most concentrated in chapters 1 and 2, while it decreases in chapters 3 and 4, and is almost non-existent in chapter 5. As a poetic device, enjambment energizes the poetry. Simultaneously, it urges the constant movement from one point to the next and through the chaotic images, confusions, repetitions and reversals to the bitter end. Enjambment participates in the poetry of Lamentations by urging the reader to move from one devastating image to another. To my mind, it functions as the means to move the interpreter quickly through the various reactions and graphic imagery to alight at the communal prayer in chapter 5, where the final verse concludes with a great pause that awaits a divine response to the aching concern of, "unless you have utterly rejected us, are wroth with us forever" (5:22) (my translation, see the discussion in Middlemas 2004: 97).

Qînah metre or rhythm

The nineteenth-century study of Hebrew poetry and Lamentations by Karl Budde found that a poetic line divided naturally into two parts (two cola) according to sense with the second part consisting of more than one word (Budde 1882). According to this view, the poetic lines in the biblical Lamentations tend to correspond to a 3:2 metre, although other metrical sequences, like 3:3, 4:2 and even 2:3, are also found. Based on his observation that the 3:2 pattern is found elsewhere in (some) dirges in the Hebrew Bible, Budde characterized the metre as a *qînah*, the Hebrew technical term for 'dirge' or 'funeral song'. On a literary level, the *qînah* metre serves as the equivalent of a limping beat in which three beats of weeping appear in the first colon of the verse and are followed by two beats of short, punctuating sobs in the second colon. In its cadence, then, the *qînah* conveys the expression of great emotion that lessens and fades away into despair. The third chapter represents the clearest example of the *qînah* metre because the 3:2 beat is most consistently found therein. Instances of the *qînah* beat are also found to some extent in chapters 1, 2 and 4. In sharp contrast, the verses of the fifth poem are evenly balanced lines.

Budde's categorization of the metre of the poems as a *qînah* still remains influential in studies of Lamentations; however, a growing number of interpreters prefer to speak of rhythm rather than metre. At one time, Hebrew poetry was delineated from prose on the basis of metre determined by an assessment of the number of syllables or accents in a line. Many interpreters today question the application of the concept of metre to Hebrew poetry and prefer, instead, to speak of rhythm. They point out that the concept of metre has been appropriated from Greek and Latin conceptions of poetic literature. Moreover, the attribution of syllables or stress remains hotly contested and varies according to the interpreter. A succinct definition of Hebrew poetry serves as our general guide, "Poetic expression constitutes a subtle interplay of the rhythmic expression of carefully crafted human speech wrought with special attention to artistic effect. Hebrew poetry constitutes these features along with a perceptible, elastic parallelism" (Petersen and Richards 1992: 14).

The words and the rhythm of Lamentations evoke a sense of deep emotion and the *qînah* offers a meaningful way to characterize the sound of the poetry. However, it is now recognized that not all dirges are written in the *qînah* rhythmic pattern, including David's lament over Saul and Jonathan (2 Sam. 1:17-27). Moreover, other literature, not sorrowful in nature, was composed with the 3:2 beat, including part of a love song (Song of Songs 1:9-11) and an oracle of hope (Isa. 40:9-11). Nevertheless, the *qînah* rhythm corresponds well to the contents of the book of Lamentations and is a helpful way to think of its recital (Hillers 1992: 15–31; Salters 2010: 15–17; but see de Hoop 2000). In particular, the mournful question of 'how' that opens the poems of Lamentations is reinforced by the solemn march of the dirge (Shea 1979; Garr 1983) as is the lingering question of the deity's intentions at its end.

INTERNAL STYLISTIC FEATURES

Speaking voices

All of the poems offer snapshots of a great disaster from multiple perspectives that are conveyed through speech interwoven throughout the poems from individuals and groups as well as from outsiders who are referred to in the third person. The various speakers actually convey anthropological and theological interpretations because, as one interpreter puts it, "Lamentations has as its medium dramatized speech" (Mintz 1984: 4). Suitably, then, the book of Lamentations is a collection of voices from men, women and children who lift up and interweave their testimonies and reactions in a series of accounts that detail suffering, tragedy and reflection.

The number of different speakers has been variously counted as three (Provan 1991: 6–7), five (Lanahan 1974) or seven (Heim 1999). The use of different speakers gives the impression that the words include the raw reactions of an entire community reeling from catastrophic political and societal collapse as well as the observations of outsiders.

Recounted in the poems are also the perspectives of foreign nationals who disparage or mock the downfall of the city and the nation-state as well as the cries of babes and children (Heim 1999). Notably, no single voice dominates over the others. With the exception of the fifth and final chapter in which a communal 'we' pertains throughout, each poem includes speaking voices that alternate between different individuals in chapters 1 and 2 or between an individual and a group in chapters 3 and 4.

In the first two chapters of the collection, two individual speakers recount their perspectives and even interact with each other (Conway 2012). Chapter 1 opens with the almost dispassionate account of a third person eyewitness who speaks like a reporter and recounts the events that have unfolded as well as the scenes of disaster around him or her (1:1-9b, 10-11b, 17). In the first chapter, the reportage is interrupted on two occasions by the personified city of Jerusalem who speaks in the first-person singular of her distress (vv. 9c, 11c). The testimony of Jerusalem is so urgent, in fact, that her voice finally overtakes that of the dispassionate eyewitness and her testimony concludes the first chapter (vv. 12-16, 18-22). Personified as a female speaker (see below under *Personification*), Jerusalem bemoans her, her inhabitants and her city's fate, and rails against excessive brutality.

The reporter reappears in the second chapter as a less dispassionate observer who details at length the aggressive attack of the deity and the actions of human enemy combatants against the city and its inhabitants (2:1-19). At the urging of the narrated voice, a perceptibly more downtrodden Lady Jerusalem interrupts once again to account for her descent into despair (v. 11) and her voice fades away at the conclusion of the chapter as she calls for revenge (vv. 20-2). Jerusalem is the first speaker to accuse God and hold the deity to account for maltreatment, brutality and even capriciousness.

In the third and fourth chapters the speech of an individual is augmented or echoed by that of a community which speaks in the first-person plural, 'we'. The third poem includes the personal lament of a soldier, strong man, superior or nobleman (all possible meanings of the Hebrew *geber*), who speaks of his downfall, tragedy and sense of abandonment in a plaintive personal lament that begins with a focus on his own circumstances 'I, myself, am the one who has seen affliction' (3:1, my translation). The individual's very personal concerns (vv. 2-21) are interrupted with the abrupt intrusion of a wisdom-like refrain, as if spoken by a sage, on reasons to hope in the merciful intervention of God (vv. 22-39). Following the wise counsel that interjects most unexpectedly into its surroundings, a community raises its voice in tone and outlook quite similar to that of the individual sufferers in chapters 1 and 2 (vv. 40-7). The chapter then concludes with the focus on individual suffering and reasons to regard divine retribution on behalf of the lamenter, seemingly articulated by the individual met already at the beginning of the chapter (vv. 48-66).

To a certain extent, the fourth chapter mirrors the first two chapters in the appearance of two principal speaking voices. It is distinctive, nevertheless, in that the speech of a third-person eyewitness interchanges with that of a first common plural 'we' voice whose short call for revenge contrasts the lengthy speeches of the personified city (as in 1:12-22; 2:20-2). The individual either represents the reporter encountered already in the first two chapters or a member of the *bourgeoisie* who focuses more attention on issues related to economics and status (so Lanahan 1974) (vv. 1-16). Presumably, the eyewitness can report on different aspects of the tragedy – the downfall of the city in the first chapter, the nature of the enemy attack in the second chapter and the dire circumstances of the community in the fourth chapter, which would suggest that a single reporter appears throughout as a witness to the catastrophe. The fourth chapter, though, concludes with an intrusive 'we' who complain of the terror of pursuit and miserably call out for vengeance (4:17-22). Their voices thus presage the communal lament that closes the collection of Lamentations with the mournful lament of the people. With their very personal 'we', a despairing people pray over its ignoble fate and petition God to hear and respond. Alas, they conclude all of the voiced laments, protests, complaints, confessions of trust and sin, calls for revenge, and sorrowful musings with a burning question about divine intention and commitment.

In Lamentations, a variety of speakers capture the enormity of the disaster and witness to the tragedy and misery that surround them. In addition, the use of the different speaking voices heightens the sense of emotion and makes the various experiences of affliction and misfortune more compelling. A devastating calamity has happened that affects real people. At the same time, we know from studies of victims of trauma that survivors of disaster or abuse have the urgent need to tell of their pain, to acknowledge it and to organize it as part of their sense-making in order to begin to exert control and move past its lingering effects. The tragedy of Lamentations is that the different speakers are not in a position to correct the disaster around them. They present testimonies of the abject distress they feel and their hopelessness in the face of the many horrors they see and experience in order to re-organize their pain. The damage to each person, the community, their city and their nation is so significant that they can only imagine that its reversal will be accomplished through divine feât. They express tentative hope in God to bring recompense, retribution and reconciliation. So, on the one hand, the various speakers vividly depict a painful present as part of their witness to tragedy, but, on the other hand, in so doing, they ultimately aim to motivate God to do something constructive about it.

Alas, the speaking voice most urgently sought in the series of personal and communal complaints is the one that never answers. Indeed, God remains hidden or clouded over as the narrator so eloquently conveys at the beginning of chapter 2, "How the LORD in anger beclouded Daughter Zion" (2:1, my translation). The painful protests and exclamations of brutality and affliction, although voiced, linger without answer and remain unresolved. God never responds, except perhaps in chapter 3 in quoted speech, "You have drawn near on the day I called you and you have said, 'Do not fear'" (3:57), which can also be understood as a divine word from the past (O'Connor 2002: 15). The faint echo of a divine response as though long past and the striking omission of God's voice among those raised so sorrowfully and courageously in Lamentations situate the emphasis on the voices of a multitude of sufferers. The biblical Lamentations is a very human book that places great value on the accounts of victims by including and even forefronting the sorrowful, angry and dissenting contributions of people sunk in a painful present. As Kathleen O'Connor captures so beautifully in her sensitive analysis of the survivors, "because God never speaks, the book honors voices of pain. Lamentations is a house for sorrow because there is no speech for God." In this way, scripture offers and provides a space for the expression of human suffering and so validates its unique cry and role in religion and society.

Although the deity never responds, Lamentations as public recital urges the reader to join his or her voice to those of the anguished members of the community and augment their cries for help, restoration and restitution so poignantly captured in the poems. Through personal reading and communal recital in worship, the reader or congregation becomes part of the drama of Lamentations (cf. Heim 1999). In so doing, he or she not only witnesses to the horrors experienced by a community that considers itself victimized by real human enemies and abandoned by its God, but also participates in the observations and testimonies that are made. The reader thus joins his or her voice to the speakers of Lamentations and even responds to the cries of anguish, hope and doubt. The intermingling of the speaking voices, then, fosters engagement with, rather than cool detachment from, the concerns expressed by the community's erstwhile prayers captured in the poetry of Lamentations.

Personification

Closely related to the inclusion of speaking voices to convey the message of Lamentations is the poet's use of personification. Personification is the use of imagery associated with persons and human actions or qualities for inanimate objects or things for poetic effect. In Lamentations, objects are personified to illustrate the extent and execution of the disaster (see Frevel 2017: 27–34). For example, the roads to Zion mourn (1:4), rampart and wall lament (2:8), and the sword bereaves (1:20).

The sense of tragedy and suffering becomes more poignant when the poet supplies a human face through the personification of the city of Jerusalem as a vulnerable woman. At the very outset of the poems, the city is a widow and an enslaved former princess (1:1), but later she is the survivor of sexual assault or rape (1:8, 10; see also 1:12b, 13c, 22b) (Dobbs-Allsopp and Linafelt 2001). In addition, the city personified as a human being does things that humans do; she sits (1:1), weeps (1:2, 16), groans (1:8, 21), feels pain (1:12, 18, 20) and remembers (1:7). She also has body parts including cheeks (1:2), a face (1:8), bones (1:13), feet (1:13), a neck (1:14), eyes (1:16), hands (1:17), a stomach (1:20) and a heart (1:20, 22). Like different members of society or in a family, Jerusalem has not only lovers (1:2, 19), friends (1:2), children (1:5), admirers (1:8), but also pursuers (1:3), foes (1:5) and enemies (1:2, 5, 21). More striking still, people and things are spoken of with reference to her. The poet writes of 'her lovers' (1:2), 'her friends' (1:2), 'her priests' (1:4), 'her young girls' (1:4), 'her children' (1:5) as well as 'her gates' (1:4), 'her lot' (1:4) and 'her sanctuary' (1:10) (Dobbs-Allsopp 2002: 62). The poet also attributes activity to the city in conjunction with 'her transgressions' (1:5) and 'her downfall' (1:7). As a pitiful and disheartened woman, the city speaks in her own voice (1:9c, 11c, 12-22; 2:20-2, perhaps also v. 11) and uses the first-person possessive to speak of 'my sorrow' (1:12), 'my transgressions' (1:14, 22), 'my strength' (1:14), 'my children' (1:16), 'my suffering' (1:18), 'my lovers' (1:19), 'my priests and elders' (1:19), and 'my groans' (1:22).

The poet employs the use of titles as another means to personify the city and the nation-state in order to generate empathy. Strikingly, more metaphorical epithets of the city and the nation-state are found clustered in Lamentations than anywhere else in the Old

Testament literature. Out of a total of forty-five appearances within the Old Testament, the city is referred to twenty-two times with the designation 'daughter of a geographical place or name (abbreviated GN)' or 'maiden daughter of GN' in Lamentations, with the next closest usage being sixteen times in the book of Jeremiah. The titles for the city include *bath ṣîôn* 'Daughter Zion' (1:6; 2:1, 4, 8, 10, 13, 18; 4:22), *bᵊthûlath bath ṣîôn* 'Maiden Daughter Zion' (2:13) and *bath yᵊrûšālaim* 'Daughter Jerusalem' (2:13, 15). The nation-state appears as *bath yᵊhûdâ* 'Daughter Judah' (2:2, 5), *bᵊthûlath bath yᵊhûdâ* 'Maiden Daughter Judah' (1:15) and with reference to its inhabitants as *bath ʾammî* 'the Daughter of My People' (2:11; 3:48; 4:3, 6, 10). The use of personification for a geographical entity is also found employed for the neighbouring nation-state of Edom, termed *bath ʾᵉḏôm* 'Daughter Edom' (4:21, 22). The figuration of Edom as a young maiden heightens the sense of doom so hoped for by the lamenters for their enemies.

There remains some debate on the translation of the phrase 'daughter/maiden daughter (of)' that hinges on whether it should be considered a genitive 'daughter of' or as an appositional genitive 'daughter GN'. Clearly the phrases are in the construct state, which is used in Classical Hebrew to connote the genitive or possession 'of' yielding Daughter of Zion, Daughter of Judah and so forth, and many interpreters prefer the translation 'Daughter of' or 'Maiden Daughter of' (Dobbs-Allsopp 1995: 469–70; and recently, Floyd 2008). When understood in this way, the expression conveys the sense that Jerusalem functions as a representative of the inhabitants of the city drawn from older mythology and the literature of the ancient Near East (ANE) in which the patron goddess and daughter of the chief god in the pantheon stands in as a representative of the city (Fitgerald 1972). The epithet harks back to older traditions of patron goddesses in the ANE who wept over the destruction of their cities and even interceded on their behalf with the other gods in literature concerned with the destruction of cities and/or their principal sanctuaries (Kramer 1983). The theology of ancient Israel would seemingly avoid such ideology, so the city itself is depicted in the guise of a woman lamenting over the destruction and the suffering of its citizens, without reference to the goddess.

At the same time, the phrase can also represent a rare type of Classical Hebrew usage in which one word describes a second word through possession called the appositional genitive (Stinespring 1965). As an appositional genitive, the phrasing would mean that Zion as a type of daughter is respected and dear, which yields a sense that is more or less equivalent to the metaphorical sense for which Magnar Kartveit has recently argued (Kartveit 2013). In such usage, the poet depicts the city as a vulnerable and devastated young woman, thus heightening once again the pathos of the poetry. Its use intends to evoke emotion rather than description (Berges 2002: 56; Maier 2008; recently, Bosworth 2013). The use of an epithet in conjunction with the neighbouring nation-state of Edom seemingly supports a metaphorical sense (4:20-2). In an oracle that announces the certainty of recompense for actions in wartime that countermanded treaty loyalty, a suffering people call for revenge and focus their attention on the defencelessness and vulnerability of the city to the avenging deity. By expressing the surety of divine recompense, they emphasize helplessness in the expression of 'Daughter or tender Edom'. A translation more along the lines of 'tender or dearest Jerusalem/Zion', then, captures well the vulnerability and defencelessness of the city. At the same time, understanding the expression with a metaphor does not exclude that there may be faint echoes of the mythology of the city goddesses who mourn the loss of their cities and shrines lingering in the background of the depiction.

At times, the city of Jerusalem takes on characteristics of a woman in various guises in the poems, but references also attest to the edifices of a city, such as its walls, buildings and streets. When seen in this way, the personified Jerusalem is equivalent to the City-Woman (Seidman 1992: 285) or a woman and city figured as one. Nevertheless, she represents a literary persona who is a mother, a daughter, a wife, a rape victim and perhaps also a menstruous woman, when the reference 'her uncleanness was in her skirts' is understood to be made to blood (1:9) (so Kaiser 1987). In the context of Lamentation, though, the reference to being unclean more likely stems from contact with another type of contamination, either from the corpses lying about unburied in the streets as the sorry emblems of the ferocity of war (Linafelt 2000) or through the institution of mourning rituals and sitting in ashes and dust (Pham 1999).

The presentation of the city as a woman appears in highly emotive texts and helps the reader or hearer to identify with the suffering experienced. In addition, the interplay of the speaking voices in Lamentations and the city personified creates drama, even dramatic action between the characters (Heim 1999; Lee 2002: 40–5). Through the personified city, the poet creates links to the prophetic literature, in which the city is found as a woman (Boase 2006: ch. 2). Speaking in her own voice, the personified Jerusalem also seemingly counters and rebuts traditions about her as the disobedient daughter and adulterous wife promulgated in the prophetic literature (Mandolfo 2007: 79–102). If such a conception of the personified city as the harlotrous wife appears in Lamentations, and Carleen Mandolfo argues that it does not, the criticism is certainly minimized and found only in faint echoes as in the complaint about lovers who have abandoned personified Jerusalem and provide no assistance to her in a time of need (1:2). By focusing on the survivors, the poems of Lamentations express great empathy with those who suffer and only rarely apportion blame.

Through the personification of the city of Jerusalem the poet offers a persuasive contrary perspective to conceptions found within the poems as well as within the biblical tradition itself. More importantly, perhaps, the figuration of a young and vulnerable woman who speaks for the city and its inhabitants with the heart-wrenching and moving vocabulary of loss, devastation and sorrow adds pathos so that the reader or hearer mourns with her and for her.

Figurative language and imagery

The language of poetry is evocative. One of the features of Lamentations that makes the poems difficult to assign to any specific historical period is the use of imaginative and figurative language that can be attributed to any place and time. Moreover, the chapters are full of similes, metaphors, comparisons and pictures. Among others, Christian Frevel has drawn attention to much of the figurative language of the collection (Frevel 2017: 19–21). From the opening comparison of the city 'like a widow' (1:1), similes abound. People are often compared, such as the princes who 'have become like stags' (1:6), starving children faint 'like the wounded' (2:12), cruel people are 'like the ostriches in the wilderness' (4:3), mothers 'are like widows' (5:3) and enemies make joyful noise 'as on a festival day' (2:7, 22). Other similes portray abstract ideas like 'in the house it is like death' (1:20). Jerusalem is told to cry tears 'like a torrent' (2:18) and pour out her heart 'like water' (2:19). God is portrayed in various guises as an enemy combatant who burns 'like a flaming fire' (2:3), cocks the bow 'like an enemy' (2:4, see also 3:12, 13) and generally acts 'like a foe' (2:4, 5). In the fourth chapter, the comparative is used with great effect, for example, to speak of reversal; such as, the ferocity of the disaster being 'greater than the punishment of Sodom' (4:6) or the outer appearance of nobility once 'purer than snow, whiter than milk' (4:7) has become 'blacker than soot' (4:8). Actual metaphors of the A is B type are rather rare, but found in conjunction with the deity who is said to be 'a bear lying in wait … a lion in hiding' (3:10).

In addition to figurative language use, the poet also employs vivid speech to convey the suffering and the consequences of disaster. The city 'weeps bitterly in the night' (1:2), 'God has made my teeth grind on gravel, and made me cower in ashes' (3:16), '[the soldier's] soul is bowed down' (3:20), and 'the tongue of the infant sticks to the roof of its mouth' (4:4). The demolition of once-sturdy and trusted buildings or parts of the city's infrastructure is also portrayed with graphic, even dramatic, detail, such that the city's gates 'have sunk into the ground' (2:9) and the stones of the temple 'are scattered at the head of every street' (4:1). The agony of human suffering is vividly portrayed with body imagery; Jerusalem agonizes that 'my stomach churns, my heart is wrung within me' (1:20), the eyewitness narrator reveals 'my eyes are spent with weeping; my stomach churns; my [liver] is poured out on the ground' (2:11), and the community echoes 'our hearts are sick … our eyes have grown dim' (5:17). The poet's graphic portrayal and thorough description depict destruction and its real consequences to a world without television. In this way, the vividness of language draws the reader into the disaster in order to urge recognition and acknowledgement and to elicit a passionate response. Ultimately, the imagery is so alive and rich that it conveys a sense of urgency to the deity, in order to provoke God to see, intervene and remedy the distress as well as appeal to human witnesses.

The poets of Lamentations have generated a depth of heartfelt poetry that only begins to assemble the variety of emotional responses, seasoned reflection and earnest supplication possible from the accounts or memories of survivors of some unnamed, comprehensive catastrophe. Its poetry creates a vivid space that invites the observance of and participation in searing accounts of suffering and disaster by drawing the reader or hearer into the drama of grief as a participant, as a witness and perhaps also as a fellow sufferer and comforter. The biblical Lamentations wields beauty in the face of dark despair by collecting swirling and disjointed reactions, feelings, memories and thoughts, and gathering them together in order to value them and offer a word for present and future generations. Further attention to its poetic composition and organization offers greater insight into the community responsible for the production of the poems and is the focus of the next chapter.

THE LITERATURE OF LAMENTATIONS: COMPOSITION HISTORY AND MATTERS OF FORM

Literary compositions provide the reader with clues to guide interpretation. When a reader encounters a document that starts with an address "Dear Jane" and continues with a number of lines or paragraphs, and then subsequently concludes with a salutation "Yours sincerely" followed by another name, he or she knows that the item at hand represents a letter and reads accordingly. Interpreters have isolated a number of genres in the biblical literature that guide reading and interpretation, such as legal material, genealogies, historiography, prophecy, love songs, prayers, proverbial sayings and poetry. Knowing the genre of a piece of biblical literature enables us to understand it better. Imagine the confusion and frustration that could result from reading a love song as a prophecy or a historical report instead of a prayer. Since knowing the genre of a piece of literature enables greater appreciation of its message, we will focus on matters related to genre in this chapter in order to provide a deeper and richer interpretive experience. At the same time, the poems of Lamentations have been gathered into a collection so the conclusion of the chapter focuses on its composition history in order to lay the groundwork for a consideration of the provenance of the material, which will be the focus of the next chapter.

THE GENRE OF LAMENTATIONS

It is generally agreed that the book of Lamentations represents a high mark in ancient Hebrew poetry as preserved in the Bible whose artistry and message can be better appreciated by attention to the generic elements of its poetry. In many respects, the poems of Lamentations correspond most closely to the lament psalms, which make up nearly one-third of the Psalter as the German scholar Hermann Gunkel suggested already in the early twentieth century (Gunkel and Begrich 1933). Gunkel's other observation that the psalms could further be classified according to whether the speaker was an individual or a group also informs interpretations of the book of Lamentations. Nevertheless, with the exception of the fifth chapter, which corresponds closely to a Communal Lament also spoken of as the Complaint of the People, the other chapters evidence the intermingling of different genres and thus represent mixed forms. In what follows, we will survey the debate about the genre of Lamentations as a means to better regard its impact on our interpretation of the individual poems and the book as a whole.

Laments and dirges

The poems of Lamentations represent the complaints and sorrowful musings of a number of people to disaster. At times they stem from an individual who complains vociferously about rampant devastation or his or her present ignominy (Lam. 1, 2 and most of 3 and 4), while at other times they flow forth from a community that expresses its public loss (3:40-7; 4:17-22; ch. 5). As a whole, the outlook and perspectives of the interweaving voices of the different personae correspond well to the lament genre, especially to the communal lament composed of the prayerful complaints and protests raised by a number of people (Gunkel and Begrich 1933: 136, 397–403; Ferris 1992; Miller 1994: 55–134; Westermann 1994; Gerstenberger 2001).

Communal laments are thought to have originated in public outcry over a natural or national disaster. Generally speaking, grief in the biblical literature and the ancient Near East (ANE) tends to find its expression in outward gestures – tearing the clothes, changing into sackcloth, strewing ashes or dust on the head, wailing, and sometimes cutting the body. In the book of Esther, for example, when Mordecai hears of the edict authorizing the slaughter of the Persian Jews, he "tore his clothes and put on sackcloth and ashes, and went through the city, wailing with a loud and bitter cry" (Est. 4:1). By comparison, words of prayer or laments tend to accompany organized and public responses to disaster in addition to outward signs of grief. So, while Mordecai protests a looming death sentence through loud wailing, the Jewish community prays together in a more organized manner, "there was great mourning among the Jews, with fasting and weeping *and lamenting,* and most of them lay in sackcloth and ashes" (Est. 4:3, italics added for emphasis). A public and communal response requires the articulation of grief, and poetry is the biblical vehicle for such expression (Berlin 2002: 22–3).

Communal laments capture the complaints of a group of people or the nation (Middlemas 2005: 144–70). In so doing, they contain details that align them with actual events that occurred in the history of ancient Israel, such as a great military defeat (Ps. 44), the desecration of the temple (Pss. 74, 79), the desolation of Judah (Isa. 63:7-64:11) and the loss of the Davidic king (Ps. 89). Communal laments almost always exhibit three main elements that have no consistent order of appearance in the poem:

(a) lamentation over a disastrous circumstance that has dire consequences for the community or nation

(b) a confession of trust otherwise known as the certainty of a hearing which outlines mythical or historical reasons to believe in the intervention of the deity to overturn said disaster

(c) an appeal or petition by which the community asks for divine help, rescue and restitution.

When regarded more generally, then, the biblical book of Lamentations which responds mournfully and painfully to a socio-political disaster as well as to a human catastrophe represents a lengthy example of the communal lament genre that is found elsewhere in the Old Testament.

Closely related to the lament of the people is the *qînah*, which is another form of poetry common to the ANE as well as to ancient Israel that captures the outpouring of the grief of individuals and communities over the death of a loved one and also the collapse of a city or nation. From its very outset, the book of Lamentations begins with a technical expression that has clear associations with funeral ceremonies, that is, the plaintive *ʾêkah* 'ah', 'how' or 'alas' that echoes the shocked and sombre responses made to the death of a loved one (Lam. 1:1). The mournful exclamation *ʾêkah* also provides the first word for chapters 2 and 4, which suggests that three of the five poems in Lamentations are biblical examples of the funeral dirge. We have discussed the *qînah* already in conjunction with the metre or rhythm of the poetry, but in this context the term indicates an additional *literary genre* that appears in the poems. According to Hedwig Jahnow's thorough study of the funeral song in ANE, biblical and contemporary folk literature, the dirge actually best captures the genre of the biblical Lamentations (Jahnow 1923: 168–91; cf. Lee 2002: 12–18).

In the simplest terms, the dirge "proclaims a death, announces a funeral, and summons a community to mourn" (Westermann 1994: 8–11). It is characterized by a series of motifs consistent with the context of a funeral, including a proclamation of death, an account of illness when it led to death, a retrospective look back at the life of the deceased, the expression of grief over the transitoriness of life, and the expression of bitter loss made through weeping and other physical reactions. When death was not by natural causes, funeral dirges also commonly included accusations against the perpetrator as well as caustic calls for justice or revenge. In the biblical literature as well as down through the ages and across cultures, women played prominent roles in the mourning rituals over the dead (Jer. 9:17-19; Ezek. 32:16; 2 Chron. 35:25) (Olyan 2004: 49–51). Nancy Lee provides a list of the many cultures where there is evidence of a recognized, even professional, role for women mourners and includes ancient Mesopotamia, Ugarit, ancient Israel, Egypt, Rome, ancient and modern Arabia as well as other contemporary cultures and nations (Lee 2002: 18). In the book of Lamentations a funeral eulogy is raised over the personified city of Jerusalem by an eyewitness who is usually identified as male, but could equally be a female given the prominent role professional women played as temple and funerary singers in ancient times (Lam. 1:1-11; 2:1-19). Poignantly, a speaker recounts, mourns and seems deeply resigned to the downfall of Jerusalem, the capital city of the kingdom of Judah, depicted as a figurative death. Nevertheless, the city of Jerusalem is also portrayed as a woman, as a widow and as a mother bereft of her children who herself grieves over the deceased (1:12-22; 2:20-2).

Many of the themes found in examples of funeral dirges intertwine in the poems of Lamentations, especially in chapters 1, 2 and 4, where they convey a sense of the devastating loss that accompanied the destruction of the city of Jerusalem. The attribution of the dirge genre to the poems of Lamentations has resulted in a lively debate about whether the elements of the eulogy override the notable features of the lament as well as the relationship of the various thematic elements. Claus Westermann has conducted one of the most thorough studies of genre as it pertains to the poems of Lamentations and he argues that the dirge ultimately fails to dominate the public lamentation that characterizes its poetry (Westermann 1994; see also Ferris 1992; Bouzard 1997). A way out of the impasse has been offered by Nancy Lee who regards the poems as examples of a genre made up of the deliberate intermingling of both types. She terms the mixed genre a communal dirge (Lee 2002: 1–37), which is one helpful way to understand the distinctive poetry of chapters 1, 2 and 4.

The elements of the communal lament intermingle with those of the funeral dirge in the poems of Lamentations, which perceptibly alters the meaning of the poems. As Adele Berlin helpfully characterizes, "A *qînah* is an outpouring of grief for a loss that has already occurred, with no expectation of reversing that loss; a communal lament is a plea to prevent a calamity or reverse it" (Berlin 2002: 24). The combination of a backward, mournful glance with a forward-looking, hopeful outlook in the poetry of Lamentations suggests that the collection addresses a crisis of unimaginable proportions in a creative and meaningful way. Notably, the interweaving of the dirge and the lament is not consistent in the poems in which the elements are found. As Tod Linafelt notes in his analysis of the genre of the poems, chapter 1 contains the greatest amount of dirge motifs. Otherwise, the elements consistent with the backward glance of the funeral song gradually decline over the course of the collection and the form beginning to dominate is that of the communal lament, which suggests a turn away from the retrospective, mournful glance to death toward life, survival and hope for the future (Linafelt 2000). When seen in this way, language consistent with the dirge and the lament appears as contributions from different community members who seek the means to express their loss, but fails to positively determine the genre of the poetry itself.

The city lament

With their focus on the destruction of the city of Jerusalem and the accompanying disasters that struck its physical structures and people, the poems of Lamentations, with the exception of the third and fifth chapters, also correspond closely to a type of literature known from the wider ANE known collectively as the Mesopotamian City Laments (MCL). Mesopotamian examples of city laments include a series of poems written after the fall of a city or the destruction of a local shrine and were recited at the point of restoration or on the occasion of the rededication of the temple. The MCL, which are dated to the end of the third millennium BCE, originated in ancient Sumer and include the five classic poems of the Lament over the Destruction of Ur, the Lament over the Destruction of Sumer and Ur, the Nippur Lament, the Eridu Lament, and the Uruk Lament. The Curse of Agade is sometimes included in the MCL, but it is slightly different in its formal elements. A series of daughter texts that are similar in form and content, but more formulaic in nature, are the *balags* and *eršemmas*, which were used in Mesopotamia as part of the temple liturgy from the first millennium BCE and well into the Greek period. The classic study of the relationship between the MCL and the biblical Lamentations is that of F. W. Dobbs-Allsopp (1993), who traces knowledge of the MCL within traditions of the Old Testament, especially within prophecies of judgement and some Psalms.

There remains a vigorous and heated debate about the relationship between the MCL genre and the biblical book of Lamentations with scholars tending to argue either for or against awareness and direct dependence (see the recent list in Salters 2010: 13–15). In general, the similarity of themes has been used to argue that the biblical poets borrowed directly from the Mesopotamian poems (Gwaltney 1983). Although the details of expression vary, interpreters point to thematic overlap – the total destruction of a city and its temple; divine intentionality and causality of the destruction; the prominent role attributed to a female speaker, who is represented by a goddess in the ANE city laments, but personified Jerusalem in keeping with biblical tradition; the abandonment of the city by the chief deity of the pantheon in the MCL and Yahweh in Lamentations; and the desire for restoration. At the same time, there are distinct differences between the Mesopotamian examples and the biblical Lamentations that could equally suggest that similarities arose from correspondences in the subject matter – the destruction of a city and its chief shrine (classically, McDaniel 1968).

A way out of what appears to be an impasse on this point has been offered by Dobbs-Allsopp, who argues for a city lament genre already evidenced within the biblical tradition in the prophetic literature and some of the psalms (Dobbs-Allsopp 1993). He finds that ancient Israel had knowledge of the various motifs and themes of the MCL long before the composition of Lamentations which were taken up and fashioned in a distinctive biblical ideology. The awareness of motifs consistent with the MCL would then come about through the use of themes found already in other biblical literature rather than from direct dependence on the ANE examples of lamentation over fallen cities. Also worthy of note in the discussion is a point raised by Adele Berlin. The themes and motifs shared between the MCL and the biblical Lamentations also appear in other types of literature as in treaty curses and the curses listed in Deuteronomy 28 (Berlin 2002: 28). Certainly, the poets of Lamentations had a wealth of literature to draw upon in the articulation of their grief over the fall of Jerusalem and how they explore and develop those motifs, rather than their origin, is of more interest to the task at hand.

There are telling differences between the MCL and Lamentations. For one, the MCL serve as a justification for the destruction of a city, while the Jerusalem laments find the loss incomprehensible and seek restoration (see Berlin 2002: 28–30). In addition, the MCL end on a positive note in which restoration is made possible through the good will of the gods. The lack of a hopeful conclusion in the biblical Lamentations offers one argument against the knowledge of and direct borrowing from the MCL. However, the lack of restoration or a hopeful outlook may not be decisive in determining whether or not there was direct dependence on the Mesopotamian examples. As Edward Greenstein points out the motif of the joyful ending evidenced in the MCL pieces corresponds with the return of the gods which would have been symbolized in cultic ritual with the parading and restoration of the divine statues of the relevant deities (Greenstein 2008). Arguably, the biblical Lamentations does not include the motif of God's return and the celebrations that took place at that time because there was no divine statue of the deity in ancient Israel. According to this view, the poems of Lamentations avoid the restoration so typical of the MCL in order to remain consistent with the biblical position on aniconism. Another striking difference between Lamentations and the MCL is the puzzling lack of the dominant image associated with the god's destruction of the city in the Mesopotamian examples – the violent storm. The image of a violent, swirling storm appears to inform the shaping of the book rather than signify the complete execution of divine wrath as in the

MCL (Middlemas 2004). In keeping with biblical tradition, the deity's wrath in the book of Lamentations is more closely aligned with the image of the deity as the divine warrior.

Certainly, a number of connections between the biblical Lamentations and the MCL suggest strong correspondence to, even knowledge of, the Mesopotamian examples. In addition to the weeping goddess who laments the destruction of her city as an obvious parallel to the grieving Jerusalem personified as a woman in the biblical Lamentations, the depiction of the former city as a ruin upon which wild animals roam, "May foxes that frequent ruined mounds sweep with their tail" (Curse of Agade l. 257), is strikingly similar to a motif in the fifth chapter, "Mount Zion, which lies desolate; jackals prowl over it" (5:18). At the same time, direct dependence should not be the exclusive talking point in the debate. Surely, the similarity of the circumstances that led to the composition as well as the subject matter – themes of human suffering, feelings of punishment and abandonment by the deity, and the destruction of beloved and revered symbols of governance, society, and religious observances – that is common to the poems of Lamentations as well as to the MCL suggests awareness of the poetry of the loss of a beloved city and its symbolic physical structures, when not direct dependence. In crafting their own response to the fall of their chief city and the destruction of their central shrine, the poets of Lamentations possibly not only drew on Mesopotamian examples that may or may not have been mediated within the biblical tradition, but they also faithfully and emphatically composed their reactions and sense of loss in ways consistent with expressions of tragedy found elsewhere in the biblical literature.

The biblical Lamentations probably does not represent examples of direct borrowing from the literature of the ANE, but rather innovative adaptations consistent with the theology and traditions of ancient Israel. So, on the one hand, the poems of Lamentations provide reflections on a tragedy that attest to the cross-fertilization and cultural contact that often took place in the ancient world. On the other hand, there are striking differences between the Mesopotamian laments over cities and temples and the biblical Lamentations. Notably, interpreters regard the biblical poems to be more graphic and even gruesome in their portrayal of the lingering effects of the catastrophe and more focused on the suffering of the members of society than on the destruction of the temple when compared to Mesopotamian examples (Linafelt 2000: 49–61). Moreover and in sharp contrast to the MCL, the poems of Lamentations conclude with a haunting question related to whether Yahweh will ever adhere to the covenant, choose to return to the people, and bring about recompense and restoration. The lingering and agonized communal query at the conclusion of the work begs the question once again of the genre of the whole.

Penitential prayer

The communal laments, the funeral dirge and the MCL certainly contribute important generic elements to the poetry of Lamentations. However, with greater attention to the centre rather than the periphery, it is equally possible to argue that the poems align better to a different genre altogether, that of penitential prayer. Examples of penitential prayer stem from the Second Temple period and represent a type of communal lamentation that focuses less on complaint and more on seeking an end to the desolation and ruination of the city of Jerusalem that is accompanied by the ongoing suffering of the community in exile (Ezra 9; Neh. 1:5-11, 9; cf. Ps. 106). An example of the sentiments expressed in penitential prayer appears in Nehemiah 1 (the classic study is Boda 1999: 21–73);

> O LORD God of heaven, the great and awesome God who keeps covenant and steadfast love with those who love [god] and keep the commandments … We have offended you deeply … Remember the word that you commanded your servant Moses, 'If you are unfaithful, I will scatter you among the peoples; but if you return to me and keep my commandments and do them, though your outcasts are under the farthest skies, I will gather them … to the place at which I have chosen to establish my name.' They are your servants and your people ….
>
> (Neh. 1:5-10 selected)

The defining element of penitential prayer as opposed to a communal lament is the inclusion of an admission of past and present sin. Examples of the genre also include a statement of faith focused on the greatness and grace of God, who steadfastly abides by the covenant and acts righteously on behalf of and for the covenant people.

According to a close analysis of Lamentations, language consistent with penitential prayer is particularly noticeable in the third chapter (Lam. 3:28-9, 48-51), although statements reminiscent of the genre appear scattered elsewhere (1:2, 16, 17, 19; 2:10, 11) (Boda 2008). Close correspondence between Lamentations and penitential prayer has tended to be overlooked, perhaps because some of its elements are more general in nature (Cooper 2001) and have thus been mistakenly attributed to the lament genre. Correspondences between the two genres are so close, in fact, that penitential prayer is thought to represent a subcategory of the overarching genre of the communal lament (Bautch 2003).

The genre of penitential prayer, which is also found more widely in the ANE and in Mesopotamian petitions and literature (Cooper 2001), is most apparent in the third chapter where the complaint of an individual sufferer is transformed into a call for communal repentance (3:40-8) that leads to a new realization of divine intervention or at least urgent calls for such by the lamenter (esp. vv. 52-66). Lamentations 3 aligns with penitential prayer through the significance placed on the grace of God in a section of instruction placed in the exact centre of the collection (in vv. 22-39). The core belief in the central verses articulates hope in Yahweh and outlines the appropriate human response, and can be delineated thus (from Middlemas 2006: 521).

Verses 22-4   Reasons to hope in Yahweh: characteristics that support belief in divine restoration and redemption

Verses 25-30   Human Response: how to respond to and be the recipient of the merciful intervention of the deity

Verses 31-9   Reasons to hope in Yahweh: characteristics that support belief in divine restoration and sovereignty.

Through the didactic section set at the heart of Lamentations, the poet focuses attention on the need and importance of the human being positioned faithfully and respectfully before a good and merciful God.

The central chapter of Lamentations transforms the complaints that surround it into advice to the individual petitioner to hold onto faith in the character of God while in the midst of suffering. The lone petitioner of chapter 3 models what is considered to be the proper and sanctioned response to cataclysmic disaster (Middlemas 2006). Similarly, Mary Conway finds:

> The role of the female voice of Zion is primarily to give voice to the suffering and evoke sympathy, appealing to the mercy of God, whereas the male voices of the Speaker and *Geber*, while honouring the expression of pain, are intended to emphasize the need to accept responsibility and to find a way forward.
>
> (Conway 2012: 116–17)

Finally, Boda emphasizes the role of penitential prayer and asserts, "Through its didactic style it questions the dominance of lament over penitence, calling the community to a confessional penitence and providing a liturgical template for their communal response" (Boda 2008: 95). The central section of Lamentations 3 transforms the individual lament into an example of penitential prayer and also the laments assembled in the collection. Suitably, then, the community's laments conclude with penitence (in ch. 5), while awaiting divine restorative intervention like that attested to by the *geber* at the close of his prayer in chapter 3 (vv. 49-66).

As oft noted, the third chapter is at odds with the other poems, generically and thematically. Chapter 3 is distinguished by an interplay of genres, including the complaint of an individual to which a wisdom-like didactic lesson, a confession of sin and a lament that in outlook verges on a prayer of thanksgiving are appended. Notably, attention to the fate of the city of Jerusalem as a physical location and as the despairing personified city so prominently displayed in chapters 1, 2, 4 and 5 is almost non-existent in the third chapter (but see vv. 48-51). There is also the noticeable lack of attention to traditions associated with the city of Jerusalem as found in Zion theology, which is characterized by the divine choice of the city and its inviolability as well as the selection of the Davidic king. Instead of attention to Jerusalem, the promises made to Zion and a marked concern about human misery, the third chapter focuses almost myopically on a single suffering individual who is moved from despair and anguish to not only recognize God's saving nature and activity, but to also confess his own sins. When seen in this way, the ascription of the city lament genre to Lamentations fails to account for the distinctive message of the third chapter, which not only shifts away from the focus on Zion, but also mutes, perhaps even corrects, the complaint. The distinctive third chapter and its possible relation to the final poem suggest the need for a wider perspective on considerations of the genre of Lamentations.

City lament over Zion

A number of different generic elements from the lament, the dirge, the MCL and the penitential prayer intertwine in the biblical Lamentations, but as yet do not provide "a" single genre for the poems. Instead, the intermingling suggests that no single literary genre was felt adequate to convey the tragedy captured so poignantly in Lamentations, in particular:

It had to do with the devastation of a confident people, the loss of statehood, the collapse of the economy, the destruction of social structures, the relocation of many families, the removal of religious props, and the dashing of theological positions.

(Salters 2010: 13)

At the background of Lamentations is catastrophic collapse that reverberates in every facet and on every level of society. The devastation in and surrounding Jerusalem that is so movingly, painfully and evocatively described through the imagery of the poems suggests that a tremendous socio-political disaster served as the catalyst for the creation of a totally new genre in which a variety of poetic, literary and prayerful elements were drawn upon in its fashioning.

In this vein, Adele Berlin has argued that the various generic elements intertwine in a great Lament for Zion (Berlin 2002: 22–6) that is essentially the poetic inversion of a series of psalms that celebrate the beauty and choice of Jerusalem. A number of psalms in the Psalter are classified as the Songs of Zion (Pss. 46, 48, 50, 76, 84, 87 and 122). In the Songs of Zion, the psalmists rejoice over Jerusalem as the location from whence Yahweh chooses to rule as well as the home appointed by the deity for the reign of the Davidic kings and the earthly temple, as in the hymn, "Great is the LORD … in the city of our God. [God's] holy mountain, beautiful in elevation, is the joy of all the earth, Mount Zion … the city of the great King." (Ps. 48:1-2, selected). In stark contrast, the poems of Lamentations contain expressions of shock and horror at the dissolution of the edifices and religious, political, and social symbols of the capital city of Jerusalem and the loss of the Davidic king. Without recourse to a historical discussion, it is, nevertheless, possible to assert that Lamentations inverts the themes found in the celebrations of Zion in the Psalter. Following great systemic and societal collapse as well as the emotional and physical suffering of an innumerable amount of people, including those who remained among the ruins and those deported from a native homeland, the survivors grasped for a means to express individual and communal grief. Moreover, the Songs of Zion fell silent in the aftermath of disaster (see Ps. 137). Cut off from God, "A mourner or penitent was not permitted to engage in public joy" (Berlin 2002: 26) and had to invent a new expression, which seems to be reflected in the compact collection of Lamentations.

To Berlin, then, the book of Lamentations represents an innovative and new genre fashioned from various examples of poetry and literary types found in the tradition of biblical Israel and in the ANE – the great Lament over Zion. Perhaps no genre alone was felt adequate to express the unfathomable loss of the city that was once considered and celebrated as the beauty of all the earth (see also Berges 2002: 50–1). The poems of Lamentations memorialize siege, invasion and downfall as well as the immeasurable grief that accompanied destruction, illness, maiming and death in a series of moving and lengthy poems that allow a grieving people to express their sorrow at the fate of Jerusalem, their beloved city.

Penitential lament over Zion

The carefully argued theses of Berlin, Boda and Dobbs-Allsopp are not mutually exclusive. Dobbs-Allsopp has shown that there is more than a passing correspondence to the imagery and motifs of the MCL in the biblical Lamentations. At the same time, he suggests that Lamentations represents an internal Hebrew example of a city lament, which corresponds well to Berlin's argument for the emergence of a distinctive genre that acts as a counter to the Hymns to Zion in the Psalter. For Berlin, Lamentations represents a City Lament over Zion, which is clearly a poem relevant to the situation in Judah, but it may share, nevertheless, images, motifs and themes with the MCL, which were pertinent to the communities in which they arose. It is also relevant that the city lament genre fades into the background in the third poem, which focuses on and uses the figure of a suffering individual to call a broken community to reflect on its loss in worship through petition, prayer and confession. When seen this way, the persuasive argument of Boda to better account for penitential prayer adds a nuance to the emphasis on the city lament. Notably, the collection ends with a lengthy prayer of people who mention past and present sin amid their complaints at an ignoble present. They pray and hope for the divine intervention that the *geber* had already sensed at the conclusion of his penitential prayer in the third chapter. After all, it is only a small step from the Jerusalem lament to post-exilic penitential prayer like those lifted up by Ezra and Nehemiah (Ezra 9; Neh. 1 and 9) (Berlin 2002: 26).

What has been less accounted for is the shaping of the collection as a whole and its contribution to the debate about the literary genre of Lamentations. Berlin has drawn attention to the fashioning of a new genre to speak of the loss of the city and the use of various elements of different motifs therein. In the early days of attributing genre, what is also spoken of as the form category of a work, the debate centred on relatively clear examples of different genres, the communal lament or the funeral dirge. Through close analysis, the genres applicable to the crafting of Lamentations became more numerous and other examples are thought to represent the mix of elements in the poems, a wisdom didactic interlude, the MCL and the penitential prayer. None of the different genres determine each poem of Lamentations or even the whole work. To this debate belongs brief consideration of the last chapter, which has tended to be thought of as an almost pure communal lament (so also in my own work, Middlemas 2007: 38–40), but which includes elements not consistent with the genre. The book of Lamentations ends with a prayer in chapter 5 and the ascription of its form or genre influences or should influence an interpretation of the whole composition.

Like chapter 3, the fifth and final chapter is at odds with the other poems in Lamentations in its form and content. In form, it deviates from the acrostic and evidences single evenly balanced lines in each of its twenty-two verses. Furthermore, the poem contains no elements of the funeral dirge, scarce traces of the MCL and almost no attention to the infrastructure or institutions of the city of Jerusalem. Instead, the fifth poem commences by addressing the deity and calling for attention to a dire situation of communal concern, "Remember, O LORD, what has befallen us; look and see our disgrace" (5:1). In content, the final poem contains a lengthy section of complaint that is at variance with examples of the Communal Lament in its length and sustained focus on the present misery of the people (vv. 2-18). The lengthy lament includes a complaint about foreign sovereignty and the suffering of various members of society from famine, sexual assault and oppressive labour demands. Notably, the form of the poem is slightly different than other laments in that it opens with a call to God to remember, concludes with urgent questions to the deity and the fear of sustained divine rejection, contains only a brief statement of a reason to believe in divine relief, and the lament itself is broken by two statements that attest to or confess sin or wrongdoing. Because Lamentations 5 does not correspond so closely to the genre of the communal lament as often argued (compare Pss. 44, 74, 79), the confusion noted between communal laments and penitential prayer comes to mind (e.g. Cooper 2001).

Very preliminarily, I would like to suggest that Lamentations ends with a penitential prayer that has already been presaged by the petition of the third chapter. Boda isolated five elements that appear in penitential prayer: expression of and the request for divine recognition of a great distress, the recollection of examples of divine intervention or promises, the admission of past and present sin, a theological orientation to God who keeps the covenant, and less concern with the concept of divine discipline and favouring instead expressions of trust in God's grace or might. The fifth chapter contains all of these elements. Attention to present misery occupies lengthy sections (vv. 2-6, 8-16a, 17-18, 20). The request for divine recognition opens the chapter (v. 1), and the poem also contains a brief statement of theological orientation that confirms trust in God's eternal reign (v. 19). Confessions of sin, past and present, interrupt the lament of distress in two places (vv. 7, 16b), but the focus is not on the weight of the sin, but rather on hope in the fulfilment of divine promises made possible through divine restoration (v. 21).

What sets chapter 5 off from other examples of penitential prayer is that it includes the people's fear that God's rejection will continue indefinitely. The uncertainty expressed about the return of the deity to the covenant and the people suggests at least to me that chapter 5 is an earlier or alternative example of the type of penitential prayer isolated by Boda. At the same time, the poem is a bulwark of steadfast trust in God's might because it ascribes the present misery to divine determination. It is not that God cannot overturn the present distress, but rather the community lingers on the painful query that relates to whether the deity will choose to do so. Although the petitioners of the poem pray to God, acknowledging wrongdoing by former and current generations, the focus is not on sin, but rather on the inaction or inattentiveness of the deity. In this way, it comes closest in sentiment to a penitential prayer found in Trito- or Third Isaiah (Isa. 63:7–64:11) (Gregory 2007; Middlemas 2005: 156–8 and 2007: 41–3).

Alan Cooper conducted a short but important examination of Mesopotamian examples of penitential prayer that he compared with Lamentations, especially chapter 3 (Cooper 2001). In distinction to the penitential prayers that are the focus of Boda's work and that stem from the mid- to late Persian period (including Ezra 9; Neh. 1, 9; Dan. 9; Ps. 106), the Mesopotamian examples focus on human suffering as a means to motivate divine favour. The correlation to sin and its consequences is downplayed or omitted entirely with preference given to the incomprehensibility of God's anger in the Mesopotamian prayers. The only hope for the community then is to "evoke God's mysterious love" (Cooper 2001: 15). I would argue that the whole shape of Lamentations corresponds to a lengthy penitential prayer that is punctuated with different generic forms to capture a sense of the loss with which it deals. The showcase chapter 3 draws attention to the importance of penitential prayer and pushes towards the concluding prayer 5, which is also an example of the genre appropriately placed on the lips of the grieving community. Regarding

Lamentations as an example of penitential prayer that shares some commonality with Mesopotamian examples helps to explain the overwhelmingly lengthy and graphic presentation of human suffering therein, the association of the wrath of God with the actions of the divine warrior fighting brutally against god's own people, and the yearning need for and anxiety about divine recognition of the present distress and the possibility of salvific intervention in the future.

As a whole, the poems of Lamentations create one long, extended and unified penitential lament prayer over Zion. The Penitential Lament over Zion responds to a unique event in the history of ancient Israel, the fall of Jerusalem, with a new expression produced by the intermingling of different genres. The crisis at its background is related to a great catastrophe that has struck the city of Jerusalem and the kingdom of Judah, which threatens the enduring commitment of God's promises to a chosen people and a sacred place. In so doing, the dramatic political circumstances raised questions about the efficacy of the covenant and God's loyalty to the covenant people, which are essentially encapsulated in the questions raised in the very last verses of the whole collection;

> Why have you forgotten us completely?
> Why have you forsaken us these many days?
> … Unless you have utterly rejected us,
> are angry with us beyond measure. (5:20, 22)

The book of Lamentations in its entirety, then, represents a mixed genre and a new expression that can be characterized fruitfully as a Penitential Lament over Zion.

THE FORMATION OF GRIEF

The consideration of the shape of Lamentations as a lengthy penitential prayer draws attention to the fact that a number of biblical books are organized to convey meaning. Form, content and message intertwine. A number of scholars have worked out the relation of the form and function of the psalms, particularly with respect to the laments (Brueggemann 1995; see the discussion in Middlemas 2005: 220–6). Walter Brueggemann speaks of a formfulness to grief when he shows how lament psalms with the exception of Psalm 88 move through situations of disorientation captured by the lamenter to reorientation to the deity vocalized in praise or confessions of trust. For all the chaotic images, shifts in speaker and points of view, and different themes, the five seemingly independent poems of Lamentations also cohere. When considered holistically, the poems correspond to a concentric pattern like that of a centrifuge (Grossberg 1989: 83–104). Differently conceived, the wisdom interlude that focuses on hope in the centre of the collection serves as the peaceful eye around which storm winds of tragedy and suffering swirl (Middlemas 2004). As a whole, then, the book of Lamentations is unified in its diversity, which betrays a sense of purpose to its composition.

Meaning is also thought be expressed in the shape of the biblical book. William Shea argued that in its entirety the collection corresponds to a funeral dirge (Shea 1979). Attention to the use of the acrostic and number of lines suggests that the book of Lamentations is actually shaped to correspond to and evoke a *qînah* or the 3:2 limping rhythm of the dirge in which 3 beats represent uncontrollable weeping and 2 beats the slippage into despair. When seen this way, the first three chapters are lengthy recitals of personal and communal outcries that respond to tragedy in poems of sixty-six lines, while the final two chapters are shorter, punctuations of dejection and even doubt captured in forty-four and twenty-two lines, respectively. As Lamentations draws to a close the petitioners are exhausted, even despondent, towards the point of silence overwhelmed by the depth of their grief and suffering as well as the weight of the uncertainty of divine abandonment. Although compelling, Shea's suggestion of the correspondence between the overall shape of Lamentations and the dirge has not been followed by the majority of interpreters, partly because it fails to take into consideration the content and form of the chapters, which are what we shall attempt to do now.

Lamentations certainly has the feel of a constructed collection. The use of the acrostic links four of the poems as does the subject matter. In addition, the first two poems are very alike and, except for thematic differences, they correspond almost identically in terms of their structural components. Each verse contains a stanza of three cola introduced by a letter of the Hebrew alphabet beginning with the first Hebrew consonant *aleph*, continuing in sequential order, and containing twenty-two verses of sixty-six lines that correspond to the number of the consonants in the alphabet from *aleph* to *taw*. The fourth chapter follows this general pattern, except that each stanza contains two cola, so that its twenty-two verses actually equal forty-four lines. Notably, these three poems, chapters 1, 2 and 4, are further linked in that they all begin with the mournful question or exclamation of *'êkah* 'alas' and concentrate on destruction in post-war Jerusalem and to a lesser extent the territory of Judah.

In form, the *'êkah* chapters (chs. 1, 2 and 4) contain a combination of elements of the communal lament and the funeral dirge in varying amounts. As Tod Linafelt observes, the most frequent occurrence of elements of the funeral dirge appears in the first chapter, gradually lessens in the second, and is most infrequent, almost non-existent, in the fourth (Linafelt 2000: 75). The form beginning to dominate over the course of the collection is the communal lament, which is related to the penitential prayer that appears in the fifth chapter. In addition, the interaction of two principle groups of speaking voices also set apart the *'êkah* poems as a subset within the collection. In chapters 1 and 2, two speaking voices intermingle, the eyewitness and the personified city, while in the fourth chapter the testimony of an eyewitness gives way to a communal response. The 'we' voices that conclude the fourth chapter form a natural bridge to the communal 'we' that prays in the fifth chapter. In contrast to the other poems, though, the final poem is alphabetic rather than acrostic. It contains a communal penitential prayer, which was notably presaged by the communal petition in the third chapter (3:40-7).

The third chapter stands out in its use of the acrostic, its mix of formal elements and its themes. In comparison to the *'êkah* poems in chapters 1, 2 and 4, the third chapter illustrates an impressive triple acrostic. Each consonant of the Hebrew alphabet sequentially introduces three couplets a piece. Like chapters 1 and 2, the third poem contains sixty-six lines, but the number of lines in the third chapter corresponds to the number of its verses. All of the verses are bi-cola and the 3:2 rhythm of the *qînah* is most consistently found. The staccato, emphatic cry evoked is captured well in the English in Ronald Knox's translation:

> Ah, what straits have I not known, under the avenging rod!
> Asked I for light, into deeper shadow the Lord's guidance led me;
> Always upon me, none other, falls endlessly the blow.
> Broken this frame, under the wrinkled skin, the sunk flesh.
> Bitterness of despair fills my prospect, walled in on every side;
> Buried in darkness, and like the dead, interminably ….
> (Lam. 3:1-6 in Knox 1956: 734)

With its highly stylized, rhythmic triple acrostic, the third chapter represents the literary masterpiece of the collection. In addition, the intensive use of a more formal acrostic demands that it be regarded as one unit, in spite of the diversity of the material therein.

In order to consider more carefully the shape of Lamentation or the forming of its grief, it is helpful to take a deeper look at the third chapter, which is set off from the others. It contains a mixture of formal elements including an individual lament (3:1-21), a didactic interlude akin to a wisdom saying (vv. 22-39), a seemingly truncated prayer of confession by a plural subject, 'we' (vv. 40-7), and concludes with another individual lament that contains elements of or even corresponds to a prayer of thanksgiving (vv. 48-66). Equally distinctive is the focus of the poem, which narrows dramatically to concentrate almost myopically on the personal tragedy and sufferings of an individual. The speaker even introduces himself with the phrase *ʾănî haggeḇer*, which the editors of the NRSV translate as "I am the one (the man)" (3:1-3). The Hebrew term *geḇer* is used in the Old Testament with reference to a strong man, a soldier, or a person of high social or political status (v. 1). Since features consistent with a military person are not salient, the term conjures up the image of a nobleman in exile, like the king, a priest or some other member of the ruling class who was forcibly deported from Jerusalem after its defeat in battle.

The third chapter turns away from grieving the dead that so captured the outlook of the *ĕkah* poems and towards the myopic, narrow focus of a noble individual brought low. Strikingly, then, the aching question of 'how' of chapter 1, 2 and 4 is replaced by the individual 'I, myself' in the third chapter. Similarly striking is the complete loss of the communal lament and the funeral dirge so prominent in the other chapters to be replaced by a mixed composition that functions to draw attention to the need for and model penitential prayer. Finally, the individual mourner shows almost no concern for and about the city: neither its inhabitants nor its infrastructure.

The immediate impression, then, of the third chapter is that it is deliberately distinguished from the other poems. In addition to its impressive acrostic, length of verses and distinctive generic elements, it contains themes that are at odds with the other chapters. The suffering of the individual leads to a rare moment of reflection and contemplation that is akin to a wisdom teaching. In the wisdom section, the focus is on correction rather than prayer (Westermann 1994: 191–3), on silent submission rather than protest (Middlemas 2006) and on reasons to focus on the divine saviour rather than the divine warrior (Middlemas 2006). The autobiographical character functions not to situate suffering in the experiences of an individual, but rather to move the community to penitence (Boda 2008), which is notably how the prayer in chapter 5 concludes the collection.

The communal penitential lament of the final poem outlines the persistence of ongoing distress in a lengthy account (5:2-18) and brings misery to the deity's attention, mentions past and present wrongdoing, and urges God to attend to and rectify a painful present by restoring the community. All the speakers who have raged, grieved and commented heretofore gather together to convey despair coupled with deeply troubling accounts of hardship and the ongoing oppression and persecution of foreign rule and the seeming abandonment of their God. Instead of protest, the community at the conclusion of Lamentations prays. Their persistent recognition of human suffering fades away into a haunting concern about whether the deity will ever choose to respond, intervene and bring recompense in a penitential prayer that harkens back to that of the third chapter. Unlike chapter 3 which ended with the petitioner perceiving that the deity was fighting on his behalf, for example "You have taken up my cause, O Lord, you have redeemed my life" (v. 58, selected from 56–8), the final poem concludes on a note of uncertainty about whether the deity will choose to intervene. The ending leaves open the opportunity for and possibly even anticipates a new act of divine salvation.

There are reasons to believe that the third chapter stems from a different perspective that essentially "corrects" the complaints and assertions found in the other chapters (Middlemas 2006). The individual lamentation that begins chapter 3 (vv. 1-21) actually leads into a sermon-like section that incorporates wisdom-like reflections (vv. 22-39). The two different formal units, the individual lament and the wisdom interlude, are actually integrated into a distinct interpretive unit through the use of the term *geber* which appears so strikingly and startlingly at the poem's opening. In fact, the term *geber* demarcates a distinct interpretive unit (vv. 1, 39) and also punctuates its message (vv. 27, 35). Significantly, the term *geber* does not appear elsewhere outside of this unit in Lamentations. Through appending a wisdom-like sermonic reflection to an individual lament, the poet transforms the genre of complaint into the opportunity to believe and hope in the deity, and also supplies an optimistic vision for the individual as well as for the community to hold onto in the middle of the crisis.

In content and especially in conjunction with the depiction and speech of the individual lamenter, the first section in chapter 3 is also at variance with that of the other poems. While the individual lamenter is like the personified city of Jerusalem who speaks of her personal agony in the first two chapters, his speech is, nevertheless, distinguished by its very narrow focus on his own, very personal torment to the exclusion of attention to the destruction of the city and the suffering that takes place around him. Moreover, unlike the eyewitness who testified to the severity of the devastation in Jerusalem and otherwise interacted with the personified city by seeking and failing to comfort her (Middlemas 2019: 353–6), the *geber* complains about his own personal misery. The *geber* is the only explicitly individual male figure who laments and, in this, serves as a foil to personified Jerusalem who also lifts up lamentation to God. The *geber* is further distinguished from the individual figures in the other chapters in that the language he uses to relate his experiences includes images of being driven, in captivity, in a pit, and imprisoned. Figuratively, the imagery resonates with how the exiles resettled in Babylonia conceptualize their experience in the biblical tradition elsewhere (Smith 1989; Berlin 2002: 84–5). In addition, the experiences of the solitary, suffering individual are used to introduce and lead into a wisdom interlude that serves a reflective and didactic purpose. In so doing, it responds to and also corrects the protestations against affliction and the implication of divine culpability and injustice articulated, particularly, although not exclusively, by personified Jerusalem in chapters 1 and 2 (Middlemas 2006).

The strong man's meditation responds to and provides an alternative and corrective theological lesson to the doubt and emphasis on unjust suffering articulated in all the other poems. The complaint of an individual, then, is adapted to convey a credo of faith, admonition and instruction (3:1-39) and thus serves as the natural backdrop for introspection, like that for the recognition of sin and communal confession that follows (vv. 40-7). It, then, leads ultimately to the belief that in spite of evidence to the contrary the deity will intervene in a just and compassionate way to rectify the injury (vv. 48-66). When seen as a whole, the third chapter stands out within Lamentations. It emphasizes the need to stay silent and accept suffering as correction from God, advocates the confession of sin as response, and focuses on God's justice, mercy and advocacy, rather than the themes of abuse, abandonment and capriciousness so prominent in the poems outwith the central poem. These are features that at the outset suggest that the third chapter stems from a different hand, time or place than the other poems and will influence a discussion of the cultural context of the material that is the task for the next chapter.

There is an artificiality to the poems of Lamentations themselves that suggests a conscious and theological or ideological design in their composition. The use of the acrostic, the association with the alphabet, the observable parallelism between chapters, the centring of the only truly hopeful passage in the absolute middle of the collection, the swirling of images of misery, suffering, despair, horror around a meditative, peaceful core, and the hints of correction to alternative viewpoints or expressions all suggest that the book of Lamentations in its final form stems from the hand of an editor who collected and arranged the material. The final editor may also have imposed the acrostic on chapters 1–4 and arranged chapter 3 as the centrepiece of the poems, using inherited material in his or her composition of the individual lament.

The intentionality observed in the shaping of the poems helps us more clearly understand why there remains a debate about their origin. Do they represent oral compositions that were later written down as argued by some interpreters (Westermann 1994; Lee 2002; Salters 2010) or an organized, literary composition from the outset (Renkema 1998; Assis 2009)? A couple of factors may help adjudicate this debate. It is well known that the MCL, which correspond in remarkable ways to the motifs, themes and sentiments of the biblical Lamentations, were actually written at some distance, estimated at fifty or sixty years, from the events which they purport to describe. Furthermore, Trauma Studies' research has revealed that memories of traumatic events resurface chaotically, unexpectedly and sporadically over time. The process of shaping them for memory, to memorialize them, is a concerted act that often took place at some distance from the events to which they relate. The poems of Lamentations suggest that concerted attempts were made to capture the expressions of suffering and objections thereto by survivors of a great catastrophe into a meaningful interpretive whole. When this may have taken place is the topic to which we now turn.

THE HISTORICAL BACKGROUND
OF LAMENTATIONS

The biblical book of Lamentations includes various expressions of raw emotions, thoughtful reflection and prayer that at first glance stem from more than one anonymous poet. At the same time, the collection consists of a fairly homogeneous group of material that includes reactions to some unnamed disaster. The nature of the composition of the poems of Lamentations needs to be taken into consideration in any discussion of their provenance as do references, however ambiguous, to historical events. In this respect, various details emerge, many tantalizingly vague, such as a catastrophic invasion and its aftermath, the desecration of an important sanctuary, the collapse of city walls, starvation from the famine conditions associated with siege warfare, the loss of political and social independence, the imposition of foreign rule, the forced migration of a number of diverse members of the community, and death at the hands of an enemy. Among this jumble of adverse conditions, there remains no determinative detail with which to specify clearly the event to which the poems relate, although the location of Jerusalem as the site of the devastation is most probable due to copious references to the city (e.g. Lam. 1:4, 6, 7, 8, 17; 2:1, 8, 10, 13, 15) and to the temple (e.g. 1:10; 2:1, 6, 7).

The ascription of date, authorship and provenance to biblical books, especially those classified as poetry, remains contentious. The vague nature of allusions, copious figurative language use, the lack of historical reference points, and general applicability to many different events and situations present a number of difficulties for dating Lamentations (Provan 1991: 7–19). Nevertheless, this chapter concentrates on the provenance of the poems with the evidence available because the likely historical circumstances in which they arose help us to better understand the thought that took place. The discussion of provenance also tends to be linked to matters of composition, particularly to whether inherited material has been updated by an editor. Greater awareness of the history of the transmission of the material which we considered preliminarily in the last chapter in conjunction with its composition history forms part of the enquiry of the present chapter. Traditional dating and linguistic analyses also contribute constructive data for our consideration. In this chapter, then, we will look at the question of provenance according to the topics of issues of composition, socio-historical background, and mourning rituals in the Bible and the ancient Near East (ANE).

MATTERS OF COMPOSITION

Inner-biblical correspondence

Although we are not in a position to identify a particular author, like the prophet Jeremiah, for the book of Lamentations, indications from linguistic evidence and biblical correspondence bolster the association of the collection with the period of time subsequent to the downfall of Judah in 587 BCE. Close attention to linguistic and grammatical matters suggests a similarity between the language of Lamentations and the style of late biblical Hebrew that is found in biblical books from the sixth to fifth centuries BCE. Notably, Lamentations lacks features found in the books of Esther, Ecclesiastes or Qoheleth, Ezra, Nehemiah, and Chronicles, which are dated mid- to late Persian period (roughly 450–331 BCE) (Dobbs-Allsopp 1998). Commonality with the language, motifs and outlook of the books of Jeremiah, Deutero-Isaiah and Ezekiel tends to reinforce the evidence from the linguistic data, which would substantiate a time in the sixth century, extending from the Babylonian triumph over the Southern Kingdom and the fall of Jerusalem (587 BCE) into the Persian period that began with the capture of Babylon in 539 BCE by the Persian king, Cyrus.

The linguistic evidence corresponds with the thematic. Lamentations is survival literature, that is, the poetic attempt to capture the despair, turmoil, grief process, suffering, even hope, of the survivors of a great catastrophe that is widely understood to be the seminal event of the sixth century – the fall of Jerusalem in 587 BCE (Linafelt 2000). The fall of Jerusalem that marked the end of the Southern Kingdom of Judah as an event is considered the only catalyst of such consequence to have sparked the sorrow and reflection of the biblical Lamentations. The careful artistry and the sophisticated nature of its acrostic and alphabetic poems further point to literary activity at some removal from the immediate aftermath of disaster (Berlin 2002). Taken together, then, the linguistic, thematic and ideological evidence indicate the sixth to fifth centuries BCE as a general time frame for the composition of Lamentations. Attention to the individual poems provides further constructive data for consideration.

Composition history and the evidence of individual poems

In general, the book of Lamentations is considered a homogenous collection of independent poems that are unified in outlook and literary expression. Nevertheless, it is possible that certain chapters actually stem from different time periods or poets. In conjunction with chapters 1, 3 and 5, then, arguments for a different provenance, if not hand, have arisen. As an extended Penitential Lament over Zion, Lamentations is thought to belong to the period after the devastating defeat of Jerusalem in 587 BCE, which is the determinative event that many interpreters regard as the only catastrophe in ancient times to which the book with its message and odd mixture of genres can possibly relate. It is helpful, therefore, to bear in mind the fall of Jerusalem when considering arguments about the provenance of individual chapters, but we will remain open about the ultimate date of the whole collection until all the evidence has been assessed.

A series of Neo-Babylonian incursions in the sixth century BCE led to the downfall of the city of Jerusalem, the loss of independent statehood, and the forced deportation of the last Davidic king, royal family members, inhabitants of the city of Jerusalem, including the political, religious and social leaders of the nation as well as the demolition of the king's palace and national sanctuary, the infrastructure of the city of Jerusalem, and other towns in Judah. With this in mind, the first chapter has been attributed to a different time, but not setting, within this general period. To the historian and exegete Wilhelm Rudolph, the composition of chapter 1 belonged not to the time after the fall of Jerusalem in 587 BCE, but rather to the period subsequent to the first Babylonian incursion in 598 and thus stemmed from roughly a decade earlier than the other chapters (Rudolph 1962: 190–9). In his view, an earlier date commends itself because the poet makes no clear reference to the destruction and fall of Jerusalem or the temple. Instead, the poet focuses on forced deportation and the desecration of the sanctuary in the first chapter.

However, various allusions in the first chapter can be translated or interpreted in a way that would suggest that the poem stemmed from after the second Babylonian incursion and thus coterminous with the fall of Jerusalem. Enno Janssen notes for example that the verb used in the description of the desolation of the gates of Zion (*šmm* in Lam. 1:4) equally conveys the idea of 'ruination' or 'torn down' and the presence of priests still in the city would also have been the situation after the ultimate downfall of the state. Chapter 1 could easily stem from the period after the actual downfall of the city in 587 BCE (Janssen 1956: 10–12). Although differing in their interpretations of the historical circumstances to which the poetic details relate, both Rudolph and Janssen would still agree, however, that the composition of the first chapter stems from the events that took place around the collapse of the kingdom of Judah in the sixth century BCE.

The debate about how to precisely interpret and then ascribe dating to the references in the poems illustrates how difficult it is to use biblical allusions to pinpoint specific historical events, particularly, but not exclusively, in poetic literature. Because vague allusions to social or historical circumstances have been used to posit various mutually exclusive dates for the different poems, the discussion has shifted in recent years to focus on issues of form and content. Based on this criteria, chapters 3 and 5 have the most reason to be attributed to a different date or author than the rest of the poems in Lamentations.

The form and content of chapter 3 certainly suggest a different hand than the other poems of Lamentations (Westermann 1994: 191–3; Albertz 2003: 161–5; Middlemas 2006). The third chapter is remarkably different in its mix of formal elements and it alone evidences the intensification of the acrostic such that each letter of the Hebrew alphabet introduces three short lines apiece. In addition, the form category of chapter 3 aligns most closely with the individual lament rather than the dirge that is found in chapters 1, 2 and 4. It begins with the myopic mournful reflection of an individual who plaintively opines, *'ănî hageḇer'* 'I am the one/the man' (3:1), who is roughly equivalent to a strong man, soldier or nobleman, instead of the funeral term *ēkah* 'alas' that opens chapters 1, 2 and 4. Perhaps even more strikingly still, the chapter contains a number of different formal units, including the individual lament (vv. 1-21), a communal petition that functions like a confession of sin (vv. 40-7), the only articulation of hope in the whole collection as a wisdom interlude that teaches and preaches the correct understanding of God to a suffering individual (vv. 22-39), and closes with an individual lament that verges on a prayer of thanksgiving (vv. 48-66). Finally, the elements of the Mesopotamian City Laments (MCL), so prominent especially in chapters in 1 and 2, but found to some extent also in chapter 4, are almost entirely absent.

In form and content, then, the third chapter is at odds with the other poems which on a surface level suggests a different hand or a different provenance altogether. In Lamentations, the individual's complaint leads to theological reflection on divine goodness, justice and mercy that in turn moves the community to a confession of wrongdoing, and then ultimately to the petitioner's affirmation of divine intervention and restoration on his or her behalf. In content, then, the third poem echoes the sequential emphasis on sin, repentance, confession and rehabilitation as featured in the theological traditions that remain consistent with the book of Deuteronomy or deuteronomic ideology (for consideration of this pattern within the Deuteronomic History,[1] see Middlemas 2007: 52–63). In its message and mixture of formal elements, the third chapter prescribes behaviour that aligns well with the themes and emphases that are found in literature, such as the final forms of the Deuteronomistic History and the book of Jeremiah, which have been attributed to the Judahites exiled to Babylonia, referred to as the *Golah*, that returned and steered the course of the reconstituted community from the end of the sixth century (compare Nicholson 1970; Seitz 1989; Albertz 2003).

Although difficult to assert with any degree of certainty, it is important that a growing body of evidence has documented correspondences between the presentation of the *geber* of chapter 3 and the Suffering Servant of Deutero-Isaiah (Isa. 40–55) (Gottwald 1962: 44–6, 106–7; Sawyer 1989; Newsome 1992; Willey 1997: 215–20, 226–7; Sommer 1998; Linafelt 2000: 62–79; Tiemeyer 2011: 311–32). Moreover, just as Lamentations evidences the interchanging voices of a male and a female speaker, the Suffering Servant of Isaiah alternates in speech and appearance with the city of Zion portrayed as a mother and a woman in Isaiah 46–55. The Suffering Servant (Isa. 49:1-13; 50:4-11; 52:13–53:12) alternates three times with personified Zion (49:14–50:3; 51:17–52:12; 54:1-17). Two juxtaposed figures – the Suffering Servant and Mother Zion – appear together in Isaiah in a similar way to the interchange of the voices of the individual sufferer (Lam. 3:1-21, 48–66) and personified Jerusalem in Lamentations (Lam. 1:9c, 11c, 12-22; 2:20-2). Arguably, the figures of the Suffering Servant and Mother/Daughter Zion represent the two main groups of the former Judahite community – those who were forcibly deported to Babylonia and the remnant who stayed in the homeland (Middlemas 2006). The poems of Lamentations and the prophecy of Deutero-Isaiah are aligned in the use of community representatives, the personified city of Jerusalem and the suffering man, which suggests a rhetorical strategy shaped around including personae who stand in for the two main

---

[1]The Deuteronomistic History refers to books of Joshua through 2 Kings introduced by parts of the book of Deuteronomy. Biblical scholars have long thought of this as disparate material edited to convey a unity of message about divine intentionality and the downfall of the kingdoms of Israel and Judah because of human sin and the abrogation of the covenant.

communities that survived the catastrophic invasion and systemic collapse of Jerusalem, those that remained in the homeland and those exiled to Babylonia.

However, in distinction to Deutero-Isaiah, the suffering individual of Lamentations 3 provides a correction to the perspective of the personified city. The *geber* corrects the sense of inexplicable tragedy, vociferous complaint and hints of divine culpability associated with the speech of personified Jerusalem in the first two chapters of Lamentations (Middlemas 2006). For example, although Jerusalem complains about a yoke being placed on her (1:14), the sage of the wisdom section teaches that it should be regarded and accepted as correction, "It is good for a man that he bear a yoke in his youth" (3:27) and "let him sit alone in silence when [God] laid it [the yoke] upon him" (3:28). Moreover, the emphasis in the first two chapters on protesting and drawing attention to extraordinary suffering is counterbalanced in the wisdom section through the importance placed on silent submission (3:28-30) (see Westermann 1994: 168–9, 192–3; Middlemas 2006). The direct use and indeed inversion and contradiction of Jerusalem's vocabulary by the *geber* suggest that the author of the third chapter was responding to prayers to which he or she had access and was thus writing on the basis of them, which would suggest the work of a redactor.

Commonality between the figuration of the suffering strong man in Lamentations and Isaiah's Suffering Servant raises new possibilities for the provenance of the material. The Suffering Servant of the Isaianic material promotes an ideology of silent submission to affliction and the redemptive nature of suffering that is consistent with the thought of the exiles in Babylonia, also referred to as the *Golah*. The placement and themes of the third poem would suggest that either communication took place between the Judahites in exile and those in the land as indicated by Jeremiah's letter to the *Golah* community (Jer. 29) (so Gottwald 1962: 44–6) or repatriated exiles updated and compiled Lamentations upon their return to the homeland in conjunction with material from Deutero-Isaiah (Middlemas 2006). An alternative point of view has been offered more recently by Lena-Sofia Tiemeyer that places the provenance of Deutero-Isaiah in the land of Judah, which if correct would suggest different perspectives on disaster took place within the same geographical location (Tiemayer 2011).

Continuing a tradition on the basis of inherited material is consistent with biblical writing elsewhere and provides some evidence of the hand of a redactor in the final composition that makes up the book of Lamentations. It should be noted in this context that biblical scholars do not devalue the work of redactors and regard them as in any way less faithful or inspired than biblical authors because they used poetic licence to update traditions for new circumstances. The redactor may have gathered together and organized poems that reflect actual prayers related to the fall of Jerusalem in order to point to possibilities of divine renewal consistent with deuteronomic and *Golah* thought more generally. The placement of the third poem with its emphasis on repentance and the redemptive nature of suffering suggests that in the final composition it commends a core belief that once held has the potential to move the community beyond its experience of hardship.

The other obvious distinctive chapter in terms of form is the fifth, where the acrostic fails to appear, although it is still associated with the alphabet because its twenty-two verses equal the number of letters in the Hebrew alphabet. The lament in chapter 5 is at odds with the other communal complaints because it contains an extensive section outlining the suffering of a despairing people (vv. 1-18) in terms of length like no other example of its genre found in the Psalms (compare Pss. 44, 74, 79, 89, 137). Other distinguishing features of the last chapter include a brief, seemingly truncated, confession of trust based on assertions of God as king (Lam. 5:19) and an appeal that ends on a note of depressing uncertainty rather than with the expectation of divine intervention (vv. 20-2). In addition, although two acknowledgements of sin appear, "Our ancestors sinned; they are no more" (v. 17) and "woe to us, for we have sinned" (v. 16b), the statements correspond more to components required by the lament form because of their abbreviated and general nature, rather than actual, heartfelt confessions. In their lack of specificity, the "confessions" lie close in thought to what is otherwise characteristic of ANE penitential prayers in which "the speaker acknowledges guilt, and recognizes that s/he is suffering on account of divine wrath. But those are merely the existential facts of the situation – part of its 'background,' as it were" (Cooper 2001: 13). In tone and outlook, then, the fifth chapter fits well with the poems of Lamentations, but it could have arisen in a different provenance and been joined to the collection to conclude the book on a note of penitence.

Certainly, the lack of an optimistic ending and what was perceived as the confessional nature of the poem led commentators to consider the last chapter later than the others in Lamentations. In his study of the situation and literature of the homeland after the fall of Jerusalem in the sixth century BCE, Janssen, for example, pronounced chapter 5 "indisputably from the time of temple reconstruction" (Janssen 1956: 9), which he understood as related to the activities of Haggai and Zechariah in 520–518 BCE. Moreover, it stands apart from the other poems in being the only one in which no corresponding allusions or comparable expressions appear in Deutero-Isaiah (here regarded as Isa. 40–66), which certainly hints at a later date of composition than the other chapters (Sommer 1998: 130). At the same time, arguments made on the basis of the lack of biblical allusion are notoriously difficult to substantiate as omission could also be the result of other factors such as ideological, that is, it did not serve the theological purposes of the prophet of Deutero-Isaiah, or logistical, that is, the compositions could have been written within communities at a physical distance from one another.

Although the fifth poem may stem from a different hand and a date somewhat later than the other poems of Lamentations, it contains internal details that suggest a high degree of affinity with the language and sentiments expressed therein – the concern with the suffering of the inhabitants of Jerusalem and Judah as well as its persistence. Moreover, its albeit vague historical allusions to either the collection of tribute or taxes by which an undisclosed overlord siphons off food and goods from an already strained community certainly resonate with the depiction of Jerusalem as a 'vassal' (Lam. 1:1) and also the general socio-historical background of chapters 1–4.

Thematic links with the other poems, then, suggest that chapter 5 functions as a concluding prayer for the whole collection. For instance, the community calls out for divine attention in a way that resonates with appeals made elsewhere in the poetry. The cry, "look, and see our disgrace!" (5:1), echoes the language used by the personified city as she calls out for the deity to attend to her distress. Although it is not so clear in translation, the verbs are *nābaṭ* 'to look at' and *rāʾah* 'to see' in that order. Elsewhere, Lady Jerusalem urges Yahweh to 'see' (*rāʾah*) her distress (1:9c, 20a) and to 'see' (*rāʾah*) and 'look at' (*nābaṭ*) her misery (1:11c; 2:20a). The exact phrasing used by the communal voice at the beginning of chapter 5, though, is found in Zion's appeal to passers-by to witness to her suffering when she says, "look (*nābaṭ*) and see (*rāʾah*), if there is any sorrow like my sorrow" (1:12b). In this way, the community reiterates Zion's urgent appeal to witnesses, but situates it in a petition to the deity rather than in the language of protest that characterized the first two chapters of Lamentations. Indeed, the beginning of the fifth chapter with the imperative or command form of *zākar* 'remember' addressed to God (5:1) effectively turns complaint into petition, which reinforces the turn to prayer at the conclusion of the collection. Finally, the lack of a clear articulation or vision of salvation, the awareness of divine wrath and unresponsiveness, and the intense focus on human suffering in the last chapter align Lamentations as a whole with ANE penitential prayers that "seek to put an end to god's wrath by the presentation of the penitent's wretched state" (Cooper 2001: 14).

The outlook of the fifth chapter fits with the other poems of Lamentations because its details align with the circumstances thought to lie at the background of the collection as a whole. In this respect, the grounds for the prayer of the concluding chapter commend themselves to a socio-historical setting like that of the other poems of Lamentations. The community presents details that suggest that they continue to endure the hardships of foreign rule: "Our inheritance has been turned over to strangers" (v. 2), "We must pay for the water we drink;/the wood we get must be bought" (v. 4), "With a yoke on our necks we are hard driven" (v. 5), "Slaves rule over us" (v. 8) and "We get our bread at the peril of our lives" (v. 9). These references suggest that the community languishes under a foreign power, which could very well suggest Judah under Babylonian or Persian imperial oversight in the post-collapse situation. In general, the fifth chapter may represent the work of a separate author or a time later than the other poems, but it remains, nevertheless, consistent in thought and circumstances with the rest of the collection. The conclusion of Lamentations on a note of penitential prayer consistent with ANE examples and foreshadowed by the third chapter points once again to the work of a final redactor and leads us to consider the composition of the book as a whole.

Composition history and the role of a redactor

Whether a biblical book stems from one author or from an editor who inherits and updates religious literature makes a difference in how we understand the period of time to which it relates. For example, various reasons were given for why Lamentations as a whole seems to stem from a final hand in terms of its organization, especially with the placement of its theological highpoint in the central chapter and the importance ascribed to communal petition in the concluding poem. Biblical interpreters use the terminology of editor slightly differently than what is common in modern usage; such that, an editor functions (and is often spoken of) as a redactor, who compiles material, adds phrases here and there, and composes longer passages. For example, Hugh Williamson has argued that the individual who composed the material called Deutero-Isaiah (Isaiah 40–55) inherited the work of the prophet Isaiah (much of chapters 1–39), added editorial connections between the works and also wrote original prophecy in chapters 40–55 (Williamson 1994). An editor in this sense is also an author, and thus we use the terminology of redactor to signal the difference. Awareness of the work of a redactor who fashioned the final form of Lamentations from inherited traditions or prayers contributes to how we think about the time frame to which the collection relates and in which the individual poems took shape.

Before turning to discuss the *Sitz im Leben*, that is, the setting in life or the cultural context to which the origin of the poems can likely be attributed, it is worthwhile to draw together the various arguments related to matters of composition that we have surveyed in the last chapter and in this one. Traditionally, the book of Lamentations is attributed to the period after the fall of Jerusalem in 587 BCE. Certainly, the Hebrew language of Lamentations is consistent with literature of the sixth to fifth centuries BCE, but divergent from works that appeared from the mid-fifth century onwards like those of Ezra and Nehemiah. In addition, biblical allusions resonate with a number of lament psalms (Pss. 74, 79, 89) and prophetic books associated with the Templeless period, such as Deutero-Isaiah, Jeremiah and Ezekiel. Especially noteworthy is the appearance of the alternating figures of a suffering male individual (Deutero-Isaiah's Suffering Servant and Lamentations Suffering Individual) and the personified female Jerusalem (as Mother and Daughter Zion) that further links Lamentations and Deutero-Isaiah.

The order of the poems of Lamentations, shaped with hope at the centre of raging suffering, draws attention to the perception of the continuation and persistence of divine wrath in which the community languishes under extraordinary and unabated hardship. In this way, its shape may be theological rather than historical (Middlemas 2004). The distinctive chapter 3, distinguished by form, content and message, is certainly a key to understanding the composition of Lamentations. Its placement before the heartbreaking and graphic details of ongoing tragedy related in chapter 4 and the depressing end of the collection that functions as penitential prayer in chapter 5 suggests that the overall shape of the composition belongs to a time after a great disaster and before any real sense of renewal emerged, as if the community illustrated in the literature is waiting for restoration to appear on the horizon.

It is worth noting that the final form of the biblical Lamentations as a compositional unit corresponds to other biblical books or collections, namely Isaiah 56–66, Amos, Zechariah 1–8, Proverbs and Job, which evidence a concentric shape. Concentrically shaped biblical books or collections exhibit what appears to be material sometimes inherited from an honoured and respected source or which should be highlighted and emphasized surrounded by a framework of interpretive material (Middlemas 2011). In these biblical examples, interpretation surrounds a core of material, whereas the biblical Lamentations evidences an interpretive section placed at the centre of disorderly traumatic reactions and complaints. Although slightly different in terms of its shape, Trito-Isaiah (Isa. 56–66) corresponds thematically to the biblical Lamentations. Both pieces of literature evidence a section of positive material focused on divine restoration and mercy (compare Isa. 60–2 and Lam. 3:22-39) called into question or re-interpreted in the light of ongoing hardship in the community in the outer material. Shaping collections according to a centre and a periphery is a feature of biblical literary works that have been dated at the earliest to the Templeless period. The organization of the biblical Lamentations around a core, then, supports associating the poems with the period of time following the collapse of the Southern Kingdom of Judah and the fall of Jerusalem and before political, social and economic rejuvenation and reconstruction took place.

The details that emerge in the fifth poem, which is arguably the last composition of the five chapters, which in my order is chs. 1, 2, 4 together and 3 and 5 possibly together, indicate a lengthy and protracted period of social, political and economic devastation. Furthermore, the reference to the prowling of jackals on Mount Zion (Lam. 5:18) commends itself to a time before the reconstruction of the temple, which the biblical literature posits to 515 BCE (Ezra 6:15) and coterminous with the period of the activity of the prophets of the restoration, Haggai and Zechariah. It is true that the phrasing is almost equivalent to language found in the MCL, which might make it less useful for historical reconstruction. Nevertheless, its appearance as a motif in the concluding prayer points to a sanctuary that continues to lie in ruins or be desecrated. Somewhat differently, the mention of the sin of the ancestors being borne by the lamenting community (Lam. 5:7) suggests a period at least one generation removed from the disaster of 587 BCE. Finally, on the basis of the depressing ending of the fifth chapter and the lack of an optimistic outlook of the whole, interpreters tend to situate the composition of the poem towards the end of the sixth century BCE and before the reconstruction and dedication of the second temple in Jerusalem in 515 (arguments for the actual rebuilding and dedication of the second temple in the fifth century appear in Edelman 2005).

Notably, Ronald Clements has drawn attention to the fact that the Deuteronomistic History and a first volume of the prophecies of Jeremiah (chs. 1–25) conclude without restorative resolutions, which suggests to him that the two works were completed in the homeland in the sixth century BCE and before the restoration associated with Haggai and Zechariah (Clements 1996: 105–22). A date towards the end of the Templeless period, at the beginning of the Persian period and around the time to which the activities of Haggai and Proto-Zechariah tend to be posited corresponds with the linguistic evidence of the book as well as with allusions to or reflections of the theological ideas or images in other biblical literature from that time. My own work has pointed to the close of the Templeless period as a helpful temporal marker (Middlemas 2005 and 2007), but archaeological evidence also shows that the former nation of Judah continued to languish in adverse economic and agricultural conditions well into the Persian period. A more expansive dating that takes into account the redaction of the poems of Lamentations into a whole would correspond to sometime between the fall of the Babylonian Empire to the Persian King Cyrus in 539 BCE and the composition of Ezra and Nehemiah in the mid-fifth century.

Certainly a number of the poems stem from the period after the fall of Jerusalem and the loss of the kingdom of Judah that took place in the early sixth century BCE. However, as Berlin has shown the poems create a new literary genre to respond to the events of that time and in outlook belong at some remove from the disaster. The book of Lamentations is oriented to the fall of Jeruslalem, but the poems in their final form stem from redactional activity that likely occurred sometime late in the sixth century or early in the fifth century BCE.

SOCIO-HISTORICAL CONTEXT: THE BACKGROUND OF WAR AND SYSTEMIC COLLAPSE

The fall of Jerusalem in 587 BCE to the Babylonians ushered in the final collapse of the last Israelite kingdom, the Southern Kingdom of Judah, long associated with the rule of the Davidic kings. Almost 150 years earlier, the Northern Kingdom of Israel with its capital in Samaria had already fallen to another Mesopotamian invading force under the imperial authority of the Assyrians in 722 BCE. After the fall of Judah in the sixth century BCE, the former kingdom of Judah would never again be an independent nation-state under its own local rulers except for briefly under the Maccabees in the Greek period. The nation's collapse coincided with the destruction of the capital city and surrounding areas, the deportation on at least three separate occasions of the nation's royalty and other elites like the priests, nobility and ruling classes as well as artisans, soldiers and whole families. The territory of Judah remained devastated throughout the Templeless period (587–515 BCE) and there is no evidence of any real restoration until well into the Persian period in the late fifth or early fourth centuries BCE at the very earliest (Carter 1999; Meyers 2009; Faust 2012).

The kingdom of Judah lost its status of independent statehood, experienced significant disruption in its political, religious and intellectual life, and suffered from societal collapse. Archaeological evidence from sites and surveys indicates widespread devastation, ruin and decline in the former kingdom of Judah. At the same time, there is biblical and material evidence of renewal and restoration in the Benjamin region located north of the territory of Judah centred around an administrative capital in Mizpah after the collapse. The population of the former kingdom was dispersed widely, with exiles in Babylonia (some of whom later became known as the *Golah* and participated in the restoration of the country after their repatriation), refugees in neighbouring nation-states like Moab and Ammon as well as in Egypt, and in what remained of the homeland (for a summary overview, see Albertz 2003: 45–132; Lipschits 2005; Miller and Hayes 2006; Middlemas 2007: 9–27 and forthcoming). It is now generally accepted that the return of some of the exiles took place in waves, and the first wave was sometime subsequent to the capture of Babylon by the Persians in 539 BCE (Becking 2006; Grabbe 2012). Our survey of the history of matters of composition reveals that the collected poems in Lamentations likely stem from at least two of the Judahite communities that experienced and survived the downfall of Jerusalem – the remnant population that remained in the homeland and the exiles forcibly deported to and resettled in the heartland of Babylonia. In order to more fully understand the composition, transmission and shaping of Lamentations, we consider briefly these two formative groups, the remnant and the exiles, and ideas common to them.

The remnant in Judah

According to the biblical record of the time, the Babylonian appointee Gedaliah oversaw a return to normality among the remaining populace from a regional administrative centre established in Mizpah to the north of Jerusalem, (2 Kgs 25:22-6; Jer. 40:7–41:3). The southern part of the kingdom was especially devastated, but archaeological and biblical evidence suggest the creation of an administrative centre in Mizpah even before the downfall of Judah that offered the location for social, political and perhaps also religious renewal and oversight (Lipschits 2005). Because of ambiguity in the sources and the lack of corresponding evidence from cuneiform imperial records, the actual official position of Gedaliah remains unclear. Gedaliah was established either as a puppet king or as a governor (see the discussion in Miller and Hayes 2006: 482–5). In any case, he served in some official oversight capacity for the community that remained in the homeland after the destruction of Jerusalem and the forced deportation of its political, social and religious leaders from the capital. Those who had hidden in the areas around Jerusalem as well as the refugees who had fled to neighbouring nation-states came back to the Benjamin area under his leadership (2 Kgs 25:23; Jer. 40:7-12). For his part, Gedaliah set out to re-establish stability for the inhabitants who remained and to promote agricultural production through the distribution of land in order to generate food and tribute. Arable land was distributed among the remaining population (2 Kgs 25:12; Jer. 39:10; 52:16, see also Ezek. 33:21-7) so that agricultural activity could continue for the benefit of the remnant population, but more importantly from the perspective of their imperial overlords to provide tributary goods for transport to the Babylonian heartland.

A question remains at the present time about how much activity there was in the homeland following the downfall of Jerusalem (Lipschits 2005; Middlemas 2005: 24–71). The account of the destruction at the end of 2 Kings, echoed in the book of Jeremiah (Jer. 52), portrays a Judah devoid of its population. In addition, archaeological data of the almost complete annihilation of and lack of evidence for continued habitation in the city and its environs in the territory of Judah reinforces this picture to some extent (Blenkinsopp 2002; Lipschits 2005; Faust 2012). However, the assessment that the remnant in the land lived veritably as squatters in subsistence conditions until the repatriation of the exiles is no longer widely accepted today.

Historians point to indications of renewal in the accounts of 2 Kings and Jeremiah as well as in the material culture (Janssen 1956; Albertz 2003). There are hints in the biblical account of renewal, if not prosperity, in the devastated and depopulated Judah, as with the mention of the vine-dressers and ploughmen who tend the soil as well as the detail of an abundant harvest that took place at the time of Gedaliah in the Jeremianic account (Jer. 40:12). In addition, archaeological reconstructions based on the material culture reveal that the ferocity of the Babylonian campaign focused on the environs of Jerusalem and regions to the north remained virtually unscathed. Mizpah to the north of Jerusalem suffered no Babylonian attack and it seems to have had an administrative role before the actual fall of the city of Jerusalem. Although wine and oil production continued and seemingly flourished in Mizpah and Gibeon, the economic vitality of the period was restricted to the Benjamin region so that economic decline in the territory of Judah and in the environs of Jerusalem should not be discounted.

Although Judah was severely crippled, the appointment of Gedaliah by the Babylonians to oversee the country suggests at least a modicum of Babylonian-sponsored regeneration. Nevertheless, there is no direct evidence of Neo-Babylonian policy in Judah. Regrettably, the extant Babylonian Chronicles break off after the eleventh year of Nebuchadnezzar

(594 BCE) and resume only some thirty years later. The former kingdom of Judah could have remained a vassal. The Babylonians would have provided few resources or regional support for regeneration to a vassal state and tribute would have been exacted on a yearly basis by invading troops who continued to disrupt the local environment (Vanderhooft 1999). Alternatively, there is some indication that the imperial policies changed in the region after the fall of Jerusalem and likely in conjunction with the suppression of Egypt by the Neo-Babylonians. According to this scenario, Judah was a vassal in the early period, but became a full province of the empire after the downfall of Jerusalem and the installation of Gedaliah to oversee the region (Middlemas 2005: 48–70; Barstad 2012). As an imperial province, the former nation would have benefited from integration in the empire and from imperial support. Whatever the case, on the basis of evidence from seals and wine vats, it appears that the remnant population produced some luxury goods in surplus, wine and olive oil, that were transferred to the heartland of Babylonia, facilitated by an operative administrative centre in Mizpah.

After the untimely death of the Babylonian-appointed governor, Gedaliah, the situation in the former Southern Kingdom may have changed for the worse. However, there are indications that the country remained on a continuum and it is possible that leaders were in place to stabilize the situation after the governor's assassination. Certainly by the time of the prophets Haggai and Zechariah, governors were in place (Williamson 1988). Alternatively, it is also possible that the "people of the land", a group of land owners who typically lived outside of Jerusalem and exercised local authority, acted quickly to stabilize the situation and appoint a new civic leader (Seitz 1989: 7–102).

A remnant population remained in the land primarily in the Benjamin region to the north of the devastated Jerusalem and resumed familial and communal activities. In spite of the desecration and ruination of the temple in Jerusalem, it is generally supposed that spontaneous and sporadic worship and lamentation could have continued at the site of the sanctuary. In addition, another cultic location may have been in use for regular ritual in Mizpah or in the nearby ancient site of Bethel under the authority of the Aaronite priests that had remained in the land (Blenkinsopp 2002: 425–6; Middlemas 2007: 30–4). The pilgrimage of a group to observe the Feast of Weeks, bearing grain offerings and incense and dressed in mourning attire, suggests the continuation of sporadic and spontaneous worship (Jer. 41:4-5), while a list of fasts observed during the period points to the resumption of regular ritual observance (Zech. 7:5; 8:19) (Lipschits 2005: 112–18; Middlemas 2005: 126–30 and 2007: 16–18).

Until recently, there has been little understanding of the thought particular to and consistent with the homeland population. In my doctoral work, I considered four of the five poems of Lamentations as examples of literature from the Judahite population that remained in the homeland during the Templeless or exilic period in order to isolate themes relevant to the remnant therein (Middlemas 2005: 171–228; for a recent use of the data to posit more literature to the population in the homeland, see Tiemeyer 2011). In a close analysis of literature thought to stem from Templeless Judah, chapters 1–2 and 4–5 were regarded as authentic representatives of the remnant population. Even if this present study suggests that chapter 5 should now be considered from a later period than the three

ʾêkah poems (chs. 1, 2, 4), the isolated themes remain consistent, nevertheless, with the thought in the last chapter. The focus on human suffering and complaints about foreign oppression serves as guideposts to an ideology pertinent to the homeland.

There are five motifs that remain peculiar to the Judahite remnant population, which draw attention to a distinctive experience and thought in the literature of the time. Most notably, a value was placed on providing space for the memories of violence and the expression of human suffering. Literature from the homeland focused to a large extent on the prevalence and persistence, sometimes even the injustice, of human pain. Another distinction found in the liturgical literature of the remnant is the lack of confidence in a future restoration initiated by the deity. Interpreters speak of the sense of doubt manifest in Lamentations as well as the undercutting of any reasons for hope. A third important theme developed in a particular way among the homeland population is the undercutting and even deconstruction of sin as a valid explanation for disaster. Norman Gottwald showed that sin is attributed to the people and their leaders, but remains perplexingly vague in terms of specifics (Gottwald 1962: 69–70). Although the correlation of sin with the community's present dire circumstances is at times made, more often than not the nature of the transgression is so generalized as to be almost meaningless as an actual determinative factor. Moreover, on a couple of occasions, sin is deconstructed or contradicted within its own context (1:5, 18) and thus the force of transgression as a valid reason for the disaster is downplayed, and even negated (see also Dobbs-Allsopp 1997: 36–9). One striking point of Judahite reflection is that the amount of devastation and suffering cannot be justified by the explanation of the just punishment for sin.

A fourth concept found in Judahite literature is the authorization of protest and the vocalization of pain. Outside of the theology of chapter 3, pain never has a redemptive function in Lamentations. The poems validate protest against perceived injustice and human suffering. Complaints and laments to God were considered faithful responses that called the deity to account and urged the execution of divine righteousness to right the wrong of individual, social and systemic collapse. Finally, an importance was ascribed in the collection to the formulation of grief. The acrostic binds the articulation of suffering within twenty-two verses and limits it to the alphabet. Moreover, chapters 1, 2 and 4 evidence the intertwining of the funeral dirge and the lament, but with differing degrees of emphases. In their current order, the motifs and expressions consistent with the funeral song gradually lessen and the elements of the lament come to the fore. When seen in this way, the actual form or genre of the poems reveals the transition away from a retrospective mournful glance at death and towards the embrace of survival and life. In shaping its grief, the Judahite poets of Lamentations present a vision of hope for the future that is not so fully embraced within the language of the poems themselves. Ultimately, the remnant population throws its lot in with the deity and hopes for divine recognition and restoration:

> Faced with human suffering on a divine scale, mournful Judah does not metaphorically sit in an ash heap and ruminate, but shouts of loss and limitation. The formation of the protest of pain and its setting in worship is just as significant as that which has been said. In spite of everything, the people in Judah prayed to their God. (Middlemas 2005: 227)

The exiles in Babylonia

The Babylonians left Judah devastated and depopulated, and used forced deportation as a punitive tactic of war, much as their forbears, the Assyrians, had done. The Babylonians deported inhabitants of the Southern Kingdom of Judah and resettled them in the city of Babylon itself and on rural crown properties in the south and west of the heartland, on at least three separate occasions, 598, 587 and 582 BCE (Smith 1989; Albertz 2003; Middlemas 2007: 24–7). In general, the Babylonians seemed more selective in their choice of deportees than the Assyrians before them – choosing political, social and religious elites as well as skilled workers. In addition and again in a departure from Assyrian policy, they re-settled deported families and whole communities together in ethnic enclaves.

Our understanding of deportation as a martial tactic of war has been greatly enhanced by analyses of Assyrian records, palace iconography and inscriptions (Oded 1979: 34–41). Babylonian practices have been reconstructed on the basis of the Assyrian evidence. It is suspected that the Babylonians conscripted military personnel into their army, employed artisans in building projects and used other skilled workers as scribes for official record keeping. The king, the royal family and other palace officials were probably in the capital, where suitably educated individuals would have worked for the court as scribes and interpreters. Biblical tradition elsewhere makes reference to the service of royalty and nobility in palace positions (Isa. 39:7; Dan. 1:3-6), and Daniel and Nehemiah are reported to have held leadership roles in the court of foreign kings (Dan. 6:2; Neh. 1:11). The summaries of the fall of Jerusalem in the books of Kings and of Jeremiah conclude with a brief note marking the release of Jehoiachin in 562 BCE from imprisonment (2 Kgs 25:27-30; Jer. 52:31-3) and the food allowance allotted to him and his family;

> In the thirty-seventh year of the exile … King Evil-merodach (Amel-marduk) of
> Babylon … released King Jehoiachin of Judah from prison … Every day of his life he
> dined regularly in the king's presence … a regular allowance was given him by the king,
> a portion every day, as long as he lived. (2 Kgs 25:27-30, selected)

According to Babylonian cuneiform records, Jehoiachin was allotted a substantial amount of food and oil rations, for himself and his family until his death (ANET 308).

Other exiles were settled together in ethnic enclaves in rural areas, along the canals of the Euphrates in the region of Nippur. Reconstruction of daily life of the Judahites in Babylonia has tended to be based on the Murashu Archive, that is, a series of legal, financial and administrative texts that contain records from the fifth to the fourth centuries BCE, specifically from the reigns of Artaxerxes I (464–424 BCE) and Darius II (424–404 BCE) (Stolper 1985). In recent years, a new series of documents in a repository referred to as the Texts from al-Yahudu and Našar (the TAYN corpus) has come to light that provide information about the exiles from an earlier period (Pearce 2006; Albertz 2012). The archive contains about 100 cuneiform texts that attest to Judahite participation in legal, commercial and administrative affairs as early as 572 BCE and continuing well into the fifth century. Of about 200 local communities scattered throughout southern Mesopotamia, about twenty-eight were Judahite settlements. The archive also indicates that other displaced groups, for example, from Asia Minor, Phoenicia, Syria, Philistia, Arabia and Egypt, were settled together in villages according to ethnicity.

In this way, the Judahite communities in Babylonia seem to confirm the hopes expressed in the book of Jeremiah that they would settle down and integrate (Jer. 29). Seemingly, the Babylonians did not actively seek to assimilate the peoples of other nations into their culture. Ethnic groups were allowed relative freedom to organize and lead their daily social, religious and financial affairs. The names of sons of Judahite fathers were found listed with elements from the names of Babylonian deities such as Marduk, Bel and Nabu, which suggests accommodation to the local culture and possibly also syncretistic religious observation (Beaulieu 2011). The Judahites located in the rural areas were expected to work the land as agricultural workers. In spite of biblical assertions to the contrary, a number of Judahites exiled to Babylonia chose not to return to their homeland as the Murashu Archive attests. They had integrated successfully into Babylonia and evidently enjoyed their lives there or at least chose not to risk the uncertainty of travel to and resettlement in the homeland. In this way the exile never actually ceased to exist.

The organization of the exiles in localized communities provided the circumstances which allowed for the development of strategies to maintain a strong sense of ethnic and religious identity (Smith 1989). The arduous journey, distance from the homeland and national symbols, and the trauma of loss provided key experiences out of which the exiles sought to maintain their distinct identity tied to the traditions of the former kingdoms of Israel and Judah. A feature of the literature of this time is the use of the language of imprisonment and captivity, which illustrate the negative reactions to and even attitudes towards forced deportation and resettlement. At the same time, the resettlement of the exiles in communities provided them with the opportunity to adapt creatively to their situation in order to foster social cohesion and maintain a strong sense of group identity. The collapse of the state and loss of a native king led the elders to take on leadership roles (Jer. 29:1; Ezek. 8:1; 14:1; 20:1, 3; pointed to also in Ezra 5:5, 9; 6:7-8). Socially, the exiles were thrust among other ethnic groups in the Babylonian Empire where kinship ties became more important as well as outward signs of difference, such as the observance of the Sabbath and circumcision. The loss of the temple also led to new thinking about the importance of prayer and even praying towards Jerusalem (1 Kgs 8:44-51).

The situation for the exiles was far from ideal and various biblical texts capture a sense of the grief and trauma they experienced: "Judah has gone into exile with suffering and hard servitude" (Lam. 1:3), "By the rivers of Babylon, we sat down and wept" (Ps. 137:1), "Happy shall they be who pay you back for what you have done to us!" (v. 8), and "Our bones are dried up, and our hope is lost: we are cut off completely" (Ezek. 37:11). At the same time, there was also a significance granted to external markers of distinction as a response to loss, uprootedness and resettlement among other ethnic groups (Nicholson 2014: 61). Literature was either composed or updated from the perspective of the exile, including the books of Ezekiel, Jeremiah and Deutero-Isaiah, but all differ in their conceptions of the fall of Jerusalem and its religious or theological significance.

The book of Ezekiel places a significant amount of emphasis on the defilement of the Jerusalem Temple and idolatrous worship practices, while the book of Jeremiah focuses to a greater extent on communal and political failings with only some attention to illicit worship. Deutero-Isaiah includes prophecies of divine judgement and polemicizes against the worship of divine images as well as the restoration made possible through repentance and the homecoming of the exiles. General themes that run through the exilic literature (whether composed by the exiles in Babylonia or upon their return to the homeland) include an importance ascribed to the dangers of idolatry and the need for the purification and regulation of the cult, a high regard for true prophets who spoke of a coming judgement based on covenant infractions, the role of human sin as the basis for present states of wretchedness and oppression, the possibility of redemption and the redemptive nature of suffering, the role of repentance and confession, and the assurance of divine intervention and restoration. A number of these themes overlap with and are particularly prominent in the generic elements of the third chapter of Lamentations. The thought of the exiles, then, diverges from that of the remnant, but the two seem to have come together in the final composition of Lamentations. An exploration of its setting in life illuminates how this came to be.

SITZ IM LEBEN: MOURNING RITUALS IN THE ANCIENT NEAR EAST AND THE BIBLE

The poems of Lamentations include the prayerful reflections and words of survivors after the battle against Jerusalem and its subsequent downfall, although there is not enough evidence to adjudicate if they represent the actual petitions recited by people or are instead literary compositions based on the words of actual prayers. Certainly, the careful composition of the individual poems and the shaping of the book of Lamentations as an interpretive unit point towards the latter conclusion. As vestiges of prayers, the poems likely stemmed from worship contexts, which we will outline briefly here. Notably, though, the biblical literature is not overly concerned with filling in the details of life in the homeland or among the exiles in Babylonia. There is an oft bemoaned break in the historical record and we will need to reconstruct the religious situation based on the sparse details of the biblical material.

In the former Southern Kingdom, the Babylonians set about to re-establish a sense of continuity and normality for the population that remained in the land. The remnant in the land were clustered for the most part in the territory of Benjamin, which was organized initially under the leadership of Gedaliah. Political, societal and economic renewal took place in the homeland and it is expected, although we have not yet found evidence thereof, that at least one sanctuary was established in the Benjamin region to facilitate the continuation of worship for the remnant population. In Babylonia, the exiles were settled together and appear to have quickly established community leadership under a series of elders and possibly also religious worship through prayer and study. Although not widely accepted, the origin of the Jewish synagogue as a place for the exiled community to gather for the purposes of study, prayer and worship is sometimes posited to this time.

In the First Temple period and before the catastrophic defeat and downfall of Jerusalem in 587 BCE, public fasts were called to respond to national crises, including loss in war and drought. For instance, biblical texts attest to the public mourning that accompanied the defeat of the Israelites by the Benjaminites (Judg. 20:26) and the death of King Saul (1 Sam. 31). The laments collected together and arranged in the biblical Lamentations are thought to belong to the milieu of public mourning that took place after the loss of the Davidic kingdom. As Rainer Albertz noted in his study of the history and literature belonging to the period after the fall of Jerusalem in the sixth century BCE, "ritual lamentations became the primary locus where the people could carry out the grief work necessitated by their afflictions and learn to deal appropriately with the political catastrophe" (Albert 2003: 141). In fact, a number of communal laments in the Psalter are attributed to the *Sitz im Leben* or setting in life of mourning in the Templeless period, including very conservatively, even when not all persuasively, Psalms 44, 74, 79, 89, 102, 106, 137 (for a brief introduction to some of them and further references, see Middlemas 2005: 144–70 and 2007: 35–45).

Biblical, archaeological and imperial evidence reinforce the assessment of the almost utter devastation of Jerusalem and Judah that coincided with the Babylonian attack and questions arise as to where religious rituals could take place and by whom. The temple in Jerusalem was torn down and its altar was defiled, if not also decimated. The biblical record accounts for the slaughter of important members of the priesthood including the Chief Priest Seraiah, the second in line Zephaniah and three keepers of the threshold (2 Kgs 25:18-21; Jer. 52:24-7; see also Lam. 2:6c, 20). The destruction of the temple and the loss of significant cultic personnel resulted in the cessation of regular ritual observance in Jerusalem at least for the duration of the Templeless period. Based on analogous ANE evidence, however, it is likely that spontaneous worship took place in Jerusalem as well as some kind of regular cultic activity in the Benjamin region. Extant literary pieces from the ancient world reveal how faithful religious adherents initiated a series of mourning rituals after the loss of a sanctuary or another destructive event. For example, Adad Guppi, the mother of the Babylonian King Nabonidus and High Priestess of the Moon God Sin, maintained her service in the destroyed temple of the Moon God after its destruction and outlined the mourning rituals in which she continued to participate until its reconstruction (Longman 1997). Similarly, the Jews in the military colony of Elephantine in Egypt recount their participation in three years of lamentation and mourning following the destruction of their temple (Porten 1996: 139–47).

At least one biblical reference from the period hints that spontaneous and sporadic ritual observance took place at the Jerusalem temple (Lipschits 2005; Middlemas 2005: 122–44 and 2007: 28–35). A narrator recounts in Jeremiah that "eighty men arrived from Shechem and Shiloh and Samaria, with their beards shaved and their clothes torn, and their bodies gashed, [who were] bringing grain offerings and incense to present at the house of Yahweh" (Jer. 41:4-5). The pilgrims are travelling to observe the Feast of Weeks at 'the house of Yahweh' which has been widely regarded as a reference to the ruins of the temple in Jerusalem, although another sanctuary could be in view (so Blenkinsopp 2002). Significantly, they bring with them grain offerings and incense, but not animal sacrifices, which would support the ruined temple as their destination. At the site of the temple, the altar was at least desecrated, if not broken down, and not suitable for animal sacrifices. In addition, the outward appearance of the men with clean-shaven faces, rent clothing and self-inflicted wounds underscores that they were mourning. The account of their personal pietistic behaviour suggests that some individuals gathered together spontaneously to observe traditional rituals at the site of the temple after the destruction wrought in Judah.

There is also slight evidence of regular ritual observance in the homeland. In the concluding series of oracles in Proto-Zechariah (Zech. 1–8) dated to the end of the Templeless period by a chronological framework to 520–518 BCE, the prophet speaks of fasting that had taken place during the preceding years, "Say to the people of the land and the priests: When you fasted and lamented in the fifth month and in the seventh, for these seventy years, was it for me that you fasted?" (Zech. 7:5). This brief word of God directed at the population around Jerusalem attests not only to the presence of priests in the homeland after the fall of Jerusalem, but also to different religious activities that they led and in which the remnant community participated. In addition, a sacred, cultic site may have been established to allow for the resumption of regular ritual as hinted at in the perplexing statement, "Now Bethel had sent Sharezer and Regem-melek and their men to entreat the favour of Yahweh and to ask the priests of the house of Yahweh and the prophets" (Zech. 7:2-3a, my translation).

The NRSV actually speaks of 'the people of Bethel' here, but the reference in the Hebrew is much more ambiguous which has led to a debate about whether Bethel is the subject or object of the sentence or even part of a person's name and thereby yielding 'Bethel-Sharezer'. I have pointed out that Bethel never forms part of a name in the Old Testament, that its placement in the Hebrew syntax suggests that it is the subject of the sentence, and names of places can stand in for the people of those communities (as in Amos 5:5 and as reflected in the NRSV). Important in this context is that a delegation sets out from Bethel to Jerusalem, where they seek to adjudicate a ritual matter. In the context of First Zechariah, which is focused on reasserting Jerusalem as the central authority of the community, the reference reaffirms the priority of the leadership, the priests and prophets, at the temple in the capital city. The reaffirmation of the important role of religious and social leaders in Jerusalem also shifts the locus of authority to the capital city and away from the region of Benjamin where it had been located during the Templeless period. In so doing, it hints at regular religious activity by priests taking place at a sanctuary in Bethel during the period.

The hints of spontaneous and organized religious activity continuing in the homeland in literature written after the fall of Jerusalem raise questions about comparable activity among the exiles. Certainly, there is at least one liturgical psalm that seems to reflect the experience of the exiles in Babylonia who wondered about the possibilities of continuing worship on foreign soil, ironically phrased in the language of worship (Ps. 137). Worthy of note in this context is that provision is made within the historical record for petitions to be made outside the homeland in Solomon's temple prayer in the Kings account. Towards the conclusion of Solomon's dedication of the temple there are a series of verses that have long been thought to have been added after the downfall of Jerusalem in the sixth century BCE that attest to the efficacy of prayers made towards Jerusalem and the sanctuary. These references suggest a point in time in which the community is in exile (e.g. 1 Kgs 8:30, 44, 48) and further that organized religious observance took place among the *Golah*. The prayers include those made specifically for the return of the scattered (v. 34) and also on behalf of those "carried away captive to the land of the enemy, far off or near" (v. 46, see vv. 46-53) (Ferris 1992: 106–8).

At another point, the prophecies of Zechariah conflate the mourning activities of the homeland population with those of the exiles, "Thus says Yahweh of hosts: The fast of the fourth month, and the fast of the fifth, and the fast of the seventh, and the fast of the tenth, shall be seasons of joy and gladness; and cheerful festivals for the house of Judah" (Zech. 8:19) (Hoffman 2003: 194–7; Middlemas 2005: 128–30). The cited fasts correspond to events that took place during the Babylonian incursions – the fourth month commemorates the beginning of the siege, the fifth month the destruction of the temple and the king's palace, the seventh month the assassination of Gedaliah, and the tenth month the capture of the city of Jerusalem. The fasts represent those pertinent to all of the Judahite communities that existed after the downfall of Jerusalem, but the inclusion of the fast for Gedaliah was of particular relevance for the population that remained in the homeland and possibly also for the remnant that fled to Egypt. The inclusion of fast days relevant to all of the communities that experienced the downfall of the kingdom of Judah suggests that at least at the time associated with the prophet Zechariah attempts were made to foster a sense of commonality and forge a common identity among the various Judahite communities (Middlemas 2009: 178–83, but see recently for a different view Rom-Shiloni 2013). In so doing, the citation of the fast days attests to the importance of communal mourning by the remnant and the exiles during the Templeless period and well into the early Second Temple period.

The activity of mourning and Lamentations as part of the record of and reflection on the greatest tragedy to befall ancient Israel beg the question of the actual poets who composed the poems. There remains some debate about whether the poems of Lamentations represent oral compositions prayed by real people after the tragic events that were later written down by an author who superimposed the acrostic and alphabetic forms (so Westermann) or were originally designed as written compositions meant to cohere as a group (so Renkema). This question need not detain us and what is more important in this context is to gain some sense of who wrote these poems. Johann Renkema has presented a good case that temple singers remained in Judah who were knowledgeable of the language and theology of the Psalms as well as other ANE liturgical compositions (Renkema 1998: 44–7; cf. Berges 2002). The temple singers were minor members of the clergy who assumed greater leadership roles in the vacuum left in the homeland through the slaughter and deportation of the temple priesthood that accompanied the downfall of Judah. His argument is particularly persuasive with respect to chapters 1, 2, 4 and possibly 5, but I would add that the deuteronomic theology of confession and redemption so prominent in chapter 3 suggests that it can be attributed to a redactor who assembled the poems composed by the temple singers and ordered them according to a scheme consistent with penitential prayer and exilic thought. The final editor stems from among the repatriated exiles and the odd mix of genres in the third chapter may represent aspects of the religious liturgy that took place in Babylon. These preliminary observations will need to be tested at the point when interpreters begin to distinguish more clearly the thought relevant to the homeland, which has been the onus of much of my work (see Middlemas 2005; 2006; 2007; 2009, but see Janssen 1956; Albertz 2003: 90–111), from the ideology and compositions of the exiles, which tends to be much better reflected in the literature.

Further work on mourning as an organized religious activity in connection with the biblical Lamentations has been conducted by Xuan Pham (Pham 1999; two classic studies are Lipiński 1969; Andersen 1991). Spontaneous reactions to personal or communal disaster include weeping and wailing, the tearing of clothes, shaving the head, cutting the body, sitting in the dust or ash-heap, strewing dust or ash on the head, falling to the ground, and lying prostrate. The bodily expression of mourning was typically accompanied by fasting and prayer. In the ancient world as in ancient Israel there was also a more organized way to mourn in a ritual where a comforter or comforters participate with the mourner through their presence, adopting mourning customs, offering silence or giving advice with the intent to ease the suffering of the grieving individual (Pham 1999: 27–35). There is some suggestion that the interactions between the personified Jerusalem and the eyewitness in the first two chapters of Lamentations have elements of an organized mourning ritual, whereby a friend or family member accompanies the mourner and seeks to enable him or her to work through the grief process.

In Lamentations a repetitive refrain reinforces the isolation of the city, "[Dearest Jerusalem] has no one to comfort her" (Lam. 1:2, 9, 17, 21) and once it is stated that "there was no one to help her" (1:7). Through these statements, the eyewitness narrating reporter suggests that there is no comforter present to assist the personified city through the grief process or that no particular individual was felt to be adequate to help Jerusalem overcome her trauma. The theme of the lack of a traditional comforter fits the overall emphasis of the collection, that is, that the fateful events and the ongoing distress can only be ultimately overturned through the Divine Comforter, whose presence and voice remain painfully absent (see the interplay of this thematic with compassion in Middlemas 2019). Nevertheless, Jerusalem in her own voice seems to recognize and attest to her need for divine comfort. In one of the clearest and most emphatic statements of trust or declarations of faith in God in the whole collection, she rebuts the narrator's persistent claim of the lack of a comforter, by stating bluntly and forthrightly, "a comforter *is far from me*, one to revive my courage" (1:16, italics added for emphasis). In this way, Pham is correct to draw attention to the ANE ritual of the comforter in the grieving process, but close analysis of this theme in Lamentations actually reveals that the only comforter envisioned within the poems who can help the city of Jerusalem through the tragedy is God, even though the eyewitness certainly attempts to assume this role.

Mourning rituals ensued after the collapse of the Southern Kingdom of Judah to enable a community to mourn its loss, move through its grief and draw the attention of God to their suffering and helplessness. Entire communities who survived the catastrophe of the Babylonian defeat of Judah in the sixth century BCE captured their communal memories in lamentation, some of which appears to be remembered and recorded in the biblical Lamentations. More recent studies have started to shed light on the role of women in rituals of lamentation and mourning. Indeed, women and young girls held a respected place as musicians and singers of dirges and other cries of grief in the cult and in society more generally in the ancient world and in other cultures down to today (Meyers 1994; Bergeant 2002: 11; Lee 2002: 41–5). In addition to the female singers who lament in a tradition harking back to Jeremiah in Chronicles, "all the singing men and singing women have spoken of Josiah in their laments to this day" (2 Chron. 35:25), young women are listed among those celebrating in the cult with dance (Jer. 31:13). Furthermore, in at least one psalm, the role of young women is coordinated with that of musicians, "the singers in front, the musicians last, between them girls playing tambourines" (Ps. 68:25). The personification of the city of Jerusalem as a woman who raises her voice so poignantly certainly hints at the importance and inclusion of female responses in religious ritual to mourn and commemorate the disaster of the fall of the Southern Kingdom and its catastrophic aftermath. We would be remiss, then, not to imagine female professional or lay mourners among and even leading the temple singers whose voices are captured in the biblical Lamentations and who ritually grieved the loss of the city and the devastating consequences to its inhabitants.

In general, the book of Lamentations represents a collection of mournful prayers that stem from an unnamed catastrophe that could in the end only be the downfall of Jerusalem and Judah in the sixth century BCE. The poems attest to a lengthy, protracted, painful present and are applicable to any number of crises in the history of the Jewish people in ancient times, in antiquity, in the Middle Ages and today (for rabbinic use of the complaint genre and Lamentations, see Morrow 2006). Their use on the Ninth of Ab in Jewish tradition to remember the fall of the First and Second Temples (in 587 BCE and 70 CE, respectively) as well as other tragedies and persecutions of the Jews down through the ages speaks to the general nature of the imagery and the universal applicability of various reactions to great suffering. Indeed, the language of Lamentations stems from poetic imagination that captures hyperbolically, evocatively and, yet without any degree of specificity, a series of disasters from different perspectives that have general applicability to any number of tragedies (Provan 1991: 7–19; cf. Joyce 1999). So, although it is possible to speculate about the historical and cultural context that motivated the production of the poems, the poetry itself urges theological and ideological engagement, which is the task of the next two chapters.

THEOLOGICAL AND CONTEXTUAL READINGS IN LAMENTATIONS

Heretofore, we have used critical approaches to examine the biblical book of Lamentations as literature and as the product of a particular historical context, where we have examined the cultural contexts that are thought to lie at the background of the biblical poems. The assessment of literary and historical matters lays the foundation to consider a third prong of criticism that is more loosely associated with interpretation, that is, the endeavour to draw meaning out from the text, essentially as associated with the task of exegesis, which leads to a deeper appreciation of the message of biblical literature:

> If we allow ourselves to enter into the world created by the poet, to transcend through imagination our own temporal boundedness and learn and appreciate the customs and conventions, both literary and cultural, of the poet's time and place, then we might find that Lamentations can illuminate in its own unique way some of the questions of human existence that haunt even a generation of people about to enter the twenty-first century. (Dobbs-Allsopp 1997: 54)

The types of scholarly analyses considered in a typical introductory course to biblical studies or the Bible focus on questions that can well be classified as historical or even excavatory. A historical reading of a text excavates it as the source of information about matters related to the social, political and religious circumstances in which particular pieces of literature arose as well as the life settings of its authors, redactors and the communities in which they circulated. Such enquiries are historical in the main and sometimes referred to, therefore, as diachronic which loosely translates as 'through time'. In diachronic analyses interpreters consider the social worlds behind or related to the text and the way the material evolved. Beginning in the 1960s the dominance of the historical paradigm began to be questioned as it became clear that historical reconstructions differed from expert interpreter to expert interpreter, which marks a phenomenon that one scholar characterizes as the "collapse of history" (Perdue 1994 and 2005). Furthermore, regarding the biblical literature as a window into history was felt to be unsatisfactory for those who sought to appropriate the message of the Bible to their particular, communal and personal circumstances and otherwise find a word of God that means something in their present and culturally specific contexts.

The book of Lamentations means something to readers who come with questions from their own personal contexts or interests. In this way, it contributes a word about God with its point of departure in human experience which is the burden of theology. Concomitantly, the study of Lamentations also contributes towards conceptions of the human condition with reflections on what the texts can tell us about struggles pertinent to people, actual physical and emotional suffering, and even the types of coping mechanisms used by survivors, which tend to be matters considered within the social science disciplines of anthropology, refugee studies, and trauma studies. Readers also approach the text with questions related to gender, sexuality, and the role and agency of women which fall within the particular, but not exclusive, purview of feminist criticism. In a similar way, theologians and biblical scholars in Third World locations focus on different questions when looking at biblical texts and address issues related to systemic poverty, oppression, violent suppression and colonial strategies that overwhelm indigenous narratives in liberation and post-colonial readings. Finally, the interpretation of themes and passages of biblical literature has taken place already within the Bible, but extends well beyond it into the realm of the fine arts and music. Reception historians and exegetes consider the afterlife of Lamentations, how it survives and conveys meaning in new cultural contexts and mediums. The onus of this chapter is to focus on scholarship that has sought to bridge the often-bemoaned historical gap between the critical study of historical questions in the main and the individual social contextual questions raised by interpreters of what the text means, and we begin with attention to theological discussion.

THEOLOGICAL DISCUSSIONS

Scholarly enquiry into the question of theology and the book of Lamentations has tended to veer into two differing directions, with one branch of interpretation concerned with the theological traditions that underlie the message of the poems and a second branch focused on messages about God and the human person conveyed in and through the book. Another way to look at the history of the critical study of Lamentations in the last half century is according to three main periods of research (House 2011). Theological studies of Lamentations can be divided into eras of research that correspond to particular foci: 1954–89 evidences a focus on the explanation of suffering, 1990–9 reveals a concern with the role of the lament in calling attention to and protesting suffering, and 2000 to the present includes strategies to assist in surviving the painful human experiences outlined in the material. Here, we will consider the theological traditions thought to permeate the thought of Lamentations, the theological message of the poems and its theologies, that is, the reticence among some interpreters to isolate a central theological theme.

Lamentations and its theological traditions

The first line of enquiry is related to the theological traditions that underlie the thought of the poems of Lamentations. This type of analysis can be profitably illuminated by brief consideration of the divergent analyses of Norman Gottwald and Bertil Albrektson. On the one hand, Gottwald argued that the poems of Lamentations grapple with and even call into question the tenets of the deuteronomic doctrine of retribution that emphasized divine justice and punishment for sin (Gottwald 1954). Succinctly stated, according to the deuteronomic view God punishes covenant infractions and blesses covenant loyalty (see Deuteronomy 28 for an example of this thinking). According to Gottwald, the deuteronomic perspective failed to present an adequate and persuasive explanation for the great catastrophe that lies as the central concern of the book, which he regards as the fall of Jerusalem in 587 BCE. Earnest attempts had been made to observe the covenant, especially through the reforms enacted by two prominent kings of the Southern Kingdom, Hezekiah and Josiah, yet the downfall of the temple, city and nation took place as well as the cessation of Davidic kingship. The poets of Lamentations, then, struggled with how to understand deuteronomic explanations in the light of the eradication of the Southern Kingdom and the ongoing circumstances of hardship and imperial rule.

Noting that the people actually account for their sins, albeit only rarely and sometimes even generically (1:5, 8, 18; 2:14; 4:6, 13; 5:7, 16), Albrektson countered that a theological dilemma arose not from a mismatch between historical circumstances and deuteronomic interpretation, but, rather, from the confrontation with and the failure of the promises of Zion theology (Albrektson 1963). Zion theology represents an umbrella interpretive term that includes conceptions about the central role of the city of Jerusalem in the ideology of the Southern Kingdom, including God's delight in the city, the celebration of the deity's choice of Zion for the earthly temple and the locus of divine earthly rule, the inviolability of the city, and the location of the rule of the Davidic kings for perpetuity. In spite of belief in promises to the contrary, the city fell to an invading Babylonian army, the Davidic king was captured and forcibly deported along with a number of the nation's social, religious and political elites to the heartland of the Babylonian Empire, and the homeland was left devastated and under foreign rule, if not also occupation. For Albrektson, then, the major theological problem with which the poems grappled was the loss of the promises to David and the coterminous almost complete eradication of the city of Jerusalem along with the significant political and religious symbols of the king's palace and the Yahwistic sanctuary. In Albrektson's analysis, deuteronomic theological viewpoints interweave throughout Lamentations, but the overall thrust of the book evidences the grappling with the failure of Zion theology to provide a meaningful framework with which to interpret the loss of divine promises and divine protection.

The analyses of Gottwald and Albrektson were some of the first to really account for the traditions that lie at the heart of Lamentations. Their studies have drawn attention to the theological underpinnings of the poems, the traditions with which the poets grappled, and how in the final assessment they did not provide suitable explanations of the disaster for the poets of the literature or for the community to and for whom they wrote. In isolating deuteronomic or Zion theologies as the framework grappled with in the book of Lamentations, Gottwald and Albrektson each in his own way find a single, central message in the disparate poems. However, closer scrutiny of the various voices that intertwine in Lamentations calls into question the presence of a single, overarching theology. For example, Michael Moore presents a concentrated analysis of examples of human suffering in the book that reveals the persistence of references to and articulations of the experience of pain that ultimately detract from the presentation of any single, isolated theme or theology (Moore 1983; see also Dobbs-Allsopp 1997). Close attention to the tragedy outlined in the poems undercuts any attempt to isolate *a* theology on which they depend and provides a convenient entry to another category of research on the poems that focuses more attention on their message.

The theological message of Lamentations

The majority of interpreters have concentrated less on the traditions with which the poets grappled and more with what they sought to impart. In this respect, the theological message of Lamentations has been heavily influenced since antiquity and well into the nineteenth century by the suggestion that its author was Jeremiah (Linafelt 2000; Cooper 2001: 3–9). Jewish and Christian exegetes in antiquity, the medieval period and in pre-Enlightenment criticism regarded the theological significance of Lamentations to lie in its substantiation of Jeremiah's prophecies of doom, that is, in the just punishment of God for sin. Defenders of this type of interpretation continue in scholarship up to the present day and focus on the third chapter as the theological nub of the collection. Around the same time as the debate between Gottwald and Albrektson took shape, for example, the German scholar Hermann Wiesmann called attention to the only explicit articulation of hope in the third chapter. He pointed to confidence in God found in conjunction with the *geber* as a model of behaviour for those in the middle of suffering from war, famine, disease, injury, and persecution to hold onto and emulate (Wiesmann 1954). A good number of analyses continue in this line of thinking. The persecuted individual of the third chapter not only represents a paradigm to follow, that is, to recognize and confess rebellion and estrangement against God, but also presents reasons to hope in God based on the recognition of divine mercy, the alleviation of suffering and the forgiveness of sins (e.g. Mintz 1982; Re'emi 1984; Krašovec 1992; Hunter 1996; House 2004; Parry 2010; Thomas 2013).

The focus on the third chapter as the theological nub of the collection continues to exert a significant amount of influence on theological assessments of the book as Tod Linafelt has emphasized in his study of the figure of Zion and his effort to redraw lines of interpretation to better account for her posture of protest as a contrary and equally important theme in the poems (Linafelt 2000). Better appreciation for human suffering and misery draws attention away from the comforting message of hope in divine forgiveness and intervention, which offers another avenue for the exploration of the theological message of Lamentations. A close analysis of personified Jerusalem in the first two chapters discloses the importance of her tenacity and persistent protest in the face of the brutality of war, its aftermath and the seeming absence of God, which promotes a theology based on honest contradiction, rather than pious acquiescence.

> Emerging from this reading is an ancient text that, contrary to the consensus of biblical scholars, is more about the *expression* of suffering than the meaning behind it, more about the vicissitudes of survival than the abstractions of sin and guilt, and more about protest as a religious posture than capitulation or confession. (Linafelt 2000: 4)

Along different lines, Alan Cooper proposes to regard Lamentations in the light of the penitential prayer literature of the ancient Near East (Cooper 2001). When read this way, the theological message of Lamentations attends more to issues related to the incomprehensibility of God's wrath and the hope that through sustained and attentive focus on the misery of a suffering people, God will be moved to compassion and love (see also Greenstein 2004).

The isolation of theological centre points within Lamentations according to those that focus on the centrality of the redemptive nature of suffering or those that point to protest against the attribution of sin can fruitfully be categorized along the lines of theodic and antitheodic interpretations (Bier 2015). Theodic or God-sympathetic readings emphasize the justice of God and defend the deity's behaviour. In such a reading, as Miriam Bier points out, misdeeds or covenant violations committed by the members of Judahite society coalesce within the metaphor of the sins of Jerusalem personified as a woman and come under divine judgement. In this perspective, the book of Lamentations "explain[s] the ways of God to humanity" (as quoted by Bier 2015: 13). The suffering bemoaned in the poems is thus defended, rationalized and even dismissed. In contrast, a small, but growing, minority of scholars draw attention to elements in the poems that suggest the culpability and injustice of the deity, question the rightness of the presentation of God's actions, and attend to examples that suggest divine neglect and even abuse, and thus represent an antitheodic point of view or those perspectives that challenge perceptions about God. Interpreters who represent this line of thought focus on the amount of human suffering and Zion's protest against it. In my own research, I have tried to capture this phenomenon with the term *theodiabole*, that is, 'God accuser or challenger' to signify faithful challenges to (perceptions of) God (Middlemas 2005: 212; cf. Middlemas 2012). Analyses that are not sympathetic to the conception of the punishing God hold the deity to account and resist justifying the ways of God to humanity (see Bier 2015: 8–32).

Theologies of Lamentations

The experiences and perspectives captured in the poems of Lamentations invite and make room for many theological interpretations, and "the goal of scholarship ought to be, rather, to sustain multiple interpretations, indeed, to defend the merit of *all* serious possibilities of meaning" (Cooper 2001: 15–16). Suitably, then, arguments for dialogic (Boase 2006; Mandolfo 2007) and multivalent or polyphonic readings (Bier 2015) characterize a growing trend in interpretations of Lamentations at the present time. When understood as an open text, it is possible to value the multiple theologies that appear in Lamentations without emphasizing a single one as Heath Thomas has sensitively argued, although perhaps ultimately inadequately, given that his final assessment tends to focus on the rightness and justice of the deity (Thomas 2013; see the criticisms of Bier 2015: 27–8).

One of the first monograph-length studies to value the possibility of more than one theology in Lamentations is that of Carleen Mandolfo (2007; from a slightly differently angle, see Boase 2006). Mandolfo applied a dialogic approach to consider more thoughtfully the interaction of the different speakers that alternate as if in a dialogue in the first two chapters of Lamentations. In her analysis, personified Zion presents a counter story to that of the eyewitness in the first two chapters. The eyewitness draws on themes and interpretations found in the prophetic tradition, for example, by attributing the disaster that befell the community suffering in Lamentations to sinful behaviour. In this reading, the personified city of Jerusalem counters the eyewitness and her dialogue partner by pointing to the actual depth of human suffering and physical devastation. Ultimately,

Jerusalem persuades the eyewitness to come around to her point of view, to value her theological stance and acknowledge the extent of human suffering and divine culpability. The interaction of Jerusalem and the eyewitness in the first two chapters of Lamentations challenges traditional ascriptions of disaster to the efficacy of human sin and urges God to display a fuller and more equal justice. In this reading, the differing viewpoints expressed and in dialogue in Lamentations exemplify a dynamic theology that supports divergent and even contradictory theological perspectives by members bound together in a community of faith. The poems of Lamentations, then, invite honest debate about God instead of acquiescence to the promotion of one "correct" point of view.

Along similar lines, Miriam Bier considers the interaction of voices in the different chapters of Lamentations through a careful study that draws attention to the polyphony found in the poems (Bier 2015). A variety of speakers attest to their experiences and understandings of God and they all have equal value. The different explanations and grievances offered by the many speaking voices lack adjudication by a narrator and by God, whose voice is never heard in the poems. Significantly, the testimonies skip agilely from concerns about sin and guilt, penitence, protest and suffering, and calls for comfort, revenge and restoration. Because there is no advocate for a dominant theological interpretation, no single authoritative viewpoint overshadows or overrides the others. When seen in this way, the poems present a polyphony of speakers in conversation, rebuttal and contradiction. The diverse speakers in the poems present different perspectives about God and humankind that are never settled and adjudicated, but rather in constant negotiation through being worked out in lived experience and communication with others. The theology of Lamentations, then, values the expression of each individual's truth and so invites participation in as well as the articulation of many theologies in a community of faith.

Recent studies that focus on the possibilities of a dialogic or polyphonic faith draw attention to how Lamentations can offer more than one word about God and more than one theology. When considered holistically, then, the message of the poems lies closer to a polyphony because the different testimonies do not so much contradict or refute each other as simply commingle: "All perspectives remain together in churning, unsettled interaction" (O'Connor 2002: 84). One important perspective is the theology of witness that attests to the humanity of one's neighbour without minimizing the depth of despair experienced and expressed (O'Connor 2002: 96–109). Another theology grapples with the image of the abusing God who afflicts and injures without mercy (O'Connor 2002: 110–23). Yet another view wrestles with the image of the helpless or powerless deity, "for God does not willingly afflict or grieve anyone" (Lam. 3:33). In the very centre of the whole book, the poet raises a profound question about God by proclaiming that God does not act 'from the heart', that is, with intention to cause human suffering. God does not want to afflict or grieve anyone and seems mysteriously unable to intercede to alter the course of tragedy in the human sphere. For theologians, such a testimony must surely be startling and unsettling in equal measure as the standard view is that God is all-powerful, all-seeing and ever-present (omnipotent, omniscient and omnipresent). Nevertheless, the poet has placed exactly in the centremost verse of Lamentations a provocative statement that highlights God's own vulnerability, even powerlessness.

As a testament of multivalent accounts, the book of Lamentations speaks on a number of additional levels. The powerless and suffering God attests to the image of God as servant found in the Old Testament tradition in the image of the Suffering Servant in Isaiah (esp. in chs. 49–55), in the heroic figure brought low of Lamentations 3, and in the New Testament tradition in the servant mission embarked upon by Jesus Christ and the disciples that challenge modern notions of power in the church and in society more generally. Moreover, the concept that God is somehow removed from interference in human brutality helps to foster a theology of a vulnerable God as well as the need for human partners and witnesses in creation. The image of the powerless God is consistent with the biblical message, and also a concept that later literature sought to address and redress. In what has been considered a biblical answer to the unanswered prayers and petitions in Lamentations, the book of Job attests to a deity who fails to intervene in the face of human tragedy. But in so doing, confronts and rebuts the ideology of a powerless, even vulnerable, God. The narrator depicts the deity in control of events, who pledges only to remain removed from them for the sake of the contest with the divine adversary (Job 1:12; 2:6) and attests at the same time to divine power and incomprehensibility in lengthy speeches (Job 38–9, 40–1).

In Lamentations, the provocative trace of a theology that attests to the powerlessness of the deity appears, but biblical tradition on the whole, and certainly also the wisdom section at the centre of Lamentations itself, asserts divine power and purpose. Valuing the testimonies of the different and divergent speaking voices in Lamentations suggests that there is no resolution, no single or prevailing theme or theology in Lamentations. Hopeful testimony that attests to a merciful God in control of world events inextricably intertwines with protests and counter-stories of a suffering beyond explanation in a way that mirrors the relationship between the peaceful eye surrounded by the violent winds of a hurricane;

> The grand statement of hope in 3:22–39 stands at the centre of the work as a whole, but not as the focal point because it exists in tension with the portraits of human suffering so thoughtfully pointed out by those who stress the more negative images of the material … Like the funnel effect of a cyclone that cannot exist without the peaceful eye and raging winds, the two approaches to the book of Lamentations, through the centre and the periphery, co-exist because the very nature of the material insists that they do so. (Middlemas 2004: 94–5)

With its swarming images and cacophonous voices, the biblical book of Lamentations seems to defy a single theological message or central idea. Holding together the different theological perspectives within Lamentations and within scholarly assessments, that is, the focus on the redemptive nature of suffering, the role of penitence and confession, the articulation of pain, and protest against divine injustice, in many respects makes it difficult to discern a way forward. What I have suggested, therefore, is that the shape of the book, with its incongruous messages lying alongside each other as uncomfortable bedfellows, urges greater appreciation of the imagery of the storm. In biblical tradition, the appearance of God in human history, sometimes referred to as a theophany, tends to be accompanied by storm winds that indicate divine judgement as well as untold possibilities of divine intervention and salvation. When considered in this way, the theology of the book does not rest on the co-existence of multiple theologies, but rather conveys something about human conceptions of the current experience and hope for the future. The imagery of the violent storm conveys the community's perspective of a God who is otherwise entirely absent from the collection. They conceptualize their suffering as languishing under divine wrath, buffeted by the violent storm, while at the same time holding out hope for the possibility and power of a divine theophany that brings help for the sake of a hurting humanity.

Lamentations functions as a visual depiction in written form for use as a litany in order to encourage God to see and react to the suffering that accompanied the downfall of the kingdom. As such, it includes grounds for human faith along with the graphically honest presentation of the consequences of disaster and violence on individual members of the community who doubt. In spite of their dire circumstances as well as their individual and communal pain, the lamenters, tossed and turned by the winds of a violent storm, cling to life in what is rightly regarded as survival literature.

SOCIO-CONTEXTUAL READINGS

Trauma studies and Lamentations

A fruitful emerging sub-field in biblical interpretation falls loosely under the umbrella of trauma studies. Since the First World and the Vietnam Wars along with the clinical assessment of post-traumatic stress disorder (PTSD), a field of study related to the body and the mind has emerged that examines the experience of trauma with respect to physical as well as psychological/spiritual wounding and its aftershocks on the human person and psyche. In recent years, a growing number of biblical scholars have engaged with analyses of trauma in order to elucidate figures, themes, and the shaping of individual and communal memory in the biblical literature (see the collections edited by Kelle 2011; Becker, Dochhorn, Holt 2014; Boase and Frechette 2016). The book of Lamentations with its seething images of catastrophic societal collapse and myriad portraits of human affliction and death has naturally been ripe for such examination. Working with the recognition that traumatic experiences leave an imprint on the psyche and memory enables exegetes to be more precise in reconstructions of the emergence of biblical literature, especially with texts or collections that draw on, include and even recall painful memories. As Eve-Marie Becker notes, "Ancient texts provide cultural reservoirs in which coping with pain, fear, wounding, guilt, and shame is collected and expressed. To look for specific signs of trauma and traumatization will thus sharpen our exegetical optic" (Becker 2014: 26).

Early exploration of the power of recognizing the actuality of war and the martial tactic of deportation on its victims and the coping mechanisms of its survivors formed part of the basis for a series of studies by Daniel Smith-Christopher. For example, he reads Ezekiel and Lamentations with the awareness of the effects of state sponsored terrorism (Smith-Christopher 2002: 75–104). Interpreting the graphic portrayal of painful experiences in

Lamentations benefits from the recognition that the horrors described in conjunction with siege warfare were not mere hyperbolic threats, but actual descriptions of lived experience (see Deut. 28; Smith-Christopher 2002: 104). Furthermore, the metaphorical language of fetters, chains and swords has its basis in real-world experience and, therefore, should not be sanitized or dismissed in interpretation. Images of bonding and hardship serve more than a descriptive task that enables the modern reader to imagine the circumstances of the defeat of one kingdom by a violent, invading force. More importantly, they enable the visualization and appreciation of the actual toll of tragedy on the soul and psyche of the human person (Smith-Christopher 2002: 104).

In a different way, interpreters have drawn on studies of grief and the grieving process in order to shed light in particular on various aspects of Lamentations, including the role of human suffering (Moore 1983; cf. Johnson 1985) and the uncharacteristically chaotic structure of the collection likened to the disorientation that accompanies significant loss (Joyce 1993; Joyce and Lipton 2013: 117–20). Characteristic of this type of study is that of David Reimer who draws on the significant work on loss and bereavement conducted by Elisabeth Kübler-Ross on the psychology of the grief process to show how the themes of Lamentations correspond to the structure of grieving (Reimer 2002). Isolation stands out as a dominant theme in the first chapter, anger in the second, bargaining in the sense of drawing on good behaviour to motivate the intervention of the deity in the third, the depressive loss of hope in the fourth chapter and the correspondence in the fifth chapter to a sort of acceptance characterized by the sense of defeat or exhaustion.

Analyses of Lamentations that sketch its themes according to the process of grief or tragedy reveal a number of lines of contact with the focus on the posture of lament as a protest against a harsh reality and a call for justice (so Claus Westermann 1974). A number of interpreters have concentrated on the role of the lament in a type of research that marks another movement towards the inclusion of topics of interest in studies of trauma, but not yet classified as such. One example is found in the work of F. W. Dobbs-Allsopp, who draws attention to correspondences between the biblical Lamentations and tragic literature with their overwhelming focus on suffering (Dobbs-Allsopp 1997). In his analysis, suffering rises to the foreground in Lamentations just as the significance of sin, punishment and the ethical vision of divine mercy and goodness are downplayed. Lamentations, then, underscores how sin, suffering and evil "are the very stuff of human existence" (Dobbs-Allsopp 1997: 54), but not to concentrate exclusively on a painful present. Instead, the reality of everyday hardship in Lamentations discloses something profound about the divine-human relationship, wherein the failure to explain away or rationalize human suffering discloses a sanctity to human life that deserves greater appreciation. When suffering is given its due, faith is modelled by courageous individuals who speak up to a silent God and provide examples of relationality, comfort and action in the absence of divine compassion (see also Middlemas 2019). Healing can then take place when the honest expression of pain is named and framed in a community of faith.

In recent years, a growing number of analyses pay careful attention to expressions of actual physical pain, especially as felt by the personified city of Jerusalem (Maier 2008), but also in conjunction with the lamenting speakers in chapters 1 and 3 (Boase

2014). Elizabeth Boase points out that one prevalent reaction of a survivor to trauma is isolation, to feel alone and be isolated. In her analysis of Lamentations, she shows how the metaphors referring to bodily pain otherwise known as somatization experienced by the speakers in the first three chapters actually function to foster a sense of community cohesion. Suffering does more than create the space for empathy. The articulation of actual pain accompanied by physical and bodily reactions creates the basis for a shared experience. Individual sufferers, once alone and isolated in their very personal agonies, take the opportunity to create meaningful connections with others. On the one hand, the speaking and hearing of trauma enable different individuals to come together and re-group as a community. On the other hand, the disclosure of personal pain offers a model for and even an invitation to subsequent generations to share the very human experience of suffering through liturgical recital and communal testimony. The acknowledgement of physical affliction then allows individual survivors to share personal stories of torment, come together and promote healing.

There have been many precursors to observations of the importance of lament, protest and the human grappling with what appears at times as a god-forsaken present, but Trauma Studies, which have only been brought into dialogue with biblical studies and theology within the last decade or so, offers a way to think less abstractly about the biblical literature, its themes and figures. In general, Trauma Studies research can help us not only grasp the chaotic panoply of images of affliction and violence, the bewildering snapshots of suffering, perspectives and speaking voices as well as the mix of genres and literary categories that attempt to formulate meaning, but also simply express the depth and breadth of confusion and uncertainty. Trauma Studies sheds valuable light on the organization and disorganization of biblical literature in a way that is meaningful to individuals and communities from many different walks of life and socio-cultural contexts.

Feminist criticism and Lamentations

Just as we can approach the biblical literature with questions about what it reveals about God and the divine-human relationship, which essentially relate to questions of theology, and about what it can tell us of human experiences of wounding and the impact of lived reality on the composition of individual and communal memories, a text or a book contains information pertinent to the social location of women. As I understand it, feminist criticism arises from a methodological and critical approach to literature that aims to disclose how interpretations have been and can be harmful to the idea of women as equal partners and agents in creation as well as those that reveal the activity and fruitful construction of women in the making and shaping of familial, societal and national history. A woman's view exposes narratives that harm entire communities by covering over the significant roles women play and the contributions that they make, but also encompasses an understanding of the world that extends far beyond that which relates to, sheds light on and elevates women as equal partners in the global marketplace of ideas and activity.

Feminist criticism shares in common the goals of liberation analyses, which aim to extend full humanity in perception, activity and opportunity to disenfranchised and oppressed members of local and national communities (see Sakenfeld 1988; Ringe 1992; Brenner 1997; Fuchs 2000). At the same time, a feminist perspective encompasses more than concern with the liberation of the poor, the working class and the oppressed by drawing attention to the created order and human responsibility to creation and our fellow creatures. Feminism embraces a vision that seeks to capture a more holistic conception of the role of women while at the same time noting where harmful perspectives and structures sever the harmony of creation through the power and authority exerted by some men over other men as well as over women, children, wild and domesticated animals and the environment.

As with the other methodological approaches already surveyed in this chapter, feminist interpretation takes its starting point in reading from a particular and disclosed social location. The difference is that the social context is not consideration of God or human concerns and reactions to life-shattering experiences more broadly defined, but rather those that resonate with and arise from women's experiences. Feminist critique offers new perspectives that evaluate, supplement, challenge and contradict inherited ways of being and perceiving. A feminist theology then recognizes the harmony of the created order for the benefit of all creation and aims, thereby, to reconstruct a religious perspective that recognizes the worth and dignity of all human life created in the image of God and appointed as the caretakers and tenders, rather than the assaulters and rapists of creation, to elevate the constructive power of women for the benefit of women, gender and familial harmony, society and all living things.

A number of biblical interpreters, especially in conjunction with the use of feminist methods of reading adopted increasingly since the 1970s, have drawn attention to female characters in the Bible to shed new light on their positive contributions and roles as well as texts in which they are terrorized and mistreated (Trible 1984). The contribution by Kathleen O'Connor on Lamentations is an example of feminist exegesis conducted both sensitively and affirmatively that lies in a direct line to the original intent of *The Woman's Bible* that took place in tandem with the Suffragist movement in the United States in the late nineteenth and early twentieth centuries (O'Connor 1992). In her reading, O'Connor critically evaluates the use of female images like that of Daughter Zion as well as the structure of Lamentations. Positively, the poet seems to value female experience and perspectives by using the evocative images of vulnerable and tender Zion and Judah personified as women to convey a nation's abject sorrow, bereavement and grief. Moreover, in Lamentations personified Zion acts as an eloquent and resolute spokesperson for the community. As an advocate, she even raises questions about God's justice on the basis of the enormity and severity of destruction and suffering.

The prominence of a female religious leader who gives voice to the community is an important step towards including feminine perspectives in communities of faith and in society as well as recognizing women's humanity and autonomy, but Daughter Zion is no role model as O'Connor indicates. The five poems are structured so that God's mercy and redemptive intervention extend only to the solitary male figure of the third chapter.

Elsewhere, Jerusalem and Judah personified as female experience God's silence, feelings of despair and hopelessness, and are subject to accusations of covenant disobedience. The image of a God, who comes to the aid of a suffering male petitioner, but remains stoically far removed from a female supplicant, presents a negative theology for women. Moreover, the portrayal of the city as feminine becomes a harmful image to women because the poet depicts Daughter Zion as subordinate to the deity who is symbolized as male. In the poems of Lamentations, the personified city is an object of humiliation and mockery who attributes her suffering to her own disobedience. By so doing, the female Jerusalem effectively collaborates in her own "punishment" and abuse. The images associated with the city's feminine persona are also harmful because they (can) teach the subordination of women as well as the acceptance of their physical and mental abuse.

In a different vein, a number of feminist interpreters have drawn attention to the deity's violence perpetuated against the city of Jerusalem personified as a vulnerable woman especially in the descriptive details of the second chapter (e.g. Seidman 1995; Guest 1999; Stiebert 2003). For these critics, the text is virtually irredeemable because of the hostile actions attributed to God. Lamentations, then, seems to validate the persecution of women and other subordinate members of the community, like the children and the elderly. The promotion of violence in Lamentations makes it irredeemable to some readers, such as Naomi Seidman who imagines burning the biblical books that generate damaging images that degrade the worth of women (Seidman 1995) and Deryn Guest who highlights male complicity and advocates excising harmful books from the canon (Guest 1999). Perhaps more disturbing still is the punishing God of Lamentations who denies divine righteousness, pity, forgiveness, mercy, attentiveness and responsiveness to female Jerusalem (Stiebert 2003). The frightful image of an abusing God in studies sensitive to gender relations discloses a harmful vision for communities and simultaneously challenges us to reject God's apparent justice when perpetuated at the expense of women (and other vulnerable members of society) and when imitated by men in the home, at work and in local communities.

In general, feminist interpretation of Lamentations includes a wide range of topics of discussion, from close textual analyses that highlight gender inequality, embedded patriarchy, male (divine) violence and the role of female characters in the poems to more general regard for the distressing disharmony in which the characters of Lamentations, male and female, rich and poor, old and young, live and suffer. Female voices offer a different perspective that when heard and valued can draw attention to important new dimensions of the divine-human relationship. Thus, attention to female Jerusalem who rages as an advocate against the violence perpetrated against her community and the abject suffering of the most innocent members of society presents a foil to the suffering, submissive, thought to be rational, man of the third chapter that has received the bulk of attention from people of faith and exegetes in the Jewish and Christian traditions. Greater appreciation for the role of female Jerusalem helps us to see more clearly how the biblical witness itself advocates and sanctions the inclusion of female voices. A feminist lens reveals that Daughter Zion models how to recapture lost voices and honour protest, persuasion and persistence as well as how to grapple with and include alternative points of view in a community of faith and in society more generally.

Post-colonial criticism and Lamentations

Another type of social location reading is post-colonial criticism, which has begun generating new perspectives on the interpretation of Lamentations within the last few years. Colonialism can be characterized as efforts to colonize other nation-states in order to extract resources and use people for the benefit of the colonizer which included European countries in the sixteenth century as well as the United States, the Soviet Union and Japan in the twentieth century, and China and Russia today. Post-colonial interpretation essentially consists of two prongs. On the one hand, it understands that colonialism has exerted an interpretive, conveyed as superior, metanarrative or overarching story that favours the conquerors or colonizers at the expense, and often simultaneously belittling, of the diverse, local colonized culture and people. On the other hand, the post-colonial interpreter seeks to draw attention to the value of local traditions and culture as a means to emphasize their worth for local communities and nations. Greater appreciation for native traditions often happens at the same time as concerted endeavours are made to reframe, reinterpret and reject the stories of the colonizer in order to resist imperial economic and ideological exploitation (Sugirtharajah 2002; Moore and Segovia 2005; Perdue 2005: 280–339).

As R. S. Sugirtharajah notes, the liberatory intentions of feminist and post-colonial readings collide in their "mutual resistance to any form of oppression" (Sugirtharajah 2002: 28). At the same time, as post-colonial feminists point out, feminist criticism as practised in Western countries more often than not obscures the particular issues relevant to interpreters in Third World locations, which tends to circulate colonial ideas that are irrelevant at best and harmful at worst to the global community (Sunder-Rajan and Park 2000). In actual fact, the goals and practices of post-colonial interpreters share more in common with those of liberation theologians, in seeking to disclose oppressive and dehumanizing interpretations and to offer counter readings that celebrate and liberate the marginalized. Where the two fields differ is that post-colonial criticism scrutinizes the Bible and examples of imperial ideology therein, while also engaging in exegetical readings that draw upon an awareness of empire (Crowell 2009).

In conjunction with the book of Lamentations, Archie Lee brings together the images of the mothers wailing over their suffering and slaughtered children in Lamentations and the mothers grieving over the students killed by the Chinese military in the Tiananmen Square Massacre in 1989 (Lee 2005). When Lamentations is read in conjunction with the perspectives of the Tiananmen Square mothers, it is possible to see more clearly the importance of the suffering of women more generally and the powerful female figure represented in the first two chapters more specifically. Interpretations that focus on justifying violent retributive righteous acts attributed to God and hope in divine mercy tend to silence Zion's perspective on as well as her articulation of suffering. Just so is the whitewashing of history that is taking place in China at the present time and the political and military attempts to silence dissent. Against the obfuscation of a tragic history and military aggression, the mothers of Tiananmen continue to dissent and thus behave similarly to the community in the fifth chapter of Lamentations who petition, protest and grieve instead of settling with a hopeful outlook.

Lee's interpretation recaptures voices lost under the ideological and sometimes violent promotion of a colonizing regime and thus stands firmly within the post-colonial tradition of scholarship. In drawing attention to the ongoing, courageous cries of the mothers of Tiananmen whose voices have been silenced and whose experiences have been covered over, Lee's post-colonial reading further suggests at least to me that Lamentations offers, arguably purposefully, an open endedness that continues to reverberate through time, as an ongoing communal protest against divine and human brutality, articulated faithfully within the canon and by communities of faith and other groups who have suffered.

As with other examples of social-location readings, post-colonial criticism varies greatly from interpreter to interpreter. Another recent assessment of Lamentations by Gregory Lee Cuéllar focuses on the role of empire in an analysis that draws together insights from Trauma Studies with post-colonial critique (Cuéllar 2019). In his analysis of Lamentations, Cuéllar establishes the backdrop of imperial aggression which leaves wounds through military expansion, forced migration, and supremacist ideologies and the resulting protracted suffering from imperial oppression that continues over generations. His analysis focuses on word-objects, such as the personified raped woman of chapters 1 and 2, the captive soldier of chapter 3, and the active and attacking God of chapters 2 and 3. Through these figures, the poet presents images that run counter to the ideology of the empire and confines them or moulds them within a peculiar Judahite poetic artistry that is the acrostic poem. In this way, as I understand it, the narratives of the three figures are given a particular shape whereby the subjugated Judah reclaims its version of the story, which is at odds with, even subversive of, the ideology of the Babylonian Empire. In Cuéllar's reading the poet redeems these figures from the myth of a violent and oppressive regime. The final poem that is related to the alphabet, but released from the strict acrostic form, gathers the figures in Judahite memory and community from oppressive and exploitative governance, and re-assembles them. Lamentations, then, represents "a collective resourceful spirit that sought to reimagine [its] world differently from the reigning empire" (Cuéllar 2019: 276).

Post-colonial readings draw on individual experience and local cultural context to enrich and challenge our understanding of biblical figures and the Bible according to three prongs (Crowell 2009). The first is related to the use of the Bible by the colonizers to substantiate, codify and promulgate their authority in what corresponds to colonial purposes more broadly. The second is related to local attempts by previously colonized peoples to free readings from colonial-imposed interpretations that are ultimately hegemonic. The third sheds light on the damaging role of empires and the colonial forces within the biblical material itself. Ultimately, post-colonial criticism uncovers obscured narratives and helps us to hear marginal voices that often remain underexplored by biblical interpreters especially from the First World. At the same time, post-colonial critique sheds valuable light on the ideologies in the biblical texts themselves and in interpretations thereof, so that readers are enabled to hear and respect other voices and divergent points of view.

RECEPTION HISTORY AND LAMENTATIONS

Reception history prioritizes individual and communal exposition that took place already within the biblical period as well as in religious communities and by people of faith up unto today. Reception exegetes show how "the Bible is a pilgrim wandering through history to merge past and present" (Trible 1978: 1) and thus concentrate on post-biblical readings and artistic representations (Sawyer 2009: ix). The biblical literature has been re-contextualized in a number of different mediums, including in inner-biblical (the classic study is that of Fishbane 1988) as well as in post-biblical commentary, art, sculpture, music, film, poetry and literature, and sermons (Sawyer 2009; Joyce and Lipton 2013; Frevel 2017: 361–75).

Reception in the biblical period

A number of studies have suggested or shown that there are purposeful correspondences between the biblical book of Lamentations and the prophetic collection known as Deutero-Isaiah (Isaiah chs. 40–55). Commonality in themes and vocabulary indicates that the poet of Deutero-Isaiah responded to, reversed and overturned the sorrowful mourning of Lamentations. One of the most important strategies for understanding the reception of Lamentations in the biblical literature, then, is related to its afterlife or 'survival' in Deutero-Isaiah as Tod Linafelt has so persuasively argued.

Lamentations ends abruptly without any real sense of resolution or even hope for divine presence and salvation. Moreover, the community's deep sense of despair is partly portrayed through the figure of personified Zion grieving over the loss of her children (Linafelt 2000: 62–79). The prophet in Deutero-Isaiah directly addresses the loss of divine presence and Zion's children through a number of proclamations and promises of comfort, restoration and return. For example, the persona of Mother Zion in Isaiah employs the language of the communal lament of Lamentations 5 in her query about being forgotten and abandoned (Isa. 49:14; Lam. 5:20) only to be answered by the deity's assurances of the return of her children (Isa. 49:15-26). Personified Zion's painful exclamation, "'Yahweh has forsaken me (*škḥ*), my Lord has forgotten me (*'zb*)" (Isa. 49:14), echoes the communal complaint in Lamentations of, "Why have you forgotten (*škḥ*) us completely? Why have you forsaken (*'zb*) us these many days?" (Lam. 5:20). Whereas the communal concerns in Lamentations were left dangling without resolution, God answers Mother Zion in Isaiah and asserts divine commitment through evoking the image of the Divine Mother, "Can a woman forget (*škḥ*) her nursing child, or show no compassion for the child of her womb? Even these may forget (*škḥ*), yet I will not forget (*škḥ*) you" (Isa. 49:15).

As Linafelt shows in his close reading, the deity in Deutero-Isaiah jubilantly pronounces the return of Zion's children through the repatriation of the exiles who bring about a new beginning that will benefit the solitary city and its inhabitants struggling for survival in Lamentations (Isa. 49:15-26). The promises of the return of the exiles to Jerusalem made in Deutero-Isaiah fulfilled the hopes of the abandoned Judahites expressed in Lamentations (see also Newsome 1992). In responding to concerns about divine abandonment and the accompanying despair so profoundly expressed in Lamentations and echoed by personified Zion in Deutero-Isaiah, God emphatically confirms that it is not in the nature of the deity to forget or to abandon. Notably, the divine confirmation in the Isaiah passage omits Mother Zion's language of forsaking, which reinforces once again the nature of God who is characterized by commitment, not abandonment.

One strategy for surviving Lamentations is to provide a satisfactory conclusion within the biblical tradition, like that of Deutero-Isaiah who may have actually responded to poems to which he or she had access. Whether or not the poet of Deutero-Isaiah actually knew the actual poems of Lamentations as we have inherited them or simply some of their themes and language remains open to debate at the present time. In any event, the stress on God's fortitude and motherly compassion provides a "happy ending" that moves away from the suffering ash heap of Lamentations in an example of the early reception of the literature.

Reception in the post-biblical period

Within Jewish tradition, the book of Lamentations has an afterlife in the Targums and the Midrash. The Targums of Lamentations (TgLam) represent the circulation of the book within Jewish congregations as part of the synagogue service. Targums are Aramaic translations of the biblical literature with varying degrees of expansion. Christian Brady has argued that the TgLam represent the interpretation of, as well as responses to, concerns and issues raised in the biblical book (Brady 2003). Notably, TgLam are introduced by a lengthy prologue that expands the first four verses of the book with a theological prolegomenon that explains the disaster and defends the deity against the charge of being capricious or culpable. Part of the first verse reveals the lens through which the poems are to be interpreted:

> Jeremiah the prophet and High Priest told how it was decreed that Jerusalem and her people should be punished with banishment and that they should be mourned with 'ekah. Just as when Adam and Eve were punished and expelled from the Garden of Eden and the Master of the Universe mourned them with 'ekah. The Attribute of Justice spoke and said, "Because of the greatness of her rebellious sin, thus she will dwell alone as a man plagued with leprosy on his skin who sits alone (correlation of Lam. 1:1 and Gen. 3:9). (Brady 2003: 18–19)

The aggadic or sermonic expansion of the opening verse of Lamentations functions as a theodicy by explaining the actions of God as justified because of the enormity of the sinful behaviour that had taken place in the city. At the same time, the opening verses portray divine correction, that is punishment for sin, as an outpouring of the love of God (compare Prov. 3:11-12). In this vein, the correlation of the banishment of Adam and Eve from the Garden of Eden in Genesis with the forced migration and exile of the city of Jerusalem attested to in Lamentations reveals that the deity was not heartless or unmoved by the severity of the devastation. God laments and mourns passionately over the fate of humanity. The example of the leprous individual reveals something further about the deity by focusing on divine will and determination. In this view, the universe operates according to divine principles of organization, in which, for example, leprous individuals sit outside the normal bounds of society in order that contamination be minimized and the forces of chaos contained.

These different motifs brought together by the targumist ultimately justify the destruction of the city by depicting its downfall as the punishment for sin and within the bounds of the sure execution of God's will. TgLam mount a defence of God against the charges of injustice, capriciousness and culpability that appear scattered within the biblical Lamentations.

In a slightly different way, the rabbinic Midrash or commentary on scripture by the rabbis, Lamentations Rabbati, sought to move beyond the biblical message focused on grief, mourning and suffering, so as to "not only lament the past but also give consolation for the present and confidence for the future" (Cohen 1982: 33). According to a sensitive study of Lamentations Rabbati by Shaye Cohen one of the main themes of God's comfort is associated with the deity who not only "go[es] into exile with the Jews, but [] even cries with them and for them" (Cohen 1982: 34). The laments are overturned in Lamentations Rabbati through depictions of the deity and the Holy Spirit who grieve with the city and with her inhabitants:

> "Bitterly she weeps in the night" (Lam. 1:2). She weeps and makes others to weep with her ... Thus, she weeps, and makes the Holy One, blessed be [God], to weep with her ... She weeps and makes the ministering angels weep with her. (B 30a = S 90, cited in Cohen 1982: 34)

Instead of a suffering humanity crying out from severe affliction, the rabbinic Midrash on Lamentations presents a God who suffers and laments. In this way, as Cohen points out, Lamentations becomes a book of consolation rather than complaint, which is another point the rabbis clearly noted:

> "There is none to comfort her" (Lam. 1:2). R. Levi says, "Whenever it says 'there is none' (en lah) it indicates that there would be in the future. 'And Sarai was barren, without (en lah) child' (Gen. 11:30) but she did have one later ... Similarly, 'But Hannah had no (en lah) children' (1 Sam. 1:2) but she did have them later ... Similarly, 'Zion whom no one (en lah) seeks out' (Jeremiah 30:27), but later she will have [someone to seek her out], as it is said, 'And a redeemer shall come to Zion'. (Isaiah 59:20) ..."
> (B 31a-b and 46 a = S 96 and 141, Cohen 1982: 34)

Reception in the fine arts: Music, literature and art

The book of Lamentations has an afterlife that exists in many different mediums, including music and the fine arts. Christian Frevel rightly observes the important role that Lamentations has played in musical compositions, "in the 16th and 17th centuries there is hardly a Renaissance composer who had not concerned himself with Lamentations" (Frevel 2017: 369). In the modern period, the poetic images of Lamentations were incorporated in the a capella composition, "Wie liegt die Stadt so wüst = how the city lies so desolate/deserted", of Rudolf Mauersberger as a musical response to and lament over the destruction of Dresden by the Allied forces in February 1945 (Frevel 2017: 371–2). Mauersberger drew on scattered verses of the biblical Lamentations in order to express musically the tragedy, misery and plaintive cries for divine sympathy that accompanied the veritable eradication of his beloved city (e.g. Lam. 1:1, 4; 4:1; 1:13; 2:15; 1:9; 5:17, 20, 21; 1:9). The piece focuses on the question of why and lingers on the sense of incomprehensibility.

Another reaction to the events that preceded and accompanied the Second World War is found in the masterful composition of Ernst Krenek, an Austrian Jew, who had been pronounced a 'degenerate artist' by the Nazis and who fled his homeland and relocated to the United States in 1938. In 1941, he composed an intricate *a capella* for nine voices from a selection of texts from the biblical Lamentations used liturgically entitled, *Lamentatio Jeremiae prophetae* (Joyce and Lipton 2013: 108–10). The piece is an extremely complex and hauntingly beautiful elegy that musically captures Krenek's longing for and sorrow over the loss of his beloved Vienna that is sometimes sung during Tenebrae services in Christian churches that take place Thursday through Saturday during Holy Week. During Tenebrae services, a congregation is in mourning for the coming death of Jesus Christ and lights are gradually dimmed over the course of the service, eventually to be extinguished, in a practice that is known from as early as the sixth century CE. The Roman Catholic Church has a long tradition of using elements of Lamentations during the Tenebrae services of Holy Week. One of the better known pieces is *O vos omnes* from the Latin Vulgate edition of Lamentations 1:12, "*O vos omnes qui transitis per viam: attendite et videte si est dolor sicut dolor meus* = Is it nothing to you who pass by? Look and see, is there any sorrow like my sorrow?".

The themes of Lamentations resonate also in literature from the medieval period up to today. One of the most famous receptions of Lamentations is found in the work of St John of the Cross, a Spanish mystic from a Jewish family that converted to Catholicism before the Jews were forced from Spain in 1492 (Joyce and Lipton 2012: 103–5). The individual lament of chapter 3 clearly resonated with the personal and visionary experiences of St John of the Cross as evidenced in his allegorical poem, "The Dark Night of the Soul". The poem concentrates on the struggles of the individual who seeks to attain a sense of unity with God the Creator. One of the analogies he makes is in the soul's agonizing search for God and the need for divine empathy, which he characterizes as:

> All these complaints Jeremiah makes about these pains and trials, and by means of them he most vividly depicts the sufferings of the soul in this spiritual night and purgation. Wherefore the soul that God sets in this tempestuous and horrible night is deserving of great compassion. (cited in Joyce and Lipton 2012: 104)

Also within the Christian tradition, John Keble's collection of poetry, *The Christian Year*, published in 1827, actually begins with a morning prayer that forefronts the celebratory verses of God's mercy in Lamentations 3 (vv. 22-3) (Joyce and Lipton 2012: 125–6). Like the dawn is the love of the deity:

> New every morning is the love,
> Our wakening and uprising prove;
> Through sleep and darkness safely brought,
> Restored to life and power and thought.

In the nineteenth century, Keble's vision of divine mercy was distributed widely; "at the end of the Victorian era Christian believers from Canada to New Zealand, India to the Caribbean, began their day reflecting with Keble on the dawn of hope articulated at the heart of the book of Lamentations" (Joyce and Lipton 2012: 126).

One of the most famous pieces of art that is connected to the book of Lamentations is the painting by Rembrandt called *The Prophet Jeremiah Lamenting the Destruction of Jerusalem, 1630* (Holt 2010; Thomas 2011; Frevel 2017: 372–3). In the painting, the prophet Jeremiah is found in a cave reclining on a BiBeL, a copy of the Bible, next to what appear to be sacred objects salvaged from the Jerusalem temple, with his head sunk in repose in his left hand. His right hand is held out of view behind his back and over his right shoulder in the distance through the cave entrance is a glimpse of the city of Jerusalem in the midst of destruction. Soldiers scale its gates; its temple depicted with a cupola held up by columns is not yet destroyed, but under threat; a solitary inhabitant, possibly the last king, Zedekiah, flees from the city with his hands over his eyes, and flames rage and send smoke pluming into the sky. Jeremiah casts his gaze down rather than towards the smouldering ruin over his shoulder and appears lost in thought or in his own grief. The painting corresponds to the description of the Babylonian attack on Jerusalem and includes imagery consistent with the man of sorrows in Lamentations (3:1; but see also Lam. 2:2, 3; 4:1) as well as visual snapshots from the book of Jeremiah (ch. 39) and the depiction of Jeremiah in a cave in 2 Maccabees (2 Macc. 2:4-5).

Expositions of the painting vary by interpreter. Heath Thomas contrasts the insistence on prayer and complaint in the biblical Lamentations with the figure of Rembrandt's Jeremiah, who sits silently and in melancholy. Poignantly, he notes, "Rembrandt foregrounds the grief of the present moment, enabling the observer to embody the pain with Jeremiah the prophet" (Thomas 2011: 159). In a different way, Else Holt draws attention to parallels between God and the portrayal of the prophet in the Jeremianic tradition by focusing some attention on the significance of Jeremiah's body language. On one level, the position of Jeremiah's right arm held behind his back suggests the lack of intention to turn back or intervene for the city in its downfall. In his posture, Jeremiah accepts the fate of the city and mourns its loss. On another level, when understanding Jeremiah as a symbol for the deity, Holt draws attention to how the right hand of God is a symbol of power in the Old Testament traditions that can be wielded and withheld at the behest of the deity. Like the prophet's hand held behind his back, God's hand is seemingly withheld to allow the destruction to take place, but at the same time poised to act and intervene at a later, divinely determined, point in time. To my mind, then, the figure of Jeremiah corresponds to the uncertain conclusion of Lamentations that ends awaiting a divine response.

The poems of Lamentations inspired reception in a variety of different mediums, partly because they capture so vividly the human experience as well as the outpouring of emotion and dejected silence of despair and even depression. In this way, Lamentations presents a biblical text of power and promise for many generations that have widespread, if not also universal, appeal. When we pay attention to the inheritance of religious texts by people of faith – including Jews, Christians and Muslims who all include the traditions of the Old Testament within sacred scripture, but vary to the degree by which they are considered authoritative or inspirational – a number of additional points become clear. First of all, sacred traditions are updated by those who have a vested interest in them and therefore belong to faith communities rather than to the public at large. They can illuminate themes as part of humanity's cultural heritage, like human suffering, the validity of protest and contrary interpretations, the importance of acknowledging human misery and providing support and compassion to those who suffer, and the optimism that stems from hope and belief in God. At the same time, they provide a word about and to God that is instructive as well as authoritative for religious communities and their members.

Second, and more importantly for this study, the examples of the reception of Lamentations remain in keeping with the claims of its poems. To read and interpret the biblical literature is to be an educated critic, who wrestles with the scriptural witness rather than disregarding those bits that generate discomfort or challenging perspectives. The testimony of suffering as antithetical to God's intentions for humanity is honoured within Lamentations not only within the collection, but also in religious and cultural traditions that extend in time far beyond it. For example, the *geber* who offers a different take on the interpretation of the disaster seeks to silence complaint and protest, but does not deny the pain observed or the power of its validity, claim that human persecution is a necessary evil, and present a series of alternative facts that whitewash other claims and testimony. The *geber*'s voice lies alongside of, rather than instead of, the perspectives of those whom he contradicts and obviously values.

One of the significant messages of the *geber* (and Jesus Christ who is fashioned similarly in the New Testament tradition as well as other prominent religious and political figures who have suffered alienation and persecution) is that human pain and torment are an affront to the biblical message and contrary to God's will for humanity and creation. Human suffering exposes the schism between God and the world – the brokenness of creation and the estrangement of the human being from God. When seen in this way, it would not be in keeping with Lamentations to fashion a sermon or musical that celebrates or exalts in the hurt, persecution, rape and exploitation of real people. The poems of Lamentations in their graphic and honest depiction of survivors of a horrific catastrophe present a powerful rebuttal to theological and indeed political perspectives that disregard and diminish the humanity of other members of the community. In modern terms, Lamentations presents a biblical vision that grapples with and sharply rebukes the corruption of the good of creation for the monetary and material benefit of only a select few, especially when it is accompanied by the discrimination, oppression and exploitation of others who are denied adequate reimbursement for their work, access to health care and education, a basic quality of life, and the pursuit of happiness. Interpreters within the biblical tradition and beyond recognized human pain as contrary to a world considered part of the outworking of a good and right-enacting deity. With this in mind, the next and final chapter focuses on different readings that offer new interpretations that remain in keeping with and so honour the voices in Lamentations.

READINGS IN LAMENTATIONS

The foundation of exegesis lies in understanding the composition, provenance and theological themes of a biblical verse, story or book. The goal of exegesis is to draw out meaning that is pertinent to the concerns of the reader in his or her time and place. The different foci on which we have concentrated heretofore underscore how scripture meant something in its time and place, but can also mean something today to readers who approach it with their own concerns. Indeed, the present study illustrates how the cultural embeddedness of scripture is at a distance to and different from the context of modern readers who read and interpret from their own social and religious locations. The critical understanding of Lamentations, that is, the awareness of its composition, provenance and underlying theological traditions, effectively creates a gap. The gap of which theologians speak refers to a recognized difference in the context in which scripture was written and the audience to whom it spoke and the context of the reader, personally, confessionally, communally and socially. Because the modern reader tends to come from a vastly different world than the one in which the texts of the Bible arose, it is not advisable to simply read a verse and apply it to one's life or worldview without a critical understanding of what it meant in its own time.

At the same time, though, there are no clear indicators that confirm a definite provenance for the biblical Lamentations. The themes and figurative language of the poems have a timeless character that generates conceivably inexhaustible associations for many individuals and communities in times of suffering and trial. Loosening biblical texts from specific historical settings, but remaining cognizant of their peculiar speech, enables appropriation to new circumstances. I would argue further that the lack of concrete historical referents invites readers and hearers to become witnesses to the unfolding tragedy. The poetry of Lamentations urges its interpreters to engage with, join their voices to, and then make associations with the speakers and scenes. Moreover, the graphic details require the faithful interpreter to see and not turn away in embarrassment, disgust, judgement or self-righteousness from the despairing, depressive, and painful protests and silences. Building on the previous chapter that turned from reading the theology in the texts, that is, what theological traditions undergird the poems, to reading theology from the poems, in the sense of a word of God to readers in their contextual circumstances, the present chapter offers four short exegetical pastiches. The hope is to offer some options for how to read the text faithfully with different questions that arise from modern readers.

A TEXT OF TERROR

Phyllis Trible has offered one of the most profound studies of scripture from a literary and feminist perspective that continues to reverberate in its audacious storytelling. In the 1980s, she gave a voice to four women in the Old Testament who had been stifled, overlooked and mistreated in a compact volume that arose from a series of lectures that she called *Texts of Terror* (Trible 1984). In its early stages, feminist criticism sought to uncover the lost female characters and voices in scripture as a way to value their contribution to biblical history and to offer examples for women readers of the Bible. Since its inception, feminist criticism has branched into a number of different areas, and Trible offers a reading that aims to honour the diversity of female biblical stories by sharing those in which women were subject to violence and terror. She uses the methodological approach of rhetorical criticism to show how the text speaks and weaves its tale. The goal of her analysis is not to redeem the women or offer them a happy ending, but to restore their tragedies to the community of faith with the hope that "sad stories may yield a new beginning" (Trible 1984: 2).

The texts of terror to which Trible draws attention are stories found in the canon of the Bible that deserve attention in their own right. In her own words:

> In this book my task is to tell sad stories as I hear them. Indeed, they are tales of terror with women as victims. Belonging to the sacred scriptures of synagogue and church, these narratives yield four portraits of suffering in ancient Israel: Hagar, the slave used, abused, and rejected; Tamar, the princess raped and discarded; an unnamed woman, the concubine raped, murdered, and dismembered; and the daughter of Jepthah, a virgin slain and sacrificed. (Trible 1984: 1)

The stories of women who have been mistreated in the Bible and then further victimized through sermons about them that fail to account for their humanity and agency, or even through omission, benefit from a new reading that hears and values their experiences and suffering. On the one hand, Trible offers us a service by paying close attention to the texts about persecuted, maltreated and violated women. On the other hand, she draws in other biblical literature in order to illuminate the texts of terror in new ways with one result being the assessment that at least in these oft overlooked narratives "women, not men, are suffering servants and Christ figures" (Trible 1984: 2–3).

Texts of terror do not have happy endings. They can be read with other scripture in the Old and New Testaments as well as the Apocrypha in a type of inner-biblical exegesis which alleviates to some extent the horrors they evoke, but they also stand alone, even as their female victims were isolated and brutalized. The following sketch provides an outline that aims to promote further thinking about the readers' own texts of terror, but does not employ the sophisticated rhetorical analysis so perfected by Trible. Like the book of Lamentations, Trible values suffering, hears of it, acknowledges it, and invites the reader to sit on an ash heap and mourn with, rather than lecture to, the suffering, the persecuted and the terrorized, which is what we will attempt now.

In the second chapter of Lamentations, the eyewitness reporter focuses almost myopically on divine agency and the attack on Jerusalem and the Southern Kingdom of Judah. From beginning to end, the chapter sheds light on one ultimate, violent and brutally successful oppressor – God, alternatively spoken of as Yahweh and Adonai. As the reader is aware, in the rest of this guide, I have sought to use language for the deity that allows the interpreter to build for himself or herself a picture of God. The Old Testament literature is reticent to ascribe gender or even an anthropoid shape to the divine (see Middlemas 2014), but the picture of Yahweh in this chapter is of a male divine warrior and I have chosen to utilize where necessary male pronouns for the deity in keeping with the gender of the verbs. The use of male pronouns illustrates why using gender for the deity can be problematic, particularly in texts of terror.

The chapter begins with the startling image, 'How Adonai in his anger beclouded daughter Zion! He has thrown down from heaven to earth the splendour of Israel; he has not remembered … on the day of his anger' (2:1). At the close of the chapter, the personified city echoes the sentiments of the eyewitness and she speaks of the devastation wrought by the deity as the mother forlorn, 'You invited my enemies from all around as if for a day of a festival; and on the day of the anger of Yahweh, no one escaped or survived; those whom I bore and reared my enemy has destroyed' (v. 22). Although the chapter also details the actions of an invading army, when the city speaks in her own voice she acknowledges only one enemy – the deity horrifyingly comprehensive in the execution of his wrath. The narrator recounts passionately, but nevertheless impersonally, annihilation. In stark contrast, Jerusalem wails as a mother over her slaughtered and scattered children, the inhabitants of the city who suffered from a disaster so great that it could ultimately be attributed only to divine causality.

First, let us consider the destruction wrought. All facets of the socio-economic and political life of Jerusalem and Judah have been wiped out. Chapter 2 highlights in particular the eradication of infrastructure; all the dwellings of Jacob (v. 2), the strongholds of daughter Judah or the fortresses scattered throughout the kingdom (v. 2), the kingdom itself (v. 2), all the might of Israel (v. 3), the tent of daughter Zion or the temple (vv. 4, 6, 7), all its palaces (vv. 5, 7), the city wall and ramparts of Jerusalem (v. 8), and its gates as well as the bars that close them (v. 9). From the description of the buildings alone, the poet conveys the sense of a violent and sweeping attack, but destruction is not only of the city's infrastructure. Divine aggression is said to target all people, including the rulers (v. 2), the king and priests (v. 6), the king and princes or nobles scattered to the nations (v. 9), the priests and prophets slaughtered in the temple (v. 20), young men and young women felled by the sword (v. 21), and possibly also the reference to 'the might of Israel' listed above as the reference in its context is ambiguous in meaning and could equally refer to individual members of the ruling or priestly class rather than infrastructure (v. 3). The devastation is so encompassing that the survivors, apparently only the elderly and young girls, mourn and sit in dejected silence (v. 10) among corpses scattered and abandoned in the streets (v. 21).

The first half of the chapter is actually composed of the eyewitness reporter's depiction of the effects of what he or she attributes to God's wrath (vv. 1-12). God is the divine warrior raging in burning anger against his own people. Through the use of verbs and various ever-changing depictions the poet vividly portrays violence and brutality.

The deity has humiliated, thrown down all the way from heaven to earth, destroyed, broken down, brought down to the ground, cut down in anger, burned like a flaming fire consuming all around, killed, poured out fury like a raging fire, and decimated and shattered buildings and walls. In these descriptive verses, the eyewitness categorizes the deity's behaviour three times with verbs that connote destruction, but which convey wholesale eradication and even swallowing up (vv. 2, 6, 8). The result is so fierce and thorough that the city's gates sink into the ground (v. 9) and even the ramparts and walls lament and languish together (v. 8). In the account, God is the divine terminator who 'has bent his bow like an enemy, with his right hand set like a foe' (v. 4), who fights and rages against his own people.

In the midst of his or her reportage, the reporter breaks down and speaks of his or her own personal response at the devastation in a soliloquy that interrupts the graphic portrayal of the violence (vv. 11-17) and seeks however vainly to comfort Jerusalem, 'What can I say for you … that I may comfort you, O [tender] daughter Zion? For vast as the sea is your ruin; who can heal you?' (v. 15). The use of metaphorical epithets in Lamentations and in the speech of the eyewitness, that is, when the city is spoken of as 'daughter of geographical name [GN]' or 'virgin/maiden daughter of GN' over twenty times in the book underscores the helplessness, vulnerability and fragility of the city and correspondingly her inhabitants. A translation of 'dearest Jerusalem' or 'tender Zion' captures the sense well. Such phrasing also emphasizes, on the one hand, the male, punishing and violent deity and, on the other hand, the cowering, defenceless and terrorized young woman. In addition, the eyewitness's use of metaphorical epithets conveys a sense of his or her own emotional attachment and feeling for the city, perhaps also horror at its fate. This tender Jerusalem is the victim of divine wrath. In spite of an acute awareness of the destruction, humiliation, enemy mockery and suffering of the once-proud city, the eyewitness ends his or her passionate speech with a rational explanation of the disaster, 'Yahweh has done what he purposed, he has carried out his threat; as he ordained long ago, he has demolished without pity; he has made the enemy rejoice over you, and exalted at the might of your foes' (v. 17).

The rationale given by the reporter effectively points a finger at Jerusalem as culpable, if not also responsible, for her affliction and downfall. At the same time, the personified city also speaks, and in so doing confirms the agent and extent of the devastation. In contrast to the eyewitness, however, Jerusalem draws attention, first and foremost, to the human victims of the deity's destructive activity. At the beginning of her speech, she challenges God, 'Look, O Yahweh, and consider! To whom have you done this?' (v. 20) and then speaks not of her own personal sorrow or injury, but that of her inhabitants, including mothers who have to resort to eating their own children, and the murder of priests and prophets in the very sanctuary itself. She continues her sorry tale with a visual picture that illustrates to the deity the human devastation around her. Her depiction captures snapshots of the destruction through graphic depiction of the young and old lying dead or dying in the streets, the sword attack that left the bodies of young men and women pierced, ripped open and butchered, and the comprehensive and merciless slaughter that took place. Her caustic, lament prayer ends with attention to the enemies who were invited by the deity to participate in her downfall, but she holds God, who she calls 'my enemy' in verse 22, firmly to account for the lack of divine mercy, assistance and pardon. Ultimately, 'no one escaped or survived; those whom [Jerusalem] bore and reared [her] enemy has destroyed' (v. 22). In the midst of her beloved children lying all around her, fighter Jerusalem is cowed beneath the enemy attack, but nevertheless asserts that the amount of suffering defies rationalization. She resolutely rejects blaming the victim, and in so doing anticipates the subtle reference to the powerlessness of the deity over human violence hinted at in the very centre of the book (3:33).

The second chapter of Lamentations is a text of terror, of the terrorizer and of the terrorized. What is problematic in the poem, particularly for feminist critics, is that the deity portrayed as male brutalizes and violently abuses the city personified as female. Perhaps more egregious still is that God's abuse is explained away as the just punishment for sin. Although only metaphors, the dynamic of God as male and city as female can have negative implications for real women and their relationships. In a close analysis of the use of the metaphor of the feminine for cities in the prophetic literature (especially in Hosea, Jeremiah and Ezekiel), Renita Weems has drawn attention to how the attribution of gender roles can go awry (Weems 1995). In her study, she notes that although the figurative language of cities as female is found in ancient Near Eastern (ANE) as well as in biblical literature, the former material contains only positive connotations, while the latter contains both positive and negative depictions. In ancient Israel, then, the city is the beloved young girl who arouses care, pity and sympathy, but also the loose or wanton woman in need of correction and deserving of punishment by the male God often characterized as the city-woman's husband in the prophetic literature (Weems 1995: 44–5). Weems correctly notes that metaphors matter in how we make sense of the world around us and of our own interpersonal relationships. To imagine God as a justified abuser can on some level substantiate the abuse perpetuated by husbands and fathers who can more readily identify with God as male than female members of the family and society.

Trible was inspired to pay attention to texts of terror because 'ancient tales of terror speak all too frighteningly of the present' (Trible 1984: xiii). She illustrates poignantly what she means:

> hearing a black woman describe herself as a daughter of Hagar outside the covenant; seeing an abused woman on the streets of New York with a sign, 'My name is Tamar'; reading news of the dismembered body of a woman found in a trash can; attending worship services in memory of nameless women; and wrestling with the silence, absence, and opposition of God. (Trible 1984: 1–2)

To witness the extent and the depth of human suffering and pain in Lamentations and to place the blame on female Jerusalem for violations of the covenant likened however faintly to adultery is too facile. More disturbingly, the gender codes of the text allow for the rationalization of violence against women. Weems, too, has struggled with the image of the city as female victimized by the male deity and wonders how it enables readers to improve their world:

> When women – even for the sake of argument – are mutilated by and in religious texts, how has the kingdom of God with its promise of peace, justice, righteousness, and love been made more authentic within the world? … However enthralling and entertaining a work may be, readers have the right to reject living in worlds that in the end diminish their humanity. (Weems 1995: 104)

Feminist critics highlight how the imagery in Lamentations is not innocent, neither in its portrayal nor in its application. Like women in the texts of terror who were victims in a world in which the rules were defined by men for men, and who were subsequently despised and ultimately rejected, Tender Jerusalem represents 'a woman of sorrow acquainted with grief' whom the reader is asked to see, and in so doing understand 'the endless suffering of her present' just as the biblical exegete has done (Trible 1984: 52). The city personified as a vulnerable woman victimized by a male warrior God (in modern terminology, perhaps better regarded as the 'alpha male') reinforces male stereotypes of hierarchy, power and retribution that are damaging to the full biblical vision of the harmony, relationality and reciprocity of men and women created in the image of God and of creation itself. Reading texts of terror helps us to see through the eyes of the victims of abuse, to account better for their humanity, and to re-evaluate our own presuppositions and rationalizations.

POST-COLONIAL AWARENESS: SILENCING AND THE VOICES OF THE MARGINALIZED

Post-colonial criticism has made us aware of the damage that colonialism has done to the economic, cultural and societal fabric of local communities in countries that have been subjected to the political control of other nations through military and ideological force. The purpose of colonialism (and continued in a slightly altered form as neo-colonialism practised by multinational corporations today and by authoritarian political leaders) is to gain land and exert control over natural resources, trade and human labour for the benefit of wealthy nations and wealthy individuals (see the discussion in Perdue 2005: 280–339). In the last chapter, we showed how post-colonial interpreters draw attention to the silencing and whitewashing of native languages, values, beliefs and stories among other means employed to control local populations. Post-colonial critics, then, work to disclose the colonial efforts to silence local voices and also to recover lost narratives, 'to discover in the literature and its culture voices of the silenced and to recognize the ideologies at work in the writing of various texts' (Perdue 2005: 302). In the context of this chapter with its focus on using what we have learned of the discussion of the literature, history and theology of Lamentations, I would like to highlight two areas of study that participate in the endeavours of post-colonial analyses. The first highlights the silencing of other voices in the text, which is akin to the silencing of local cultures and expressions by colonial powers. The second seeks to recover and make space at the table for marginalized speakers who tell of their suffering under the might of an imperial power.

Silencing alternative perspectives through appeal to God

Post-colonial critique has made us more aware of attempts to silence and cover over the stories of local communities exploited for resources. Closer attention to Lamentations with sensitive post-colonial reading strategies in mind enables a better appreciation of the art of silencing. We have already discussed the uncomfortable fit generically and thematically of chapter 3 within the collection of poems otherwise focused on societal catastrophe and the evocation of human tragedy. One of the most observable and therefore striking thematic features of chapter 3 is that it advocates silent submission to suffering in a collection of poems that are otherwise focused on proclamation, complaint and protest, and the validity thereof (Westermann 1994: 79, 180, 192; Linafelt 2000: 268). That the poem begins with the plaintive complaint of an individual sufferer, 'I' or *ʾanî*, instead of the death knell of the funeral song 'alas' or *ʾêkah* of chapters 1, 2 and 4 tellingly also establishes at the forefront a shift away from attention to the destruction wrought in Jerusalem and Judah, the daily affliction of members of the community, and Zion's struggle to survive and advocate for divine care, recompense, justice and restoration on behalf of her inhabitants to the very individual concerns of the 'strong man', 'soldier' or 'nobleman' brought low.

In the peculiar chapter 3 the individual complaint (vv. 1-21) is welded to a section that serves a didactic purpose (vv. 22-39) (Westermann 1994: 192–3; Middlemas 2006), that is, it purposes to teach rather than form the basis for contemplation or meditation. The linking of the complaint with instruction is signalled through the appearance of the rare term *geber* (Hebrew for strong man, soldier or nobleman) that fails to appear elsewhere in Lamentations. Notably, *geber* demarcates the extent of the unit through its appearance in the first and last verses of the section (vv. 1 and 39, respectively) and it pointedly recurs twice within the didactic section itself at verses 27 and 35, respectively, as if to reinforce the linking of two distinct literary formal units (Middlemas 2006: 512). The addition of the wisdom section serves as admonition and teaches what is to the poet the correct understanding of and human response to God. In so doing, it stifles the validity of complaint that has formed the focus of the rest of the poems and also other interpretations of the disaster in what I consider analogous to the silencing of native ideas and values as promulgated in colonial interpretation and propaganda.

In an article otherwise focused on the strategies that form the physical and theological centre of the third poem and the book of Lamentations as a whole, I drew attention to how the wisdom interlude corrects interpretation promulgated in the other chapters (Middlemas 2006). In the course of that study, I suggested that the ideology therein is consistent with the theological perspective of the repatriated exiles and functions to overshadow the claims of the remnant – the Judahites left in the land. In this context, the historical purpose of the central verses is of little interest. Instead, what comes to light is how the unit illustrates the importance of post-colonial criticism in uncovering and disclosing strategies utilized by one interpretive lens, that of colonial propaganda, to marginalize and deny the validity of local voices. In this case, the authoritative wisdom interlude functions to correct and also stifle alternative reactions, interpretations and explanation.

An individual complains, which could otherwise verify the validity of the protests of the other chapters except that he presents how each person should respond privately and personally to disaster. The *geḇer*'s complaint, then, moves into a wisdom-like section wherein the central verses of the chapter and the whole collection focus in an 'aba' structured unit on human response (vv. 25-30) which is surrounded by two sets of verses that attend to divine promises, love and compassion (vv. 22-4 and 31-9). In an 'aba' structured literary unit, the central section b is emphasized. In this case, the poet urges silent submission and the redemptive nature of suffering:

> The LORD is good to those who wait for [God] … It is good that one should *wait quietly* for the salvation of the LORD … to *sit alone in silence* … to put one's mouth to the dust … to give one's cheek to the smiter and be filled with insults. (selected from vv. 25-30)

The conclusion of the unit, 'Why should any who draws breath complain about the punishment of their sins?' (v. 39), highlights and reinforces the central message of *silent* submission in the wisdom interlude. The 'official' way to respond to human suffering entails that victims wait, acceptingly, without protest, complaint or criticism, for divine intervention.

In a poem distinguished as the literary high point of Lamentations through the artistic use of the triple acrostic, a didactic, wisdom section appears exactly in the centre of Lamentations. It conveys a central position both literally and figuratively that the poet seeks to impart and even impose, that is, to present the 'correct' human posture before the deity. In so doing, the message stifles the laments, protests and complaints that suffuse the other chapters. In addition, it corrects statements made elsewhere by fellow sufferers, including the personified Jerusalem. For example, female Jerusalem complains about the burden of a yoke (1:14) and the hardship she has endured, but the *geḇer* teaches and admonishes, 'It is good for one to bear the yoke in youth' (3:27) and 'let him sit alone in silence when the Lord has imposed it' (3:28). In addition, the poet rebuts depictions of the divine warrior, indeed accusations of God as a brutal enemy fighting against his own people and implications of divine capriciousness with images of the divine saviour. Like the divine saviour, God's 'salvific actions … never cease, they are new every morning' (3:22, my translation to capture the plural use of *ḥesed* as divine heroic deeds on behalf of the covenant people). In addition, the sage teaches divine attributes that encourage faith in the deity, such as compassion (vv. 22, 32), faithfulness (v. 23) and steadfast love (v. 32).

The wisdom section offers a counter-testimony to that found in the outlying chapters of Lamentations and insists on an interpretation of God that the other figures in Lamentations find foreign to their experience and what they consider faithful response to tragedy. The wisdom interlude attached to the myopic lamenting of the strong man almost paternally stifles the cries of the innocents who suffer under violence and brutality. In so doing, the appended verses (vv. 22-39) call into question the validity of complaint, protest and raging against a God perceived to be unjust and capricious by promoting a vision of the deity who is omnipotent, omniscient and omnipresent. In the sanctioned view, everything happens as a result of the execution of God's plan to which the human person must acquiesce and submit without protest or complaint.

The silencing of other voices and the presentation of a persuasive counter narrative that effectively whitewashes personal articulations of experience share much in common with the tactics used by colonial representatives and even authoritarian regimes who foster their own interpretations and ideologies, while suppressing those of local communities. Sensitivity to post-colonial concerns and critique enables readers to see strategies in the presentation of theology and to better understand how debate and dialogue as well as contrary perspectives inform the composition of scripture that should be accounted for in theological interpretation today.

Lamentations captures an internal debate about the sanctioned interpretation of disaster, the right response from the individual and the correct way to address God. Notably, the perspective promoted through the figure of the *geḇer*, of silent submission and the redemptive nature of suffering, is eclipsed by real-world experience. After the third chapter, the poet resumes an outlook similar to that of the first two chapters by the focus on the actual effects of calamity on various individuals in chapter 4 and complaints thereof in chapter 5. The conclusion of Lamentations on highlighting the painful present raised in prayer and petition to God suggests that the instruction to remain silent and accept suffering does not have the final say. Comparable to a democratic process that includes and adjudicates many competing voices, a community comes together to proclaim that their pain, protests and complaints matter. The *geḇer* with his theology-light interpretation is overruled. In their reckoning, a persecuted people understand that their suffering and their troubles, however graphic and uncomfortable, are significant and matter to their God.

Honouring suffering under imperial exploitation

Post-colonial interpreters not only highlight the silencing of native stories and viewpoints, they also seek to amplify and draw attention to local voices. The stifling of difference and the containment of local cultural norms, beliefs and values dehumanize the other by shutting their perspectives out of public conversation and governance, denying their validity, and overlooking real hardship and suffering when experienced by the 'other'. Reading with the oppressed, persecuted and marginalized through a post-colonial lens is to also hear another side of the story and to erase the line separating us from the 'other' by recognizing a common humanity and accepting difference. In the interest of space, I point briefly to the fifth poem of Lamentations, which draws attention to the physical effects of the severity of imperial control in order to bring the voices of the persecuted to the public conversation and to honour their contribution.

The Mesopotamian empires long sought control of other nation-states in order to gain access to resources that were lacking in their native heartlands, to boost their labour force for construction projects and their marauding armies, and to ensure the steady flow of foodstuffs and luxury items into the empire in a way that primarily bolstered the prestige and wealth of the ruling class. The Babylonians may not have been as brutal as the Assyrians who had ruled before them and who had a reputation for punitively carting away even the top soil of defeated nation-states, but on occasion they reacted fiercely to treaty disloyalty.

For example, archaeologists have uncovered evidence of the complete annihilation and depopulation of the Phoenician city-states, Ashkelon and Ashdod, by the Neo-Babylonians (Stager 1996), which corresponds to the devastation in Jerusalem and rural areas in the territory of Judah. A glimpse of the hardship of imperial governance comes to the fore in the various perspectives of the victims who lament in the fifth chapter of Lamentations. Their accounts correct any romanticized view of colonial rule and re-balance attention to those who suffer from economic exploitation (from the oligarchs, the rulings classes, multinational corporations, dictators, and unjust political and social systems).

The fifth chapter of Lamentations is strikingly different from the other poems in form and content. It abandons the use of the acrostic and corresponds closely to the communal lament form, but has a lengthy section of complaint and no resolution unlike other examples of its genre elsewhere in the Old Testament. In diverging from the communal lament, it shares most in common with ANE penitential prayers that remain focused on the presentation of sorrow and suffering as a means to motivate the deity to see and do something. The difference in form and genre to the other poems has tended towards historical discussions about the provenance of the lament. Here, we will concentrate on the message that comes to the fore in the complaints of the people.

The community in the fifth chapter concentrates on describing the hardship and horror of imperial rule. A subjugated people no longer own their own land, 'Our inheritance has been turned over to strangers and our homes to aliens' (5:2), and are under foreign rule, 'Slaves rule over us' (v. 8). In addition, they suffer economically, 'We must pay for the water we drink, the wood we get must be bought' (v. 4) and 'With a yoke on our necks we are hard driven' (v. 5). More challenging still, they are terrorized and live in fear, 'We get bread at the peril of our lives' (v. 9). Under oppressive present circumstances that may point to the real effects of imperial control and interference, they are starving, 'Our skin is black as an oven from the scorching heat of famine' (v. 10). Finally, each member of the community faces torturous personal affliction, 'Women are raped in Zion, virgins in the towns of Judah' (v. 11), 'Princes are hung up by their hands' (thought to be from punishment or a reference to death from a type of crucifixion in v. 12a), 'no respect is shown to the elders' (v. 12b), and 'Young men are compelled to grind and boys stagger under loads of wood' (v. 13).

Economically, physically and socially the community in Lamentations 5 cries out from oppression, persecution and exploitation. In the accounts of the victims themselves, imperial governance was not benign for those subjugated to foreign rule. The subjects of the state languished under punishing conditions in which they and their resources were exploited and violated. Their persons and their property belonged to an autocratic regime. Their representation of foreign rule echoes the images associated with the city of Jerusalem that appeared at the very beginning of the collection, where she was called a widow and a vassal (1:1). The poet described Jerusalem with language that graphically depicts vulnerability and servitude to another. In Pharaoh Merneptah's victory inscription, called the Merneptah Stele (line 27), the Egyptian term for widow is used for lands that have been plundered, so the image of the city as a widow points, like the use of the terminology of vassalage, to its status under the imposition of foreign rule (Berlin 2002: 19). As a vassal,

Jerusalem experienced the imposition of forced labour, exploitation and the siphoning off of resources for the good of the empire and the enjoyment of the few – the veritable rape of the land.

One of the closest correspondences to the hardship experienced and expressed by a suffering people in Lamentations 5 that occurs to me, in addition to the treatment of the Jews and other ethnic, political and religious minorities during the Holocaust, relates to the system of slavery in the American South that existed until the mid-nineteenth century. African slaves were a people forcibly deported from their homeland to settlement in a new land. They were denied basic human rights and education, healthcare, wages and autonomy to make decisions about their own persons and movement. From another perspective:

> The conditions under which the enslaved people lived are well known. They were forced to work under inhumane conditions. They were beaten and abused. They had family members sold away. Their names and identities were erased and replaced … They had no control over their present or their future. The plight of enslaved females was even worse. Sexual abuse and humiliation were rampant both on the ships and on dry land. (Bailey 153)

Reading Lamentations 5 with an appreciation of the hardship of slavery or the economic and physical exploitation of an entire people on the basis of their skin colour uncovers the pathos of the laments. At the same time, reading the songs of the slaves as an intertext of Lamentations enables us to better regard the suffering endured and the real and lasting consequences of exploitative and dehumanizing interaction. The slaves captured their protests in songs that allowed them to express the wounding and sorrow that they experienced as in, 'Nobody knows the trouble I've had/seen' as well as their hopes for a better life in a heaven that they sought on earth away from the abusive slave master, 'Got hard trial in my way, Heav'n shall-a be my home. O when I talk, I talk with God, Heav'n shall-a be my home' (from 'Poor Rosy') (from Allen, Ware and Garrison 1867, as quoted by Bailey 2008).

An imperialistic or colonial worldview manifests itself in perceptions of the 'other' as subjects to be dominated and downplays, refracts and suppresses real experiences and eyewitness accounts of terror, oppression and persecution. In so doing, it inculcates systemic racism or ethnism through denial as well as through violent suppression. The difficulties faced by the slaves in the pre-Civil War South who were unable to claim autonomy over their physical circumstances, much less their own bodies, reverberate through the oppression of the Jim Crow era to the rampant use of extreme and/or deadly force against non-white individuals in the United States today, including members of the Black and Hispanic communities as well as Native Americans. The Black Lives Matter (BLM) movement channels the pent up and simmering hurt of persecuted and exploited individuals and communities into a resounding cry for systemic and societal change – to wrest free from subjugation and suppression and embrace autonomy and self-fulfilment.

We are in a better position to understand, appreciate and feel the hardship of marginalized communities because post-colonial critics have uncovered the voices of the oppressed and the persecuted who suffer physical and emotional harm under exploitative control. Post-colonial interpretation enables better regard for the strategies of fostering and maintaining imperial and colonial rule and its real (and harmful) consequences as well as other forms of systemic oppression by shining light on the realities of hardship for those without equal access to resources or to influence. At the same time, post-colonial research enables us to see that in some ways the vociferous complaints in Lamentations mimic the outcry of the slaves in Egypt whose plight spurred a deity to intervention, unlikely men and women to bold leadership and a people to action. By drawing attention to the cudgel of injustice and inequality wielded against people because of their ethnicity and the colour of their skin, the BLM demonstrators stand firmly in the biblical tradition that honours and values the right to protest by those burdened by oppression and who insist on a better today and tomorrow.

The preservation of the testimonies of wounded individuals and groups in the book of Lamentations evidences how the stories of unjust suffering, persecution and hardship matter to the biblical community. The protests and complaints, the bitter cries and the laments, attest to the brokenness of creation, but more significantly to the broken and downtrodden of creation, who can envision, and indeed deserve, a different and better future, and who cry out against injustice and gasp for righteousness and the enactment of right dealings in society modelled on a just deity. Ultimately, the post-colonial lens draws much-needed attention to how the vocalization of a painful present reveals the true costs of harmful attitudes and systems that can lead to transformation, reconciliation and change on the personal and societal level.

READING FOR COMFORT AND COMPASSION

The final reflection I would like to offer on the biblical book of Lamentations takes seriously the language of its poetry and the figures who appear therein. The terrible images of physical devastation and human affliction, the cacophony of voices that intrude and interrupt each other, the use of personification to evoke emotion work together not just to literarily televise images of war and its devastating consequences on real people and communities. More importantly, the images intend to highlight the dire circumstances of people in need of rescue. Lamentations yields a message about a shared humanity that is of particular relevance at the present time in which divisions of misunderstanding and skewed stories take root in communities and foster division and war – another example of people in need of rescue. An analysis sensitive to the interactions that take place between two of the personae in chapters 1 and 2 discloses the important role of compassion within the collection as well as the lack thereof, the significance ascribed to the recognition of the pain and suffering of the other, and the need for active engagement and human comfort (this section draws on Middlemas 2012 and 2019: 353–6).

Lamentations, like other examples of ANE and biblical penitential prayer, places an emphasis on divine mercy and the lack thereof. There are three different roots used in Lamentations for comfort (*nḥm*) and compassion (*rḥm* and *ḥml*) that are similar in meaning, yet also distinct. The term for comfort is found six times in Lamentations: five times with reference to a lack of comfort for Jerusalem and once in the wish of the eyewitness to offer comfort to the personified city (2:13). The term is particularly associated with rituals to aid a person or persons in mourning through the grief process on the occasion of a death, often referred to as a comforter (Andersen 1991; Pham 1999). In the first chapter, a refrain repeats, echoes and reverberates that '[Dearest Jerusalem] has no one to comfort her (lit. "there was no comforter for her" using the noun form *mənaḥēm*)' (Lam. 1:2, 9, 17, 21) and 'there was no one to help her' (lit. 'there was no helper for her' with *'zr* in 1:7). Also with a negative sense as in 'there was no', the poet employs the root *ḥml*, which points more generally to compassion or mercy, but can also connote the act of pardoning or sparing someone. Correspondingly, the poet attributes a lack of compassion to God in Lamentations because the deity in anger (1:12; 2:1-6, 21-2; 3:42-3; 4:11; 5:22) destroyed without mercy (2:2, 17, the noun *ḥml*) and without pity (2:21; 3:43, the verb *ḥml*). In conjunction with these references, the deity refrains from sparing the people destruction, demolition, slaughter and killing. The theme of mercy also echoes in conjunction with the depiction of once-compassionate mothers who boil their own children for food (4:10; cf. 2:20) and in the image of a forlorn and abandoned people who wait and watch 'vainly for help' (4:17, with the root *'zr*).

In spite of doubts to the contrary, the wisdom promise of the third chapter insists that 'The steadfast love (plural of *ḥsd*) of Yahweh never ceases, God's mercies (plural of *rḥm*) never come to an end' (3:22) and the deity 'will have compassion (verb of *rḥm*) according to the abundance of God's steadfast love (singular of *ḥsd*)' (3:32). The articulation of hope in God as compassionate and loving in the wisdom verses surely rings hollow given the overwhelming tragedy and the lack of mercy highlighted in descriptions of and statements from the intertwining voices in the poems.

The confidence of the third chapter is eclipsed by the images of trauma and reversal that suffuse the poems and provide its conclusion. In fact, the fourth chapter contains some of the most gruesome imagery in the collection and vividly portrays the ravishing effects of famine (4:2-10) and forced deportation (vv. 15-19). Correspondingly, the poet portrays the deity as an absentee overlord in the final two poems, which again reinforces the prevalent theme of the lack of divine concern and comfort in Lamentations (Middlemas 2005: 192). Finally, Lamentations ends on a doubtful note, with a question about whether God will ever intervene (Gordis 1974; Linafelt 2001 and 2008; Middlemas 2004: 97, n. 47). The swirling of horrifying images of post-war Jerusalem functions within a lengthy, almost exhausting, intercessory plea that ultimately seeks to provoke God's compassionate response and intervention, but regrettably fails to succeed. In its entirety, the book of Lamentations presents a graphic portrait of human pain and the lack of any comfort or assistance. In the final summation, the lack of divine compassion is underscored. God never answers, alleviates or spares the suffering or the sufferer.

In spite of the resounding theme of comfort and especially the emphasis placed on the (divine) lack thereof, the eyewitness reporter models the outreach and interaction so desperately sought from God. In the first two chapters, the voices of an eyewitness who I liken to a reporter and the personified mother city of Jerusalem both appear. In fact, the first two poems are aligned in length (sixty-six lines) as well as by the mournful opening of 'how' (*'ĕkah*), the inclusion of two main speaking voices (of the eyewitness and the personified city), and the order in which the voices appear – the poems open with an account of disaster presented by the reporter (1:1-11; 2:1-19) and conclude with the cries of vulnerable Jerusalem (1:12-22; 2:20-2). In the first chapter, the eyewitness's rote report of a great catastrophe was twice interrupted (1:9c and 11c) by the urgent appeal of the personified city of Jerusalem who then speaks until the conclusion of the chapter (vv. 12-22). Here, Jerusalem advocates vociferously and tenaciously as a mother fighting for her children against the terror around her and appeals for assistance (see also Linafelt 2000 and 2000).

Noticeably, in the second chapter which corresponds quite closely with the first, Jerusalem appears far less able to intercede on behalf of herself and her community. She seems to represent the figuratively dead city mourned in the eyewitness's dirge in the first chapter. An additional striking difference again to the first poem is that the eyewitness reporter and the personified city in the second chapter not only appear together, but they also interact. During a review of the ferocious divine and human enemy attack, the reporter actually breaks down and speaks directly to the personified city. He or she urges her emphatically to cease her silence or awake from the haze of death and raise her voice to protest the present misery, 'Cry aloud to the Lord! O wall of daughter Zion! Let tears stream down like a torrent day and night! Give yourself no rest, your eyes no respite! … Lift your hands to God for the lives of your children, who faint for hunger at the head of every street!' (Lam. 2:18-19). Seemingly moved by the suffering of the most innocent members of society who faint with hunger in the streets and fade away in their mother's arms (so v. 12), the reporter loses the last vestige of cool composure, seeks to remedy the distress and in the end demands that personified Mother Jerusalem resume her protest to the deity.

In the Hebrew, the first strophe attributed to the eyewitness is literally 'Their heart cried out to the Lord', but the switch from a third masculine singular verb at the beginning of the verse to direct commands to a woman in the rest of verses 18 and 19 strikes many commentators as odd. As it stands, the strophe suggests that the children who are mentioned at the end of verse 19 are crying out for survival and divine intervention with every fibre of their being. It is to their misery, then, that the reporter responds with his commands to Jerusalem. Alternatively and as indicated here, the statement is odd in its immediate and wider context because a series of imperatives to a second-person feminine character begin with the narrative description of children pleading for help, which leaves the second stich of the line, 'O wall of daughter Zion!', dangling without explanation. Many interpreters and also Bible translations, then, follow a suggested emendation to the text and understand a command to personified Jerusalem to continue her protest. Although I prefer the emendation, either understanding reveals that the reporter loses his or her objective stance and rational distance when confronted with the actual human cost of war and intervenes. Moved by the seeming frailty of personified Jerusalem and the children's acute pain, the reporter casts aside level-headed observation and for the first time he or she takes note of the desolation, feels with the afflicted and speaks directly to the city.

The book of Lamentations presents a literary visual portrait of real human tragedy that aims ultimately to move the deity to see and intervene. Given that the voice most urgently sought, that of the deity, is the one never heard, the reaction of the reporter in the second chapter becomes significant. Abject and untold misery inspired the eyewitness to lose his or her objective distance and to feel with Jerusalem and her suffering community. When confronted with the lack of divine response, the objective eyewitness refuses to look away and instead assumes or at least tries to assume the role of comforter so longed for and sought by Jerusalem and her survivors. The reporter seemingly accepts the role of the official comforter for Jerusalem, but is unable to offer constructive solutions to enable her to overcome her grief, 'What can I say for you … O daughter Jerusalem? … that I may comfort you (verb *nhm*), O virgin daughter Zion? For vast as the sea is your ruin; who can heal you?' (2:13). Truly, there is a lack of comfort in the collection when even the reporter's attempt at assistance fails to alleviate the immeasurable depth of pain. Ultimately, hope lies with a deity who will react like the eyewitness – to see, to be moved, to have compassion, to comfort and to intervene salvifically and restoratively.

The reporter becomes Jerusalem's human comforter and values her account, her experience and her suffering, but recognizes his or her inability to overturn the desperate state of affairs and offer the assistance so desperately needed. At the point when the eyewitness loses rational distance when confronted with the actual human victims of war and famine and seeks to offer comfort to Jerusalem, his or her statement 'there is no one to comfort/help her' is confirmed. However, Jerusalem at least in the first chapter reveals a significant faith and trust in God because she interrupts the account of the reporter in order to urge the deity to 'look and see' (1:9c, 11c). Truly, in the middle of abject suffering, personified Jerusalem also confidently asserts that her comforter is only at a distance, perhaps wrapped in a cloud (when taking 2:1 literally). In what is one of the most significant declarations of faith or confessions of trust in the whole collection, Jerusalem claims that 'a comforter *is far from me*, one to revive my courage' (1:16, italics added for emphasis). Although the eyewitness repeatedly stated that there is no comforter or helper for Jerusalem, the City Woman actually knows that there is indeed one, the deity, who remains far from her in her time of need.

The tragedy of Lamentations is that divine restoration remains at bay, but the attempts at comfort and compassion from the eyewitness reporter, who speaks and feels with Jerusalem, offer hope and succour. Notably in the second chapter, the eyewitness broke away from the physical distance of description and rational explanation to speak directly to the city, in order to tell her that he or she saw her misery, felt her pain, and urge her to continue her protest and her resistance. The reporter steps up. Human compassion and attempts at comfort inspired the personified city to resume her lament and her plea. Jerusalem's voice holding God to account for wanton slaughter and a raging famine then concludes the chapter.

The compassionate presence and commitment offered by the eyewitness compare favourably with the eloquent words about God's mercy and love in the central or core verses of the whole collection (3:22-39). In wisdom's interpretation, God is described as compassionate and loving at the same time (3:22, 32), which echoes a recurring biblical assertion found used only of the deity, 'Yahweh, merciful and gracious' (Trible 1978: 38–9). In a study sensitive to rhetorical use, Phyllis Trible traces the Hebrew root *rhm* 'compassion, mercy' to the noun to which it is semantically related, that is, 'womb' (Trible 1978: 31–59). Compassion is an example of Yahweh's womb-like love such that 'this metaphor suggests the meaning of love as selfless participation in life. The womb protects and nourishes but does not possess and control … Truly, it [exemplifies] the way of compassion' (Trible 1978: 33). A few biblical texts capture the depth of the intertwining connections of the Mother God's womb-like compassion and love, when God is compared to a nursing mother, 'Can a woman forget her nursing child, or show no compassion for the child of her womb? Even these may forget, yet I will not forget you' (Isa. 49:15) or when equated to one, 'As a mother comforts her child, so I will comfort you; you shall be comforted in Jerusalem' (Isa. 66:13).

It is true that the absence of the divine comforter in Lamentations created a theological challenge that is answered in the prophecies of reversal and homecoming made in Deutero-Isaiah (Isa. 40–55), in other Old Testament literature, as in the book of Job, for example, and then in the New Testament traditions about the compassion, pathos, suffering and passion of Jesus Christ. Nevertheless, the compassionate response of the eyewitness to Jerusalem's suffering models the divine character to one in great need of comfort. In so doing, I would argue that the reporter mirrors more closely the divine image and thereby exemplifies the necessity of human acknowledgement of and response to the suffering of the neighbour and the other – to mirror divine motherly compassion – for our world today. As I wrote elsewhere:

> In the absence of God and divine comfort, the prayerful poems urge a human response and set the relationship between the eyewitness and the vulnerable, personified Jerusalem as an example of the possibility, even necessity, of human compassion as well as the power and possibility of comfort in the presence of protest, untold agony, and the depressing knell of despair. The book of Lamentations serves as a litany of remembrance to remind humanity of one of the values that makes us human and which draws us together in spite or racial, ethnic, economic, and educational differences. Further, it serves as a tractate that spurs reaction and action to confront, challenge, and respond to the brutality perpetuated against (all) human beings, who are in the first and final assessment of the biblical tradition, created in the image of God. At the present time, in a conflict- and war-weary world, the book of Lamentations offers a brutal and honest look at the cost of discord and rivalry that can inspire us, like the reporter, to take a hard look and reclaim our humanity. What makes us human is to see the circumstances of our neighbour and to feel with them. (Middlemas 2019: 355–6)

One could add that by embracing our best notions, like compassion and comfort, each human person conforms more closely to the divine image in which we are constructed and so comes that little bit closer to God. And God's presence, then, is felt a little bit more on earth.

WORKS CITED BY CHAPTER

INTRODUCTION

U. Berges, *Klagelieder* (HKAT; Freiburg: Herder, 2002).

A. Berlin, *Lamentations* (OTL; Louisville, KY: Westminster John Knox, 2002).

S. J. D. Cohen, 'The Destruction: From Scripture to Midrash', *Prooftexts* 2 (1982): 18–39.

P. W. Ferris, *The Genre of Communal Lament in the Bible and the Ancient Near East* (SBLDS 127; Atlanta, GA: Scholars 1992).

H. Gunkel and J. Begrich, *Einleitung in die Psalmen: Die Gattungen der religiösen Lyrik Israels* (Göttingen: Vandenhoeck & Ruprecht, 1933).

H. Heater Jr. 'Structure and Meaning in Lamentations', *BS* 149 (1992): 304–15.

J. Hunter, *Faces of a Lamenting City: The Development and Coherence of the Book of Lamentations* (BEATAJ 39; Frankfurt am Main: Peter Lang, 1996).

E. Janssen, *Juda in der Exilszeit: Ein Beitrag zur Frage der Entstehung des Judentums* (FRLANT 51, ns; Göttingen: Vandenhoeck & Ruprecht, 1956).

B. Johnson, 'Form and Message in Lamentations', *ZAW* 97 (1987): 58–73.

R. W. Klein, 'A Theology for Exiles: The Kingship of Yahweh', *Dialog* 17 (1978): 128–34.

N. C. Lee, *The Singers of Lamentations: Cities under Siege, from Ur to Jerusalem to Sarajevo* (BIS 60; Leiden: Brill, 2002).

T. Linafelt, *Surviving Lamentations: Catastrophe, Lament, and Protest in the Afterlife of a Biblical Book* (Chicago, IL: University of Chicago Press, 2000).

M. Löhr, 'Der Sprachgebrauch des Buches der Klagelieder', *ZAW* 14 (1894): 31–50.

M. Löhr, 'Threni III und die jeremianische Autorschaft des Buches der Klagelieder', *ZAW* 24 (1904): 1–16.

J. Middlemas, *The Divine Image: Prophetic Aniconic Rhetoric and Its Contribution to the Aniconism Debate* (FAT 2/74; Tübingen: Mohr Siebeck, 2014).

J. Middlemas, 'Speaking of Speaking: The Form of Zion's Suffering in Lamentations', in *Daughter Zion: Her Portrait, Her Response* (SBLAIL 13; eds. M. J. Boda, et al.; Atlanta, GA: SBL, 2012), pp. 39–54.

J. Middlemas, *The Troubles of Templeless Judah* (OTM; Oxford: Oxford University Press, 2005).

J. Middlemas, *The Templeless Age: An Introduction to the History, Literature, and Theology of the 'Exile'* (Louisville, KY: Westminster John Knox, 2007).

M. S. Moore, 'Human Suffering in Lamentations', *RB* 90 (1983): 534–55.

K. M. O'Connor, 'The Book of Lamentations: Introduction, Commentary, and Reflections', in *NIB* (vol. 6; eds. L. E. Keck, et al.; Nashville, TN: Abingdon Press, 2001), pp. 1011–72.

J. Renkema, *Lamentations* (HCOT; Leuven: Peeters, 1998).

R. B. Salters, 'Structure and Implication in Lamentations 1', *SJOT* 14 (2000): 293–300.

N. Seidman, 'Burning the Book of Lamentations', in *Out of the Garden: Women Writers on the Bible* (eds. C. Büchmann and C. Spiegel; London: Pandora, 1994), pp. 278–88.

J. Tigay, and A. Cooper, 'Lamentations, Book of', in *Encyclopedia Judaica* (vol. 12; Detroit, MI: Macmillan Reference USA, 1972, 2nd edn, 2007), pp. 446–51.

H. G. M. Williamson, 'Laments at the Destroyed Temple', *BRev* 4 (1990): 12–17, 44.

CHAPTER 1: THE LITERATURE OF LAMENTATIONS: POETIC ART

R. Alter, *The Art of Biblical Poetry* (New York: HarperCollins, 1985).

E. Assis, 'The Alphabetic Acrostic in the Book of Lamentations', *Catholic Biblical Quarterly* 69 (2007), pp. 710–24.

U. Berges, *Klagelieder* (HKAT; Freiburg: Herder, 2002).

A. Berlin, *The Dynamics of Parallelism* (Grand Rapids, MI: Eerdmans, 2008).

A. Berlin, *Lamentations* (OTL; Louisville, KY: Westminster John Knox, 2002).

E. Boase, *The Fullfilment of Doom? The Dialogic Interaction between the Book of Lamentations and the Pre-Exilic/Early Exilic Prophetic Literature* (LHBOTS 437; New York: T & T Clark, 2006).

D. A. Bosworth, 'Daughter Zion and Weeping in Lamentations 1–2', *JSOT* (2013): 217–37.

J. Brug, 'Biblical Acrostics and Their Relationship to Other Ancient Near Eastern Acrostics', in *Scripture in Context*, vol. 3: *The Bible in the Light of Cuneiform Literature* (eds. W. Hallo, et al.; Lewiston, NY: Edwin Mellen, 1990), pp. 283–304.

K. Budde, 'Das hebräische Klagelied', *ZAW* 2 (1882): 1–52.

M. L. Conway, 'Daughter Zion: Metaphor and Dialogue in Book of Lamentations', in *Daughter Zion: Her Portrait, Her Response* (eds. M. J. Boda, et al; SBLAIL 13; Atlanta, GA: SBL, 2012), pp. 101–26.

F. M. Cross, 'Newly Found Inscriptions in Old-Canaanite and Early Phoenician Scripts', *BASOR* 238 (1980): 1–20.

F. W. Dobbs-Allsopp, *Lamentations* (IBC; Louisville, KY: Westminster John Knox, 2002).

F. W. Dobbs-Allsopp, 'The Syntagma of *bat* Followed by a Geographical Name in the Hebrew Bible: A Reconsideration of Its Meaning and Grammar', *CBQ* 57 (1995): 451–70.

F. W. Dobbs-Allsopp and T. Linafelt, 'The Rape of Zion in Thr 1,10', *ZAW* 113 (2001): 77–81.

M. H. Floyd, 'Welcome Back, Daughter of Zion!' *CBQ* 70 (2008): 484–504.

C. Frevel, *Die Klagelieder* (NSKAT 20/1; Stuttgart: Katholisches Bibelwerk, 2017).

W. R. Garr, 'The Qinah: A Study of Poetic Metre, Syntax and Style', *ZAW* 95 (1983): 54–75.

H. Heater, 'Structure and Meaning in Lamentations', *BibSac* 149 (1992): 304–15.

K. Heim, 'The Personification of Jerusalem and the Drama of Her Bereavement in Lamentations', in *Zion, City of Our God* (eds. R. S. Hess and G. J. Wenham; Grand Rapids, MI: Eerdmans, 1999), pp. 296–322.

D. R. Hillers, *Lamentations* (AB 7a; Garden City, NY: Doubleday, 1972, 2nd edn, 1992).

R. de Hoop, 'Lamentations: The Qinah-Metre Questioned', in *Delimitation Criticism: A New Tool in Biblical Scholarship* (eds. M. C. A. Korpel and J. M. Oesch; Assen: Van Gorcum, 2000), pp. 80–104.

B. Johnson, 'Form and Message in Lamentations', *ZAW* 97 (1985): 58–73.

B. B. Kaiser, 'Poet as "Female Impersonator": The Image of Daughter Zion as Speaker in Biblical Poems of Suffering', *JR*, no. 7 (1987): 164–82.

M. Kartveit, *Rejoice Dear Zion! Hebrew Construct Phrases with 'Daughter' and 'Virgin' as Nomen Regens* (BZAW 447; Berlin: de Gruyter, 2013).

S. N. Kramer, 'The Weeping Goddess: Sumerian Prototypes of the Mater Dolorosa', *BA* 46 (1983): 69–80.

W. F. Lanahan, 'The Speaking Voice in the Book of Lamentations', *JBL* 93 (1974): 41–9.

N. C. Lee, *The Singers of Lamentations: Cities under Siege, from Ur to Jerusalem to Sarajevo* (BIS 60; Leiden: Brill, 2002).

T. Linafelt, *Surviving Lamentations: Catastrophe, Lament, and Protest in the Afterlife of a Biblical Book* (Chicago, IL: University of Chicago Press, 2000).

C. M. Maier, *Daughter Zion, Mother Zion: Gender, Space, and the Sacred in Ancient Israel* (Minneapolis, MN: Fortress, 2008).

C. R. Mandolfo, *Daughter Zion Talks Back to the Prophets: A Dialogic Theology of the Book of Lamentations* (SBLSS 58; Atlanta, GA: Society of Biblical Literature, 2007).

J. Middlemas, 'The Violent Storm in Lamentations', *JSOT* 29 (2004): 81–97.

A. Mintz, *Hurban: Responses to Catastrophe in Jewish Literature* (New York: Columbia University Press, 1984).

B. Morse, 'The Lamentations Project: Biblical Mourning through Modern Montage', *JSOT* 28 (2003): 113–27.

K. M. O'Connor, *Lamentations and the Tears of the World* (Maryknoll, NY: Orbis, 2002).

D. L. Petersen, and K. H. Richards, *Interpreting Hebrew Poetry* (Minneapolis, MN: Fortress, 1992).

X. H. T. Pham, *Mourning in the Ancient Near East and the Hebrew Bible* (JSOTSup 302; Sheffield: Sheffield Academic Press, 1999)

I. W. Provan, *Lamentations* (NCB; Grand Rapids, MI: Eerdmans, 1991).

J. Renkema, *Lamentations* (HCOT; Leuven: Peeters, 1998).

R. B. Salters, *Lamentations* (ICC; London: T & T Clark, 2010).

L. A. Schökel, *A Manual of Hebrew Poetry* (SubB 11; Rome: Pontifical Biblical Institute, 1988).

N. Seidman, 'Burning the Book of Lamentations', in *Out of the Garden: Women Writers on the Bible* (eds. D. Buchmann and C. Spiegel; New York: Fawcett Columbine, 1992), pp. 278–88.

W. H. Shea, 'The *qinah* Structure of the Book of Lamentations', *Bib* 60 (1979): 103–7.

W. M. Soll, 'Babylonian and Biblical Acrostics', *Bib* 69 (1989): 305–23.

W. R. Stinespring, 'No Daughter of Zion', *Encounter* 26 (1965): 133–41.

H. A. Thomas, *Poetry and Theology in the Book of Lamentations: The Aesthetics of an Open Text* (HBM; Sheffield: Sheffield Phoenix, 2013).

W. G. E. Watson, *Classical Hebrew Poetry* (JSOTSup 26; Sheffield: JSOT, 1984, rep., 2001).

C. Westermann, *Lamentations: Issues and Interpretation* (Edinburgh: T & T Clark, 1994).

J. P. Wiles, *Half-Hours with the Minor Prophets* (London: Morgan and Scott, 1908).

CHAPTER 2: THE LITERATURE OF LAMENTATIONS: COMPOSITION HISTORY AND MATTERS OF FORM

E. Assis, 'The Unity of the Book of Lamentations', *CBQ* 71 (2009): 306–29.

R. J. Bautch, *Developments in Genre between Post-exilic Penitential Prayers and the Psalms of Communal Lament* (SBLAcB 7; Atlanta, GA: SBL, 2003).

U. Berges, *Klagelieder* (HKAT; Freiburg: Herder, 2002).

A. Berlin, *Lamentations* (OTL; Louisville, KY: Westminster John Knox, 2002).

M. J. Boda, *Praying the Tradition: The Origin and Use of Tradition in Nehemiah 9* (BZAW 277; Berlin: de Gruyter, 1999).

M. J. Boda, 'The Priceless Gain of Penitence: From Communal Lament to Penitential Prayer in the "Exilic" Liturgy of Israel', in *Lamentations in Ancient and Contemporary Cultural Contexts* (eds. N. C. Lee and C. Mandolfo; SBLSS 43; Atlanta, GA: SBL, 2008), pp. 81–102.

W. C. Bouzard Jr, *We Have Heard with Our Ears, O God: Sources of the Communal Laments in the Psalms* (SBLDS 159; Atlanta, GA: Scholars, 1997).

W. Brueggemann, *The Psalms and the Life of Faith* (Minneapolis, MI: Fortress, 1995).

M. L. Conway, 'Daughter Zion: Metaphor and Dialogue in Book of Lamentations', in *Daughter Zion: Her Portrait, Her Response* (eds. M. J. Boda, et al.; SBLAIL 13; Atlanta, GA: SBL, 2012), pp. 101–26.

A. Cooper, 'The Message of Lamentations', *JANES* 28 (2001): 1–18.

F. W. Dobbs-Allsopp, *Weep, O Daughter of Zion: A Study of the City-Lament Genre in the Hebrew Bible* (Rome: Editrice Pontificio Istituto Biblico, 1993).

P. W. Ferris, *The Genre of Communal Lament in the Bible and the Ancient Near East* (SBLDS 127; Atlanta, GA: Scholars Press, 1992).

E. S. Gerstenberger, *Psalms and Lamentations*, part 2 (FOTL 15; Grand Rapids, MI: Eerdmans, 2001).

E. L. Greenstein, 'The Book of Lamentations: Response to Destruction or Ritual of Rebuilding?' in *Religious Responses to Political Crisis* (eds. H. G. Reventlow and Y. Hoffman; New York: T & T Clark, 2008), pp. 52–71.

B. Gregory, 'The Postexilic Exile in Third Isaiah: Isaiah 64:7–64:11', *JBL* 126 (2007): 475–96.

D. Grossberg, *Centripetal and Centrifugal Structures in Biblical Poetry* (SBLMS 39; Atlanta, GA: Scholars, 1989).

H. Gunkel, and J. Begrich, *Einleitung in die Psalmen: Die Gattungen der religiösen Lyrik Israels* (Göttingen: Vandenhoeck & Ruprecht, 1933).

W. C. Gwaltney, 'Lamentations in Near Eastern Literature', in *Scripture in Context*, vol. 2: *More Essays on the Comparative Method* (eds. W. W. Hallo, et al.; Winona Lake, IN: Eisenbrauns, 1983), pp. 191–211.

H. Jahnow, *Das Hebräische Leichenlied im Rahmen der Völkerdichtung* (BZAW 36; Giessen: A. Töpelmann, 1923).

Ronald A. Knox, *The Holy Bible* (London: Burns and Oates, 1956).

N. C. Lee, *The Singers of Lamentations: Cities under Siege, from Ur to Jerusalem to Sarajevo* (BIS 60; Leiden: Brill, 2002).

T. Linafelt, *Surviving Lamentations: Catastrophe, Lament, and Protest in the Afterlife of a Biblical Book* (Chicago, IL: University of Chicago Press, 2000).

T. F. McDaniel, 'The Alleged Sumerian Influence upon Lamentations', *VT* 18 (1968): 198–209.

J. Middlemas, 'Did Second Isaiah Write Lamentations III?' *VT* LVI (2006): 505–25.

J. Middlemas, 'The Shape of Things to Come: Redaction in the Early Second Temple Period Prophetic Tradition', in *Prophecy in Its Ancient Context* (eds. M. Nissinen and L. L. Grabbe; SBLANE 4; Atlanta, GA: SBL, 2011), pp. 141–56.

J. Middlemas, 'Speaking of Speaking: The Form of Zion's Suffering in Lamentations', in *Daughter Zion: Her Portrait, Her Response* (eds. M. J. Boda, et al.; SBLAIL 13; Atlanta, GA: SBL, 2012), pp. 39–54.

J. Middlemas, *The Templeless Age: An Introduction to the Literature, History, and Theology of the 'Exile'* (Nashville, TN: Westminster John Knox, 2007).

J. Middlemas, *The Troubles of Templeless Judah* (OTM; Oxford: Oxford University Press, 2005).

J. Middlemas, 'The Violent Storm in Lamentations', *JSOT* 29 (2004): 81–97.

J. Middlemas, 'War, Comfort, and Compassion in Lamentations', *Expository Times* 130/8 (2019), pp. 345–56.

P. D. Miller, *They Cried to the Lord: The Form and Theology of Biblical Prayer* (Minneapolis, MN: Fortress, 1994).

S. M. Olyan, *Biblical Mourning: Ritual and Social Dimensions* (Oxford: Oxford University Press, 2004).

J. Renkema, *Lamentations* (Historical Commentary of the Old Testament; Leuven: Peeters, 1998).

R. B. Salters, *Lamentations* (ICC; London: T & T Clark, 2010).

W. H. Shea, 'The *qinah* Structure of the Book of Lamentations', *Bib* 60 (1979): 103–7.

D. L. Smith, *The Religion of the Landless: The Social Context of the Babylonian Exile* (Bloomington, IN: Meyer-Stone Books, 1989).

C. Westermann, *Lamentations: Issues and Interpretation* (Edinburgh: T & T Clark, 1994).

CHAPTER 3: THE HISTORICAL BACKGROUND OF LAMENTATIONS

R. Albertz, *Israel in Exile: The History and Literature of the Sixth Century B.C.E.* (trans. D. Green; SBL 3; Atlanta, GA: SBL, 2003).

R. Albertz, 'More and Less Than a Myth: Reality and Significance of Exile for the Political, Social, and Religious History of Judah', in *By the Irrigation Canals of Babylon: Approaches to the Study of Exile* (eds. J. J. Ahn and J. Middlemas; LHBOTS 526; New York and London: T & T Clark, 2012), pp. 20–33.

G. A. Andersen, *A Time to Mourn, a Time to Dance: The Expression of Grief and Joy in Israelite Religion* (University Park, PA: Pennsylvania State University Press, 1991).

H. M. Barstad, 'The City State of Jerusalem in the Neo-Babylonian Empire: Evidence from the Surrounding States', in *By the Irrigation Canals of Babylon: Approaches to the Study of Exile* (eds. J. J. Ahn and J. Middlemas; LHBOTS 526; New York and London: T & T Clark, 2012), pp. 34–48.

P. A. Beaulieu, 'Yahwistic Names in Light of Late Babylonian Onomastics', in *Judah and the Judeans in the Achaemenid Period: Negotiating Identity in an International Context* (eds. O. Lipschits, et al.; Winona Lake, IN: Eisenbrauns, 2011), pp. 245–66.

B. Becking, '"We All Returned as One": Critical Notes on the Myth of the Mass Return', in *Judah and the Judeans in the Persian Period* (eds. O. Lipschits and M. Oeming; Winona Lake, IN: Eisenbrauns, 2006), pp. 3–18.

D. Bergeant, 'The Challenge of Hermeneutics: Lamentations 1:1–11: A Test Case', *CBQ* 64 (2002): 1–16.

U. Berges, *Klagelieder* (HKAT; Freiburg: Herder, 2002).

A. Berlin, *Lamentations* (OTL; Louisville, KY: Westminster John Knox, 2002).

J. Blenkinsopp, 'The Age of the Exile', in *The Biblical World* (ed. J. Barton; London and New York: Routledge, 2002), pp. 416–39.

M. J. Boda, 'The Priceless Gain of Penitence: From Communal Lament to Penitential Prayer in the "Exilic" Liturgy of Israel', in *Lamentations in Ancient and Contemporary Cultural Contexts* (eds. N. C. Lee and C. Mandolfo; Society of Biblical Literature Seminar Studies 43; Atlanta, GA: SBL, 2008), pp. 81–102.

C. E. Carter, *The Emergence of Yehud in the Persian Period: A Social and Demographic Study* (JSOTSup 294; Sheffield: Sheffield Academic Press, 1999).

R. E. Clements, *Old Testament Prophecy: From Oracles to Canon* (Louisville, KY: Westminster John Knox, 1996).

A. Cooper, 'The Message of Lamentations', *JANES* 28 (2001): 1–18.

F. W. Dobbs-Allsopp, 'Linguistic Evidence for the Date of Lamentations', *JANES* 26 (1998):1–36.

F. W. Dobbs-Allsopp, 'Tragedy, Tradition, and Theology in the Book of Lamentations', *JSOT* 74 (1997): 29–60.

D. V. Edelman, *The Origins of the 'Second Temple': Persian Imperial Policy and the Rebuilding of Jerusalem* (London: Equinox, 2005).

A. Faust, *Judah in the Neo-Babylonian Period: The Archaeology of Desolation* (SBLABS 18; Atlanta, GA: SBL, 2012).

P. W. Ferris, *The Genre of Communal Lament in the Bible and the Ancient Near East* (SBLDS 127; Atlanta, GA: Scholars Press, 1992).

N. K. Gottwald, *Studies in the Book of Lamentations* (SBT 14; London: SCM Press, 1954, rev., 1962).

L. L. Grabbe, '"They Never Returned": Were the Babylonian Jewish Settlers Exiles or Pioneers?' in *By the Irrigation Canals of Babylon: Approaches to the Study of Exile* (eds. J. J. Ahn and J. Middlemas; LHBOTS 526. New York and London: T & T Clark, 2012), pp. 158–72.

Y. Hoffman, 'The Fasts in the Book of Zechariah and the Fashioning of National Remembrance', in *Judah and the Judeans in the Neo-Babylonian Period* (eds. O. Lipschits and J. Blenkinsopp; Winona Lake, IN: Eisenbrauns, 2003), pp. 169–218.

E. Janssen, *Juda in der Exilszeit: Ein Beitrag zur Frage der Entstehung des Judentums* (FRLANT 69; Göttingen: Vendenhoeck & Ruprecht, 1956).

P. M. Joyce, 'Sitting Loose to History: Reading the Book of Lamentations without Primary Reference to Its Original Historical Setting', in *In Search of True Wisdom: Essays in Old Testament Interpretation in Honour of Ronald E. Clements* (ed. E. Ball; JSOTSup 300; Sheffield: JSOT Press, 1999), pp. 246–62.

N. C. Lee, *The Singers of Lamentations: Cities under Siege, from Ur to Jerusalem to Sarajevo* (BIS 60; Leiden: Brill, 2002).

T. Linafelt, *Surviving Lamentations: Catastrophe, Lament, and Protest in the Afterlife of a Biblical Book* (Chicago, IL and London: University of Chicago Press, 2000).

E. Lipiński, *La liturgie pénitentielle dans la Bible* (LD 52; Paris: Cerf, 1969).

O. Lipschits, *The Fall and Rise of Jerusalem: Judah under Babylonian Rule* (Winona Lake, IN: Eisenbrauns, 2005).

T. Longman, 'The Adad-Guppi Autobiography', in *The Context of Scripture, I, Canonical Compositions from the Biblical World* (ed. W. W, Hallo; Leiden: Brill, 1997), pp. 477–8.

C. Meyers, 'Miriam the Musician', in *A Feminist Companion to Exodus to Deuteronomy* (ed. A. Brenner. Sheffield: Sheffield Academic Press, 1994), pp. 207–30.

E. M. Meyers, 'Exile and Restoration in Light of Recent Archaeology and Demographic Studies', in *Exile and Restoration Revisited: Essays on the Babylonian and Persian Periods in Memory of Peter R. Ackroyd* (eds. G. N. Knoppers, et al.; LSTS 73; London and New York: T & T Clark, 2009), pp. 166–73.

J. Middlemas, 'Did Second Isaiah Write Lamentations 3?' VT LVI (2006): 505–25.

J. Middlemas, 'Going Beyond the Myth of the Empty Land: A Reassessment of the Early Persian Period', in *Exile and Restoration Revisited: Essays on the Babylonian and Persian Periods in Memory of Peter R. Ackroyd* (eds. G. N. Knoppers, et al.; LSTS 73; London and New York: T & T Clark, 2009), pp. 174–94.

J. Middlemas, "'For Vast as the Sea Is Your Ruin" (Lam. 2:13): Exile, Migration and Diaspora after the Fall of Jerusalem in the Sixth Century BCE'. in the *New Oxford Biblical World*. Edited by K. Dell. Oxford: Oxford University Press, Forthcoming.

J. Middlemas, 'The Shape of Things to Come: Redaction and the Early Second Temple Period Prophetic Tradition', in *Constructions of Prophecy in the Former and Latter Prophets and Other Texts* (eds. L. L. Grabbe and M. Nissinen; SBLANE 4; Atlanta, GA: SBL, 2011), pp. 141–56.

J. Middlemas, 'Speaking of Speaking: The Form of Zion's Suffering in Lamentations', in *Daughter Zion: Her Portrait, Her Response* (eds. M. J. Boda, et al.; Society of Biblical Literature Ancient Israel and Its Literature 13; Atlanta, GA: SBL, 2012), pp. 39–54.

J. Middlemas, *The Templeless Age: An Introduction to the History, Literature, and Theology of the 'Exile'* (Louisville, KY: Westminster John Knox, 2007).

J. Middlemas, *The Troubles of Templeless Judah* (OTM; Oxford: Oxford University Press, 2005).

J. Middlemas, 'The Violent Storm in Lamentations', *JSOT* 29 (2004): 81–97.

J. Middlemas, 'War, Comfort, and Compassion in Lamentations', *ExpT* 130/8 (2019): 345–56.

J. M. Miller, and J. H. Hayes, *A History of Ancient Israel and Judah* (Louisville, KY: Westminster John Knox Press, 1986, 2nd edn, 2006).

W. Morrow, *Protest against God: The Eclipse of a Biblical Tradition* (HBM 4; Sheffield: Sheffield Phoenix Press, 2006).

C. A. Newsome, 'Response to Norman K. Gottwald, "Social Class and Ideology in Isaiah 40–55"', *Semeia* 59 (1992): 75–7.

E. W. Nicholson, *Preaching to the Exiles: A Study of the Prose Tradition in Jeremiah* (Oxford: Blackwell, 1970).

E. W. Nicholson, 'Deuteronomy and the Babylonian Exile', in *Deuteronomy and the Judaean Diaspora* (Oxford: Oxford University Press, 2014), pp. 41–73.

B. Oded, *Mass Deportations and Deportees in the Neo-Assyrian Empire* (Wiesbaden: Reichert, 1979).

L. Pearce, 'New Evidence for Judeans in Babylonia', in *Judah and the Judeans in the Persian Period* (eds. O. Lipschits and M. Oeming; Winona Lake, IN: Eisenbrauns, 2006), pp. 399–411.

X. H. T. Pham, *Mourning in the Ancient Near East and the Hebrew Bible* (JSOTSup 302; Sheffield: Sheffield Academic Press, 1999).

B. Porten, *The Elephantine Papyri in English: Three Millennia of Cross-Cultural Continuity and Change* (DMOA 22; Leiden: Brill, 1996).

I. Provan, *Lamentations* (NCB; Grand Rapids, MI: Eerdmans, 1991).

J. Renkema, *Lamentations* (HCOT; Leuven: Peeters, 1998).

D. Rom-Shiloni, *Exclusive Inclusivity: Identity Conflicts between the Exiles and the People who Remained (6th–5th Centuries BCE)* (LHBOTS 543; New York: Bloomsbury, 2013).

W. Rudolph, *Die Klagelieder* (KAT XVII/3; Gütersloh: Gerd Mohn, 1962).

J. F. A. Sawyer, 'Daughter Zion and Servant of the Lord in Isaiah: A Comparison', *JSOT* 44 (1989): 89–107.

C. R. Seitz, *Theology in Conflict: Reactions to the Exile in the Book of Jeremiah* (BZAW 176. Berlin: de Gruyter, 1989).

D. L. Smith, *The Religion of the Landless: The Social Context of the Babylonian Exile* (Bloomington, IN: Meyer-Stone Books, 1989).

B. D. Sommer, *A Prophet Reads Scripture: Allusion in Isaiah 40–66* (Contraversions; Stanford, CA: Stanford University Press, 1998).

M. W. Stolper, *Entrepreneurs and Empire: The Muras(h)u Archive, the Muras(h)u Firm, and Persian Rule in Babylonia* (Istanbul: Nederlands Historisch-Archaeologish Instituut, 1985).

L.-S. Tiemeyer, *For the Comfort of Zion: The Geographical and Theological Location of Isaiah 40–55* (SVT 139. Leiden: Brill, 2011).

D. S. Vanderhooft, *The Neo-Babylonian Empire and Babylon in the Latter Prophets* (HSM 59; Atlanta, GA: Scholars Press, 1999).

C. Westermann, *Lamentations: Issues and Interpretation* (Edinburgh: T & T Clark, 1994).

P. T. Willey, *Remember the Former Things: The Recollection of Previous Texts in Second Isaiah* (Atlanta, GA: Scholars Press, 1997).

H. G. M. Williamson, *The Book Called Isaiah: Deutero-Isaiah's Role in Composition and Redaction* (Oxford: Oxford University Press, 1994).

H. G. M. Williamson, 'The Governors of Judah under the Persians', *TynB* 39 (1988): 59–82.

CHAPTER 4: THEOLOGICAL AND CONTEXTUAL READINGS IN LAMENTATIONS

B. Albrektson, *Studies in the Text and Theology of the Book of Lamentations* (STL 21; Lund: Gleerup, 1963).

E-M. Becker, '"Trauma Studies" and Exegesis: Challenges, Limits and Prospects', in *Trauma and Traumatization in Individual and Collective Dimensions: Insights from Biblical Studies and Beyond* (eds. E-M. Becker, et al.; SAN 2; Göttingen, MI: Vandenhoeck & Ruprecht, 2014), pp. 15–29.

E-M. Becker, J. Dochhorn and E. K. Holt, eds., *Trauma and Traumatization in Individual and Collective Dimensions: Insights from Biblical Studies and Beyond* (Studia Aarhusiana Neotestamentica 2. Göttingen, MI: Vandenhoeck & Ruprecht, 2014).

M. Bier, *'Perhaps There Is Hope': Reading Lamentations as a Polyphony of Pain, Penitence, and Protest* (LHBOTS 603; London and New York: T & T Clark, 2015).

E. Boase, *The Fullfilment of Doom? The Dialogic Interaction between the Book of Lamentations and the Pre-Exilic/Early Exilic Prophetic Literature* (LHBOTS 437; New York: T & T Clark, 2006).

E. Boase, 'The Traumatized Body: Communal Trauma and Somatization in Lamentations', in *Trauma and Traumatization in Individual and Collective Dimensions: Insights from Biblical Studies and Beyond* (eds. E. M. Becker, et al.; SAN 2; Göttingen, MI: Vandenhoeck & Ruprecht, 2014), pp. 193–209.

E. Boase, and C. G. Frechette, eds., *Bible through the Lens of Trauma* (SBLSS 86. Atlanta, GA: SBL, 2016).

C. M. M. Brady, *The Rabbinic Targum of Lamentations: Vindicating God* (Leiden: Brill, 2003).

A. Brenner, ed, *A Feminist Companion to Reading the Bible: Approaches, Methods, and Strategies* (Sheffield: Sheffield Academic Press, 1997).

S. J. D. Cohen, 'The Destruction: From Scripture to Midrash', *Prooftexts* 2 (1982): 18–39.

A. Cooper, 'The Message of Lamentations', *JANES* 28 (2001): 1–18.

B. Crowell, 'Postcolonial Studies and the Hebrew Bible', *CBR* 7 (2009): 217–44.

G. L. Cuéllar, 'The Collecting Impulse in Lamentations: Post Colonial Traumata Made Miniature in Word-Objects', in *Postcolonial Commentary and the Old Testament* (ed. E. H. Gossai; London and New York: T & T Clark, 2019), pp. 275–89.

F. W. Dobbs-Allsopp, 'Tragedy, Tradition, and Theology in the Book of Lamentations', *JSOT* 74 (1997): 29–60.

M. Fishbane, *Biblical Interpretation in Ancient Israel* (Oxford: Clarendon Press, 1988).

C. Frevel, *Die Klagelieder* (NSKAT 20/1; Stuttgart: Katholisches Bibelwerk, 2017).

E. Fuchs, *Sexual Politics in the Biblical Narrative: Reading the Hebrew Bible as a Woman* (JSOTSup 310; Sheffield: Sheffield Academic Press, 2000, rep. 2003).

N. K. Gottwald, *Studies in the Book of Lamentations* (SBT 14; London: SCM Press, 1954, rev. edn, 1962).

E. L. Greenstein, 'The Wrath at God in the Book of Lamentations', in *The Problem of Evil and Its Symbols in Jewish and Christian Tradition* (JSOTSup 366; eds. H. G. Reventlow and Y. Hoffman; London: T & T Clark, 2004), pp. 29–42.

D. Guest, 'Hiding behind the Naked Woman in Lamentations: A Recriminative Response', *BI* 7 (1999): 413–48.

E. K. Holt, 'Jer er manden, der har oplevet lidelse (Profeten Jeremias begræder Jerusalmes Ødelæggelse, 1630)', in *Rembrandt some bibelfortolker* (ed. K. B. Larsen; Frederiksberg: Aros Forlag, 2010), pp. 60–7.

P. House, *Lamentations* (WBC 23B; Nashville, TN: Thomas Nelson, 2004).

P. House, 'Outrageous Demonstrations of Grace: The Theology of Lamentations', in *Great Is Thy Faithfulness? Reading Lamentations as Sacred Scripture* (eds. R. A. Parry and H. A. Thomas; Eugene, OR: Pickwick, 2011), pp. 26–51.

J. Hunter, *Faces of a Lamenting City: The Development and Coherence of the Book of Lamentations* (BEATAJ 39; Frankfurt am Main: Peter Lang, 1996).

B. Johnson, 'Form and Message in Lamentations', *ZAW* 97 (1985): 58–73.

P. M. Joyce, 'Lamentations and the Grief Process: A Psychological Reading', *BI* 1 (1993): 304–20.

P. M. Joyce, and D. Lipton, *Lamentations through the Centuries* (WBBC; Chichester: Wiley-Blackwell, 2013).

B. K. Kelle, et al. eds., *Interpreting Exile: Displacement and Deportation in Biblical and Modern Contexts* (SBLAIL 10; Atlanta, GA: SBL, 2011).

J. Krašovec, 'The Source of Hope in the Book of Lamentations', *VT* 42 (1992): 223–33.

A. C. C. Lee, 'Mothers Bewailing: Reading Lamentations', in *Her Master's Tools?: Feminist and Post Colonial Engagements of Historical-Critical Discourse* (eds. C. V. Stickele and T. C. Penner; Atlanta, GA: SBL, 2005), pp. 195–210.

T. Linafelt, *Surviving Lamentations: Catastrophe, Lament, and Protest in the Afterlife of a Biblical Book* (Chicago, IL: University of Chicago Press, 2000).

C. M. Maier, *Daughter Zion, Mother Zion: Gender, Space, and the Sacred in Ancient Israel* (Minneapolis, MN: Fortress, 2008).

C. R. Mandolfo, *Daughter Zion Talks Back to the Prophets: A Dialogic Theology of the Book of Lamentations* (SBLSS 58; Atlanta, GA: Society of Biblical Literature, 2007).

J. Middlemas, 'Speaking of Speaking: The Form of Zion's Suffering in Lamentations', in *Daughter Zion: Her Portrait, Her Response* (eds. M. J. Boda, et al.; SBLAIL 13. Atlanta, GA: SBL, 2012), pp. 39–54.

J. Middlemas, *The Troubles of Templeless Judah* (OTM; Oxford: Oxford University Press, 2005).

J. Middlemas, 'The Violent Storm in Lamentations', *JSOT* 29 (2004): 81–97.

J. Middlemas, 'War, Comfort, and Compassion in Lamentations', *ExpT* 130/8 (2019): 345–56.

A. Mintz, 'The Rhetoric of Lamentations and the Representation of Catastrophe', *Prooftexts* 2 (1982): 1–17.

M. S. Moore, 'Human Suffering in Lamentations', *RB* 90 (1983): 534–55.

S. D. Moore, and F. F. Segovia, eds. *Postcolonial and Biblical Criticism: Interdisciplinary Intersections* (BP 6; New York: T & T Clark, 2005).

C. A. Newsome, 'Response to Norman K. Gottwald, "Social Class and Ideology in Isaiah 40–55"', *Semeia* 59 (1992): 75–7.

K. M. O'Connor, 'Lamentations', in *The Women's Bible Commentary* (eds. C. A. Newsome and S. H. Ringe; Louisville, KY: Westminster John Knox, 1992), pp. 178–82.

K. M. O'Connor, *Lamentations and the Tears of the World* (Maryknoll, NY: Orbis, 2002).

R. A. Parry, *Lamentations* (THOTC; Grand Rapids, MI: Eerdmans, 2010).

L. G. Perdue, *The Collapse of History: Reconstructing Old Testament Theology* (OBT; Minneapolis, MN: Fortress, 1994).

L. G. Perdue, *Reconstructing Old Testament Theology: After the Collapse of History* (OBT; Minneapolis, MN: Fortress, 2005).

S. P. Re'emi, 'The Theology of Hope: A Commentary on the Book of Lamentations', in *Amos and Lamentations: God's People in Crisis* (ITC; Edinburgh: Handsel, 1984), pp. 73–134.

D. J. Reimer, 'Good Grief? A Psychological Reading of Lamentations', *ZAW* 114 (2002): 542–59.

S. H. Ringe, 'When Women Interpret the Bible', in *The Women's Bible Commentary* (eds. C. A. Newsome and S. H. Ringe; Louisville, KY: Westminster John Knox, 1992), pp. 1–9.

K. D. Sakenfeld, 'Feminist Perspectives on Bible and Theology: An Introduction to Selected Issues and Literature', *Int* 42 (1988): 5–18.

J. F. A. Sawyer, *A Concise Dictionary of the Bible and Its Reception* (Louisville, KY: Westminster John Knox, 2009).

N. Seidman, 'Burning the Book of Lamentations', in *Out of the Garden: Women Writers on the Bible* (eds. C. Büchmann and C. Spiegel; London: Pandora, 1995), pp. 278–88.

D. L. Smith-Christopher, *A Biblical Theology of Exile* (Overtures to Biblical Theology; Minneapolis, MN: Fortress, 2002).

J. Stiebert, 'Human Suffering and Divine Abuse of Power in Lamentations', *Pacifica* 16 (2003): 195–215.

R. S. Sugirtharajah, *Postcolonial Criticism and Biblical Interpretation* (Oxford: Oxford University Press, 2002, reprinted, 2009).

R. Sunder Rajan and Y-M. Park, 'Post Colonial Feminism/Post Colonialism and Feminism', in *A Companion to Post Colonial Studies* (eds. H. Schwarz and S. Ray; Oxford: Blackwell, 2000), pp. 53–71.

H. A. Thomas, 'Lamentations in Rembrandt van Rijn: "Jeremiah Lamenting the Destruction of Jerusalem"', in *Great Is Thy Faithfulness? Reading Lamentations as Sacred Scripture* (eds. R. A. Parry and H. A. Thomas; Eugene, OR: Pickwick, 2011), pp. 154–60.

H. A. Thomas, *Poetry and Theology in the Book of Lamentations: The Aesthetics of an Open Text* (HBM 2; Sheffield: Sheffield Academic Press, 2013).

P. Trible, *God and the Rhetoric of Sexuality* (OBT; Philadelphia, PA: Fortress, 1978).

P. Trible, *Texts of Terror: Literary-Feminist Readings of Biblical Narratives* (OBT; Philadelphia, PA: Fortress, 1984).

C. Westermann, 'The Role of the Lament in the Theology of the Old Testament', *Int* 28 (1974): 20–38.

H. Wiesmann, *Die Klagelieder: Übersetzt und Erklart*. Frankfurt: (Philosophisch-theologische Hochschule Sankt Georgen, 1954).

CHAPTER 5: READINGS IN LAMENTATIONS

W. F. Allen, C. P. Ware and L. M. Garrison, eds., *Slave Songs of the United States* (Bedford, MA: Applewood, 1867).

G. A. Andersen, *a Time to Mourn, a Time to Dance: The Expression of Grief and Joy in Israelite Religion* (University Park: Pennsylvania State University Press, 1991).

W. A. Bailey, 'The Lament Traditions of Enslaved African American Women and the Lament Traditions in the Hebrew Bible', in *Lamentations in Ancient and Contemporary Cultural Contexts* (eds. N. C. Lee and C. Mandolfo; Society of Biblical Literature Semeia Studies 43; Atlanta, GA: SBL, 2008), pp. 151–62.

R. Gordis, 'The Conclusion of the Book of Lamentations (5:22)', *JBL* 93 (1974): 289–93.

T. Linafelt, 'The Refusal of a Conclusion in the Book of Lamentations', *JBL* 120 (2001): 340–3.

T. Linafelt, 'Surviving Lamentations (One More Time)', in *Lamentations in Ancient and Contemporary Cultural Contexts* (eds. N. C. Lee and C. Mandolfo; SBLSS 43; Atlanta, GA: SBL, 2008), pp. 57–63.

T. Linafelt, *Surviving Lamentations: Catastrophe, Lament, and Protest in the Afterlife of a Biblical Book* (Chicago, IL: University of Chicago Press, 2000).

T. Linafelt, 'Zion's Cause: The Presentation of Pain in the Book of Lamentations', in *Strange Fire: Reading the Bible after the Holocaust* (ed. T. Linafelt; BS 71; Sheffield: Sheffield Academic Press, 2000), pp. 267–79.

J. Middlemas, 'Did Second Isaiah Write Lamentations III?' *VT* LVI (2006): 505–25.

J. Middlemas, *The Divine Image: Prophetic Aniconic Rhetoric and Its Contribution to the Aniconism Debate* (FAT 2/74; Tübingen: Mohr Siebeck, 2014).

J. Middlemas, 'Speaking of Speaking: The Form of Zion's Suffering in Lamentations', in *Daughter Zion: Her Portrait, Her Response* (eds. M. J. Boda, et al.; SBLAIL 13; Atlanta, GA: SBL, 2012), pp. 39–54.

J. Middlemas, *The Troubles of Templeless Judah* (OTM; Oxford: Oxford University Press, 2005).

J. Middlemas, 'The Violent Storm in Lamentations', *JSOT* 29 (2004): 81–97.

J. Middlemas, 'War, Comfort, and Compassion in Lamentations', *ExpT* 130, no. 8 (2019): 345–56

X. H. T. Pham, *Mourning in the Ancient Near East and the Hebrew Bible* (JSOTSup 302; Sheffield: Sheffield Academic Press, 1999).

L. E. Stager, 'The Fury of Babylon: The Archaeology of Destruction', *BAR* 22, no. 1 (1996): 56–69, 76–7.

P. Trible, *God and the Rhetoric of Sexuality* (OBT; Philadelphia, PA: Fortress, 1978).

P. Trible, *Texts of Terror: Literary-Feminist Readings of Biblical Narratives* (OBT; Philadelphia, PA: Fortress, 1984).

R. J. Weems, *Battered Love: Marriage, Sex, and Violence in the Hebrew Prophets* (OBT; Minneapolis, MN: Fortress, 1995).

C. Westermann, *Lamentations: Issues and Interpretation* (Edinburgh: T & T Clark, 1994).

BIBLIOGRAPHY

COMMENTARIES

Berges, Ulrich. *Klagelieder*. Handkommentar zum Alten Testament. Freiburg: Herder, 2002.

Berlin, Adele. *Lamentations*. Old Testament Library. Louisville: Westminster John Knox, 2002.

Dobbs-Allsopp, Frederick W. *Lamentations*. Interpretation Biblical Commentary. Louisville: John Knox, 2002.

Frevel, Christian. *Die Klagelieder*. Neuer Stuttgarter Kommentar Altes Testament 20/1. Stuttgart: Katholisches Bibelwerk, 2017.

Gerstenberger, Erhard S. *Psalms and Lamentations*. part 2. The Forms of the Old Testament Literature 15. Grand Rapids: Eerdmans, 2001.

Gottwald, Norman K. *Studies in the Book of Lamentations*. Studies in Biblical Theology 14. London: SCM Press, 1954, revised edition, 1962.

Hillers, Delbert R. *Lamentations*. Anchor Bible 7A. Garden City: Doubleday, 1972, second edition, 1992.

House, Paul. *Lamentations*. Word Bible Commentary 23B. Nashville: Thomas Nelson, 2004.

Joyce, Paul M. 'Lamentations'. Pages 528–33 in *The Oxford Bible Commentary*. Edited by J. Barton and J. Muddiman. Oxford: Oxford University Press, 2001.

O'Connor, Kathleen M. 'The Book of Lamentations: Introduction, Commentary, and Reflections'. Pages 1011–72 in *The New Interpreter's Bible: A Commentary in Twelve Volumes: Isaiah-Ezekiel*, vol. 6. Edited by Leander E. Keck, et al. Nashville: Abingdon Press, 2001.

O'Connor, Kathleen M. 'Lamentations'. Pages 178–82 in *The Women's Bible Commentary*. Edited by C. A. Newsome and S. H. Ringe. Louisville, KY: Westminster John Knox, 1992.

O'Connor, Kathleen M. *Lamentations and the Tears of the World*. Maryknoll, New York: Orbis, 2002.

Parry, Robin A. *Lamentations*. The Two Horizons Old Testament Commentary. Grand Rapids: William B. Eerdman's Publishing Company, 2010.

Provan, Iain W. *Lamentations*. New Century Bible. Grand Rapids: Eerdmans, 1991.

Re'emi, S. P. 'The Theology of Hope: A Commentary on the Book of Lamentations'. Pages 73–134 in *Amos and Lamentations: God's People in Crisis*. International Theological Commentary. Edinburgh: Handsel, 1984.

Renkema, Johann. *Lamentations*. Historical Commentary of the Old Testament. Leuven: Peeters, 1998.

Rudolph, Wilhelm. *Die Klagelieder*. Kommentar zum Alten Testament XVII/3. Gütersloh: Gerd Mohn, 1962.

Salters, Robert B. *Jonah and Lamentations*. Old Testament Guides. Sheffield: Sheffield Academic Press, 1994.

Salters, Robert B. *Lamentations*. International Critical Commentary. London: T & T Clark, Intl, 2010.

Westermann, Claus. *Lamentations: Issues and Interpretation*. Translated by C. Muenchow. Minneapolis: Fortress, 1994.

Wiesmann, Hermann Die. *Klagelieder: Übersetzt und Ërklart*. Frankfurt: Philosophischtheologische Hochschule Sankt Georgen, 1954.

OTHER MONOGRAPH STUDIES

Albertz, Rainer. *Israel in Exile: The History and Literature of the Sixth Century B.C.E.* Translated by D. Green. Studies in Biblical Literature 3. Atlanta: SBL, 2003.

Albertz, Rainer. 'More and Less than a Myth: Reality and Significance of Exile for the Political, Social, and Religious History of Judah'. Pages 20–33 in *By the Irrigation Canals of Babylon: Approaches to the Study of Exile*. Edited by J. J. Ahn and J. Middlemas. Library of the Hebrew Bible/Old Testament Studies 526. New York and London: T & T Clark, 2012.

Albrektson, Bertil. *Studies in the Text and Theology of the Book of Lamentations*. Studia Theologica Lundensia 21. Lund: Gleerup, 1963.

Allen, William F., Charles P. Ware and Lucy M. Garrison (editors). *Slave Songs of the United States*. Bedford, MA: Applewood, 1867.

Alter, Robert. *The Art of Biblical Poetry*. New York: HarperCollins, 1985.

Andersen, Gary A. *A Time to Mourn, a Time to Dance: The Expression of Grief and Joy in Israelite Religion*. University Park: Pennsylvania State University Press, 1991.

Bautch, Richard J. *Developments in Genre between Post-exilic Penitential Prayers and the Psalms of Communal Lament*. Society of Biblical Literature Academia Biblica 7. Atlanta: SBL, 2003.

Becker, Eve Marie, Jan Dochhorn and Else K. Holt (editors). *Trauma and Traumatization in Individual and Collective Dimensions: Insights from Biblical Studies and Beyond*. Studia Aarhusiana Neotestamentica, vol. 2. Göttingen: Vandenhoeck & Ruprecht, 2014.

Bedford, Peter R. *Temple Restoration in Early Achaemenid Judah*. Supplements to the Journal of Jewish Studies 65. Leiden: Brill, 2001.

Berlin, Adele. *The Dynamics of Parallelism*. Grand Rapids: Eerdmans, 2008.

Bier, Miriam. *'Perhaps There Is Hope': Reading Lamentations as a Polyphony of Pain, Penitence, and Protest*. Library of the Hebrew Bible/Old Testament Studies 603. London & NY: T & T Clark, 2015.

Boase, Elizabeth. *The Fulfilment of Doom? The Dialogic Interaction between the Book of Lamentations and the Pre-Exilic/Early Exilic Prophetic Literature*. Library of the Hebrew Bible/Old Testament Studies 437. New York: T & T Clark, 2006.

Boase, Elizabeth, and Christopher G. Frechette (editors). *Bible through the Lens of Trauma*. Society of Biblical Literature Semeia Studies 86. Atlanta: SBL Press, 2016.

Boda, Mark J. *Praying the Tradition: The Origin and Use of Tradition in Nehemiah 9*. Beihefte zur Zeitschrift für die alttestamentliche Wissenschaft 277. Berlin: de Gruyter, 1999.

Bouzard, Walter C. Jr. *We Have Heard with Our Ears, O God: Sources of the Communal Laments in the Psalms*. Society of Biblical Literature Dissertation Series 159. Atlanta: Scholars, 1997.

Brady, Christian M. M. *The Rabbinic Targum of Lamentations: Vindicating God*. Leiden: Brill, 2003.

Brandscheidt, Renate. *Gotteszorn und Menschenleid: Die Gerichtsklage des leidenden Gerechten in Klgl 3*. Trier Theologische Studien 41. Trier: Paulinus, 1983.

Brenner, Athalya (editor). *A Feminist Companion to Reading the Bible: Approaches, Methods, and Strategies*. Sheffield: Sheffield Academic Press, 1979.

Brueggemann, Walter. *The Psalms and the Life of Faith*. Minneapolis: Fortress, 1995.

Brueggemann, Walter. *Theology of the Old Testament: Testimony, Dispute, Advocacy*. Minneapolis: Fortress, 1997.

Carter, Charles E. *The Emergence of Yehud in the Persian Period: A* Social *and Demographic Study*. Journal for the Study of the Old Testament Supplement Series 294. Sheffield: Sheffield Academic Press, 1999.

Clements, Ronald E. *Old Testament Prophecy: From Oracles to Canon*. Louisville: Westminster John Knox, 1996.

Dobbs-Allsopp, Frederick W. *Weep, O Daughter of Zion: A Study of the City-Lament Genre in the Hebrew Bible*. Rome: Editrice Pontificio Istituto Biblico, 1993.

Edelman, Diana V. *The Origins of the 'Second Temple': Persian Imperial Policy and the Rebuilding of Jerusalem*. London: Equinox, 2005.

Faust, Abraham. *Judah in the Neo-Babylonian Period: The Archaeology of Desolation*. Society of Biblical Literature Archaeology and Biblical Studies 18. Atlanta, GA: SBL, 2012.

Ferris, Paul W. *The Genre of Communal Lament in the Bible and the Ancient Near East*. Society of Biblical Literature Dissertation Series 127. Atlanta: Scholars Press, 1992.

Fishbane, Michael. *Biblical Interpretation in Ancient Israel*. Oxford: Clarendon Press, 1988, reprinted, 2004.

Fuchs, Esther. *Sexual Politics in the Biblical Narrative: Reading the Hebrew Bible as a Woman*. Journal for the Study of the Old Testament Supplement Series 310. Sheffield: Sheffield Academic Press, 2000. reprinted, 2003.

Gottwald, Norman K. *Studies in the Book of Lamentations*. SBT 14. London: SCM Press, 1954, revised edition, 1962.

Grossberg, Daniel. *Centripetal and Centrifugal Structures in Biblical Poetry*. Society of Biblical Literature Monograph Series 39. Atlanta: Scholars, 1989.

Gunkel, Hermann, and Joachim Begrich. *Einleitung in die Psalmen: Die Gattungen der religiösen Lyrik Israels*. Göttingen: Vandenhoeck & Ruprecht, 1933.

Hunter, Jannie. *Faces of a Lamenting City: The Development and Coherence of the Book of Lamentations*. Beiträge zur Erforschung des Alten Testaments und des antiken Judentums 39. Frankfurt am Main: Peter Lang, 1996.

Jahnow, Hedwig. *Das Hebräische Leichenlied im Rahmen der Völkerdichtung*. Beihefte zur Zeitschrift für die alttestamentliche Wissenschaft 36. Giessen: A. Töpelmann, 1923.

Janssen, Enno. *Juda in der Exilszeit: Ein Beitrag zur Frage der Entstehung des Judentums*. Forschungen zur Religion und Literatur des Alten und Neuen Testaments 69, ns. Göttingen: Vandenhoeck & Ruprecht, 1956.

Joyce, Paul M., and Diana Lipton. *Lamentations through the Centuries*. Wiley-Blackwell Bible Commentaries. Chichester: Wiley-Blackwell, 2013.

Kartveit, Magnar. *Rejoice Dear Zion! Hebrew Construct Phrases with 'Daughter' and 'Virgin' as Nomen Regens*. Beihefte zur Zeitschrift für die alttestamentliche Wissenschaft 447. Berlin: de Gruyter, 2013.

Kelle, Brad E., et al. (editors). *Interpreting Exile: Displacement and Deportation in Biblical and Modern Contexts*. Society of Biblical Literature Ancient Israel and Its Literature 10. Atlanta, GA: SBL, 2011.

Knox, Ronald A. *The Holy Bible*. London: Burns and Oates, 1956.

Lee, Nancy C. *The Singers of Lamentations: Cities under Siege, From Ur to Jerusalem to Sarajevo*. Biblical Interpretation Series 60. Leiden: Brill, 2002.

Lee, Nancy C. and Carleen Mandolfo (editors). *Lamentations in Ancient and Contemporary Contexts*. Society of Biblical Literature Semeia Studies 43. Atlanta: Society of Biblical Literature, 2008.

Linafelt, Tod. *Surviving Lamentations: Catastrophe, Lament, and Protest in the Afterlife of a Biblical Book*. Chicago: University of Chicago Press, 2000.

Lipiński, E. *La liturgie pénitentielle dans la Bible*. Lectio Divina 52. Paris: Cerf, 1969.

Lipschits, Oded. *The Fall and Rise of Jerusalem: Judah under Babylonian Rule*. Winona Lake, IN: Eisenbrauns, 2005.

Maier, Christl M. *Daughter Zion, Mother Zion: Gender, Space, and the Sacred in Ancient Israel*. Minneapolis: Fortress, 2008.

Mandolfo, Carleen. *Daughter Zion Talks back to the Prophets: A Dialogic Theology of the Book of Lamentations*. Semeia Studies 58. Atlanta: SBL, 2007.

Mandolfo, Carleen. *God in the Dock*. Journal for the Study of the Old Testament Supplement Series 357. Sheffield: Sheffield Academic Press, 2002.

Middlemas, Jill. *The Divine Image: Prophetic Aniconic Rhetoric and Its Contribution to the Aniconism Debate*. Forschungen zum Alten Testament 2/74. Tübingen: Mohr Siebeck, 2014.

Middlemas, Jill. *The Templeless Age: An Introduction to the History, Literature, and Theology of the 'Exile'*. Louisville: Westminster John Knox, 2007.

Middlemas, Jill. *The Troubles of Templeless Judah*. OTM. Oxford: Oxford University Press, 2005.

Miller, J. Maxwell and John H. Hayes. *A History of Ancient Israel and Judah*. Louisville, KY: Westminster John Knox Press, second edition, 2006.

Mintz, A. *Hurban: Responses to Catastrophe in Jewish Literature*. New York: Columbia University Press, 1984.

Miller, Patrick D. *They Cried to the Lord: The Form and Theology of Biblical Prayer*. Minneapolis: Fortress, 1994.

Mintz, Alan L. *Hurban: Responses to Catastrophe in Jewish Literature*. New York: Columbia University Press, 1984.

Moore, Stephen D. and Fernando F. Segovia (editors). *Postcolonial and Biblical Criticism: Interdisciplinary Intersections*. The Bible and Postcolonialism 6. NY: T & T Clark, 2005.

Morrow, William. *Protest against God: The Eclipse of a Biblical Tradition*. Hebrew Bible Monographs 4. Sheffield: Sheffield Phoenix Press, 2006.

Nicholson, Ernest W. *Preaching to the Exiles: A Study of the Prose Tradition in Jeremiah*. Oxford: Blackwell, 1970.

O'Connor, Kathleen M. *Jeremiah: Pain and Promise*. Minneapolis: Fortress, 2011.

Oded, Bustenay. *Mass Deportations and Deportees in the Neo-Assyrian Empire*. Wiesbaden: Reichert, 1979.

Olyan, Saul M. *Biblical Mourning: Ritual and Social Dimensions*. Oxford: Oxford University Press, 2004.

Perdue, Leo G. *The Collapse of History: Reconstructing Old Testament Theology*. Overtures to Biblical Theology. Minneapolis: Fortress, 1994.

Perdue, Leo G. *Reconstructing Old Testament Theology: After the Collapse of History*. Overtures to Biblical Theology. Minneapolis: Fortress, 2005.

Petersen, David L. and Kent H. Richards. *Interpreting Hebrew Poetry*. Minneapolis: Fortress, 1992.

Pham, Xuan H. T. *Mourning in the Ancient Near East and the Hebrew Bible*. Journal for the Study of the Old Testament Supplement Series 302. Sheffield: Sheffield Academic Press, 1999.

Porten, Bezalel. *The Elephantine Papyri in English: Three Millennia of Cross-Cultural Continuity and Change*. Documenta et Monumenta Orientis Antiqui 22. Leiden: Brill, 1996.

Rom-Shiloni, Dalit. *Exclusive Inclusivity: Identity Conflicts between the Exiles and the People who Remained (6th–5th Centuries BCE)*. Library of Hebrew Bible/Old Testament Studies 543. New York: Bloomsbury, 2013.

Sawyer, John F. A. *A Concise Dictionary of the Bible and Its Reception*. Louisville: Westminster John Knox, 2009.

Schökel, Luis Alfonso. *A Manual of Hebrew Poetics*. Subsidia Biblica 11. Rome: Pontifical Biblical Institute, 1988.

Seitz, Christopher R. *Theology in Conflict: Reactions to the Exile in the Book of Jeremiah*. Beihefte zur Zeitschrift für die alttestamentliche Wissenschaft 176. Berlin: de Gruyter, 1989.

Seitz, Christopher R. *Word without End: The Old Testament as Abiding Theological Witness*. Grand Rapids: Eerdmans, 1998.

Smith, Daniel L. *The Religion of the Landless: The Social Context of the Babylonian Exile*. Bloomington: Meyer-Stone Books, 1989.

Smith-Christopher, Daniel L. *A Biblical Theology of Exile*. Overtures in Biblical Theology. Minneapolis: Fortress, 2002.

Sommer, Benjamin D. *A Prophet Reads Scripture: Allusion in Isaiah 40–66*. Contraversions. Stanford: Stanford University Press, 1998.

Stolper, M. W. *Entrepreneurs and Empire: The Muras(h)u Archive, the Muras(h)u Firm, and Persian Rule in Babylonia*. Istanbul: Nederlands Historisch-Archaeologish Instituut, 1985.

Sugirtharajah, R. S. *Postcolonial Criticism and Biblical Interpretation*. Oxford: Oxford University Press, 2002, reprinted, 2009.

Thomas, Heath A. *Poetry and Theology in the Book of Lamentations: The Aesthetics of an Open Text*. Hebrew Bible Monographs. Sheffield: Sheffield Phoenix, 2013.

Tiemeyer, Lena Sofia. *For the Comfort of Zion: The Geographical and Theological Location of Isaiah 40–55*. Supplements to Vetus Testamentum139. Leiden: Brill, 2001.

Trible, Phyllis. *God and the Rhetoric of Sexuality*. Overtures to Biblical Theology. Philadelphia: Fortress, 1978.

Trible, Phyllis. *Texts of Terror: Literary-Feminist Readings of Biblical Narratives*. Overtures to Biblical Theology. Philadelphia: Fortress, 1984.

Vanderhooft, David S. *The Neo-Babylonian Empire and Babylon in the Latter Prophets*. Harvard Semitic Monographs 59. Atlanta: Scholars Press, 1999.

Watson, Wilfred G. E. *Classical Hebrew Poetry*. Journal for the Study of the Old Testament Supplement Series. 26. Sheffield: JSOT, reprinted, 2001.

Weems, Renita J. *Battered Love: Marriage, Sex, and Violence in the Hebrew Prophets*. Overtures to Biblical Theology. Minneapolis, MN: Fortress, 1995.

Westermann, Claus. *Praise and Lament in the Psalms*. Translated by K. R. Crim and R. N. Soulen. Atlanta: John Knox, 1995.

Wiles, J. P. *Half-Hours with the Minor Prophets*. London: Morgan and Scott, 1908.

Willey, Patricia T. *Remember the Former Things: The Recollection of Previous Texts in Second Isaiah*. Society of Biblical Literature Dissertation Series 161. Atlanta: Scholars, 1997.

Williamson, Hugh G. M. *The Book Called Isaiah: Deutero-Isaiah's Role in Composition and Redaction*. Oxford: Oxford University Press, 1994.

Yansen, James W. W. *Daughter Zion's Trauma: Reading Lamentations with Insights from Trauma Studies*. DPhil dissertation. Boston University, 2016.

Yansen, James W. W. *Daughter Zion's Trauma: A Trauma Informed Reading of Lamentations*. Biblical Intersections 17. Piscataway, NJ: Gorgias Press, 2019.

ARTICLES, BOOK CHAPTERS AND ESSAYS

Assis, Elie. 'The Alphabetic Acrostic in the Book of Lamentations'. *Catholic Biblical Quarterly* 69 (2007): 710–24.

Assis, Elie. 'The Unity of the Book of Lamentations'. *Catholic Biblical Quarterly* 71 (2009): 306–29.

Bailey, Wilma A. 'The Lament Traditions of Enslaved African American Women and the Lament Traditions in the Hebrew Bible'. Pages 151–62 in *Lamentations in Ancient and Contemporary Cultural Contexts*. Edited by N. C. Lee and C. Mandolfo. Society of Biblical Literature Semeia Studies 43. Atlanta: SBL, 2008.

Barstad, H. M. 'The City State of Jerusalem in the Neo-Babylonian Empire: Evidence from the Surrounding States'. Pages 34–48 in *By the Irrigation Canals of Babylon: Approaches to the Study of Exile*. Edited by J. J. Ahn and J. Middlemas. Library of Hebrew Bible/Old Testament Studies 526. New York and London: T & T Clark, 2012.

Beaulieu, Paul-Alain. 'Yahwistic Names in Light of Late Babylonian Onomastics'. Pages 245–66 in *Judah and the Judeans in the Achaemenid Period: Negotiating Identity in an International Context*. Edited by O. Lipschits, G. N. Knoppers and M. Oeming. Winona Lake: Eisenbrauns, 2011.

Becker, Eve-Marie. '"Trauma Studies" and Exegesis: Challenges, Limits and Prospects'. Pages 15–29 in *Trauma and Traumatization in Individual and Collective Dimensions: Insights from Biblical Studies and Beyond*. Edited by E-M. Becker, et al. Studia Aarhusiana Neotestamentica, vol 2. Göttingen: Vandenhoeck & Ruprecht, 2014.

Becking, Bob. '"We All Returned as One": Critical Notes on the Myth of the Mass Return'. Pages 3–18 in *Judah and the Judeans in the Persian Period*. Edited by O. Lipschits and M. Oeming. Winona Lake: Eisenbrauns, 2006.

Bergeant, D. 'The Challenge of Hermeneutics: Lamentations 1: 1–11:A Test Case'. *Catholic Biblical Quarterly* 64 (2002): 1–16.

Berlin, Adele. 'Introduction to Hebrew Poetry'. Pages 301–15 in the *New Interpreters Bible* IV. Edited by R. Doran, et al. Nashville: Abingdon Press, 1996.

Blenkinsopp, Joseph. 'The Age of the Exile'. Pages 416–39 in *The Biblical World*. Edited by J. Barton. London & NY: Routledge, 2002.

Boase, Elizabeth. 'Constructing Meaning in the Face of Suffering: Theodicy in Lamentations'. *Vetus Testamentum* 58 (2008): 449–68.

Boase, Elizabeth. 'The Traumatized Body: Communal Trauma and Somatization in Lamentations'. Pages 193–209 in *Trauma and Traumatization in Individual and Collective Dimensions: Insights from Biblical Studies and Beyond*. Edited by E-M. Becker, et al. SAN 2. Göttingen: Vandenhoeck & Ruprecht, 2014.

Boda, Mark J. 'The Priceless Gain of Penitence: From Communal Lament to Penitential Prayer in the "Exilic" Liturgy of Israel'. Pages 81–101 in *Lamentations in Ancient and Contemporary Contexts*. Edited by N. C. Lee and C. Mandolfo. Society of Biblical Literature Semeia Studies 43. Atlanta: Society of Biblical Literature, 2008.

Bosworth, D. A. 'Daughter Zion and Weeping in Lamentations 1–2'. *Journal for the Study of the Old Testament* 38 (2013): 217–37.

Brueggemann, Walter. 'The Costly Loss of Lament'. *Journal for the Study of the Old Testament* 36 (1986): 57–71.

Brug, J. 'Biblical Acrostics and Their Relationship to Other Ancient Near Eastern Acrostics'. Pages 283–304 in *Scripture in Context*, vol. 3: *The Bible in the Light of Cuneiform Literature.* Edited by W. Hallo, et al. Lewiston, NY: Edwin Mellen, 1990.

Budde, Karl. 'Das hebräische Klagelied'. *Zeitschrift für die alttestamentliche Wissenschaft* 2 (1882): 1–52.

Cohen, Shaye J. D. 1982. 'The Destruction: From Scripture to Midrash'. *Prooftexts* 2 (1982): 18–39.

Conway, Mary L. 'Daughter Zion: Metaphor and Dialogue in Book of Lamentations'. Pages 101–26 in *Daughter Zion: Her Portrait, Her Response.* Edited by M. J. Boda, C. J. Dempsey and L. S. Flesher. Society of Biblical Literature Ancient Israel and Its Literature 13. Atlanta: SBL, 2012.

Cooper, Alan. 'The Message of Lamentations'. *Journal of Ancient Near Eastern Studies* 28 (2001): 1–18.

Cross, Frank M. 'Newly Found Inscriptions in Old-Canaanite and Early Phoenician Scripts'. *Bulletin of the American Schools of Oriental Research* 238 (1980): 1–20.

Crowell, Bradley. 'Postcolonial Studies and the Hebrew Bible'. *Currents in Biblical Research* 7 (2009): 217–44.

Cuéllar, G. L. 'The Collecting Impulse in Lamentations: Post Colonial Traumata Made Miniature in Word-Objects'. Pages 275–89 in *Postcolonial Commentary and the Old Testament.* Edited by E. H. Gossai. London and NY: T & T Clark, 2019.

Demsky, A., and M. Kochavi, 'An Alphabet from the Days of Judges'. *Biblical Archaeology Review* iv (1978): 23–30.

Dobbs-Allsopp, Frederick W. 'Darwinism, Genre Theory, and City Laments'. *Journal of the American Oriental Society* 120 (2000): 625–30.

Dobbs-Allsopp, Frederick W. 'The Effects of Enjambment in Lamentations (Part 2)'. *Zeitschrift für die alttestamentliche Wissenschaft* 113 (2001): 370–85.

Dobbs-Allsopp, Frederick W. 'The Enjambing Line in Lamentations: A Taxonomy (Part 1)'. *Zeitschrift für die alttestamentliche Wissenschaft* 113 (2001): 219–39.

Dobbs-Allsopp, Frederick W. 'The Syntagma of *bat* Followed by a Geographical Name in the Hebrew Bible: A Reconsideration of Its Meaning and Grammar'. *Catholic Biblical Quarterly* 57 (1995): 451–70.

Dobbs-Allsopp, Frederick W. 'Tragedy, Tradition, and Theology in the Book of Lamentations'. *Journal for the Study of the Old Testament* 74 (1997): 29–60.

Dobbs-Allsopp, F. W., and T. Linafelt, 'The Rape of Zion in Thr 1,10'. *Zeitschrift für die alttestamentliche Wissenschaft* 113 (2001): 77–81.

Fitzgerald, Aloysius. 'The Mythological Background for the Presentation of Jerusalem as Queen and False Worship as Adultery in the OT'. *Catholic Biblical Quarterly* 34 (1972): 403–16.

Floyd, Michael H. 'Welcome Back, Daughter of Zion!' *Catholic Biblical Quarterly* 70 (2008): 484–504.

Freedman, David N. 'Acrostic Poems in the Hebrew Bible: Alphabetic and Otherwise'. *Catholic Biblical Quarterly* 48 (1986): 408–31.

Garr, W. Randall. 'The Qinah: A Study of Poetic Metre, Syntax and Style'. *Zeitschrift für die alttestamentliche Wissenschaft* 95 (1983): 54–75.

Gordis, Robert. 'The Conclusion of the Book of Lamentations (5:22)'. *Journal of Biblical Literature* 93 (1974): 289–93.

Grabbe, Lester L. '"They Never Returned": Were the Babylonian Jewish Settlers Exiles or Pioneers?' Pages 158–72 in *By the Irrigation Canals of Babylon: Approaches to the Study of Exile*. Edited by J. J. Ahn and J. Middlemas. Library of Hebrew Bible/Old Testament Studies 526. NY and London: T & T Clark, 2012.

Greenstein, Edward L. 'The Book of Lamentations: Response to Destruction or Ritual of Rebuilding?' Pages 52–71 in *Religious Responses to Political Crisis*. Edited by H. G. Reventlow and Y. Hoffman. NY: T & T Clark, 2008.

Greenstein, Edward L. 'The Wrath of God in the Book of Lamentations'. Pages 29–42 in the Problem of Evil and Its Symbols in Jewish and Christian Tradition. Edited by H. G. Reventlow and Y. Hoffman. Journal for the Study of the Old Testament Supplement Series 366. NY: T & T Clark, 2004.

Gregory, Bradley. 'The Postexilic Exile in Third Isaiah: Isaiah 64:7–64:11'. *Journal of Biblical Literature* 126 (2007): 475–96.

Guest, Deryn. 'Hiding behind the Naked Woman in Lamentations: A Recriminative Response'. *Biblical Interpretation* 7 (1999): 413–48.

Gwaltney, Walter C. 'Lamentations in Near Eastern Literature'. Pages 191–211 in *Scripture in Context*, vol. 2: *More Essays on the Comparative Method*. Edited by W. W. Hallo, et al. Winona Lake: Eisenbrauns, 1983.

Heater, Homer Jr. 'Structure and Meaning in Lamentations'. *Bibliotheca Sacra* 149 (1992): 304–15.

Heim, Knut. 'The Personification of Jerusalem and the Drama of Her Bereavement in Lamentations'. Pages 296–322 in *Zion, City of Our God*. Edited by R. S. Hess and G. J. Wenham. Grand Rapids: Eerdmans, 1999.

Hoffman, Yair. 'The Fasts in the Book of Zechariah and the Fashioning of National Remembrance'. Pages 169–218 in *Judah and the Judeans in the Neo – Babylonian Period*. Edited by O. Lipschits and J. Blenkinsopp. Winona Lake, IN: Eisenbrauns, 2003.

Holt, Else K. 'Jer er manden, der har oplevet lidelse (Profeten Jeremias begræder Jerusalmes Ødelæggelse, 1630)'. Pages 60–7 in *Rembrandt some bibelfortolker*. Edited by K. B. Larsen. Frederiksberg: Aros Forlag, 2010.

Hoop, Raymond, de, 'Lamentations: The Qinah-Metre Questioned'. Pages 80–104 in *Delimitation Criticism: A New Tool in Biblical Scholarship*. Edited by M. C. A. Korpel and J. M. Oesch. Assen: Van Gorcum, 2000.

House, Paul R. 'Outrageous Demonstrations of Grace: The Theology of Lamentations'. Pages 26–51 in *Great Is Thy Faithfulness? Reading Lamentations as Sacred Scripture*. Edited by R. A. Parry and H. A. Thomas. Eugene, OR: Pickwick, 2011.

Johnson, Bo. 'Form and Message in Lamentations'. *Zeitschrift für die alttestamentliche Wissenschaft* 97 (1985): 58–73.

Joyce, Paul M. 'Lamentations and the Grief Process: A Psychological Reading'. *Biblical Interpretation* 1 (1993): 304–20.

Joyce, Paul M. 'Sitting Loose to History: Reading the Book of Lamentations without Primary Reference to Its Original Historical Setting'. Pages 246–62 in *In Search of True Wisdom: Essays in Old Testament Interpretation in Honour of Ronald E. Clements*. Edited by E. Ball. Journal for the Study of the Old Testament Supplement Series 300. Sheffield: JSOT Press, 1999.

Kaiser, Barbara B. 'Poet as "Female Impersonator": The Image of Daughter Zion as Speaker in Biblical Poems of Suffering'. *Journal of Religion* ns 7 (1987): 164–82.

Klein, Ralph W. 'A Theology for Exiles: The Kingship of Yahweh'. *Dialog* 17 (1978): 128–34.

Kramer, Samuel Noah. 'The Weeping Goddess: Sumerian Prototypes of the Mater Dolorosa'.*Biblical Archaeologist* 46 (1983): 69–80.

Krašovec, Joze. 'The Source of Hope in the Book of Lamentations'. *Vetus Testamentum* 42 (1992): 223–33.

Lanahan, William F. 'The Speaking Voice in the Book of Lamentations'. *Journal of Biblical Literature* 93 (1974): 41–9.

Lee, Archie C. C. 'Mothers Bewailing: Reading Lamentations'. Pages 195–210 in *Her Master's Tools?: Feminist and Post Colonial Engagements of Historical-Critical Discourse*. Edited by C. V. Stickele and T. C. Penner. Atlanta: SBL, 2005.

Lee, Nancy C. 'The Singers of Lamentations: (A)Scribing (De)Claiming Poets and Prophets'. Pages 33–46 in *Lamentations in Ancient and Contemporary Cultural Contexts*. Edited by N. C. Lee and C. Mandolfo. Society of Biblical Literature Semeia Studies 43. Atlanta: SBL, 2008.

Linafelt, Tod. 'The Refusal of a Conclusion in the Book of Lamentations'. *Journal of Biblical Literature* 120 (2001): 340–3.

Linafelt, Tod. 'Surviving Lamentations'. *Horizons of Biblical Theology* 17 (1995): 45–61.

Linafelt, Tod. 'Surviving Lamentations (One More Time)'. Pages 57–63 in *Lamentations in Ancient and Contemporary Cultural Contexts*. Edited by N. C. Lee and C. Mandolfo. Society of Biblical Literature Semeia Studies 43. Atlanta: SBL, 2008.

Linafelt, Tod. 'Zion's Cause: The Presentation of Pain in the Book of Lamentations'. Pages 267–79 in *Strange Fire: Reading the Bible after the Holocaust*. Edited by T. Linafelt. Biblical Seminar 71. Sheffield: Sheffield Academic Press, 2000.

Max, Löhr. 'Der Sprachgebrauch des Buches der Klagelieder'. *Zeitschrift für die alttestamentliche Wissenschaft* 14 (1894): 31–50.

Max, Löhr. 'Threni III und die jeremianische Autorschaft des Buches der Klagelieder'. *Zeitschrift für die alttestamentliche Wissenschaft* 24 (1904): 1–16.

Longman, Tremper. 'The Adad-Guppi Autobiography'. Pages 477–8 in *The Context of Scripture, I, Canonical Compositions from the Biblical World*. Edited by W. W Hallo. Leiden: Brill, 1997.

McDaniel, T. F. 'The Alleged Sumerian Influence upon Lamentations'. *Vetus Testamentum* 18 (1968): 198–209.

Meyers, Carol. 'Miriam the Musician'. Pages 207–30 in *A Feminist Companion to Exodus to Deuteronomy*. Edited by A. Brenner. Sheffield: Sheffield Academic Press, 1994.

Meyers, Eric M. 'Exile and Restoration in Light of Recent Archaeology and Demographic Studies'. Pages 166–73 in *Exile and Restoration Revisited: Essays on the Babylonian and Persian Periods in Memory of Peter R. Ackroyd*. Edited by G. N. Knoppers, et al. Library of Second Temple Studies 73. London & NY: T & T Clark, 2009.

Middlemas, Jill. 'Dating Esther: Evaluating the Criteria for a Persian or Hellenistic Provenance'. Pages 149–68 in On Dating Biblical Texts to the Persian Period: *Discerning Criteria and Establishing Epochs*. Edited by R. J. Bautch and M. Lackowski. Forschungen zum Alten Testament 2/101. Tübingen: Mohr Siebeck, 2019.

Middlemas, Jill. 'Did Second Isaiah Write Lamentations III?' *Vetus Testamentum* LVI (2006): 505–25.

Middlemas, Jill. 'Going beyond the Myth of the Empty Land: A Reassessment of the Early Persian Period'. Pages 174–94 in *Exile and Restoration Revisited: Essays on the Babylonian and Persian Periods in Memory of Peter R. Ackroyd*. Edited by G. N. Knoppers, et al. Library of Second Temple Studies 73. London & NY: T & T Clark, 2009.

Middlemas, Jill. 'The Shape of Things to Come: Redaction and the Early Second Temple Period Prophetic Tradition'. Pages 141–56 in *Constructions of Prophecy in the Former and Latter Prophets and Other Texts*. Edited by L. L. Grabbe and M. Nissinen. Society of Biblical Literature Ancient Near East Monographs 4. Atlanta: SBL, 2011.

Middlemas, Jill. 'Speaking of Speaking: The Form of Zion's Suffering in Lamentations'. Pages 39–54 in *Daughter Zion: Her Portrait, Her Response*. Edited by M. J. Boda, C. J. Dempsey and L. S. Flesher. Society of Biblical Literature Ancient Israel and Its Literature 13. Atlanta: SBL, 2012.

Middlemas, Jill. '"For Vast as the Sea Is Your Ruin" (Lam. 2:13): Exile, Migration and Diaspora after the Fall of Jerusalem in the Sixth Century BCE'. in the *New Oxford Biblical World*. Edited by K. Dell. Oxford: Oxford University Press, Forthcoming.

Middlemas, Jill. 'The Violent Storm in Lamentations'. *Journal for the Study of the Old Testament* 29 (2004): 81–97.

Middlemas, Jill. 'War, Comfort, and Compassion in Lamentations'. *Expository Times* 130/8 (2019): 345–56.

Miller, C. W. 'Reading Voices: Personification, Dialogism, and the Reader of Lamentations 2'. *Biblical Interpretation* 9 (2001): 393–408.

Moore, Michael S. 'Human Suffering in Lamentations'. *Revue Biblique* 90 (1983): 534–55.

Morse, Benjamin. 'The Lamentations Project: Biblical Mourning through Modern Montage'. *Journal for the Study of the Old Testament* 28 (2003): 113–27.

Newsome, Carol A. 'Response to Norman K. Gottwald, "Social Class and Ideology in Isaiah 40–55"'. *Semeia* 59 (1992): 75–7.

Nicholson, Ernest W. 'Deuteronomy and the Babylonian Exile'. Pages 41–73 in *Deuteronomy and the Judaean Diaspora*. Oxford: Oxford University Press, 2014.

O'Connor, Kathleen M. 'How Trauma Studies Can Contribute to Old Testament Studies'. Pages 210–22 in *Trauma and Traumatization in Individual and Collective Dimensions: Insights from Biblical Studies and Beyond*. Edited by E-M. Becker, et al. Studia Aarhusiana Neotestamentica, vol. 2. Göttingen: Vandenhoeck & Ruprecht, 2014.

O'Connor, Kathleen M. 'Voices Arguing about Meaning'. Pages 27–32 in *Lamentations in Ancient and Contemporary Cultural Contexts*. Edited by N. C. Lee and C. Mandolfo. Atlanta: Society of Biblical Literature, 2008.

Pearce, Laurie. 'New Evidence for Judeans in Babylonia'. Pages 399–411 in *Judah and the Judeans in the Persian Period*. Edited by O. Lipschits and M. Oeming. Winona Lake: Eisenbrauns, 2006.

Provan, Iain W. 'Reading Texts vs an Historical Background: The Case of Lamentations 1'. *Scandianavian Journal of the Old Testament* 1 (1990): 130–43.

Reimer, David J. 'Good Grief? A Psychological Reading of Lamentations'. *Zeitschrift für die alttestamentliche Wissenschaft* 114 (2002): 542–59.

Renkema, Johan. 'The Literary Structure of Lamentations (I–IV)'. Pages 294–396 in *The Structural Analysis of Biblical and Canaanite Poetry*. Edited by W. van der Meer and J. C. de Moor. Journal for the Study of the Old Testament Supplement Series. 74. Sheffield: JSOT, 1988.

Renkema, Johan. 'The Meaning of the Parallel Acrostics in Lamentations'. *Vetus Testamentum* 45 (1995): 379–83.

Renkema, Johan. 'Theodicy in Lamentations?' Pages 410–28 in *Theodicy in the World of the Bible*. Edited by A. Laato and J. C. de Moor. Leiden: Brill, 2003.

Ringe, Sharon H. 'When Women Interpret the Bible'. Pages 1–9 in *The Women's Bible Commentary*. Edited by C. A. Newsome and S. H. Ringe. Louisville, KY: Westminster John Knox, 1992.

Sakenfeld, Katherine D. 'Feminist Perspectives on Bible and Theology: An Introduction to Selected Issues and Literature'. *Interpretation* 42 (1988): 5–18.

Salters Robert, B. 'Structure and Implication in Lamentations 1'. *Scandianavian Journal of the Old Testament* 14 (2000): 293–300.

Sawyer, John F. A. 'Daughter Zion and Servant of the Lord in Isaiah: A Comparison'. *Journal for the Study of the Old Testament* 44 (1989): 89–107.

Seidman, Naomi. 'Burning the Book of Lamentations'. Pages 278–88 in *Out of the Garden: Women Writers on the Bible*. Edited by C. Büchmann and C. Spiegel. London: Pandora, 1994.

Shea, William H. 'The *qinah* Structure of the Book of Lamentations'. *Biblica* 60 (1979): 103–7.

Soll, William M. 'Babylonian and Biblical Acrostics'. *Biblica* 69 (1989): 305–23.

Stager, Lawrence E. 'The Fury of Babylon: The Archaeology of Destruction'. *Biblical Archaeology Review* 22/1 (1996): 56–69, 76–7.

Stiebert, Johanna. 'Human Suffering and Divine Abuse of Power in Lamentations: Reflections on Forgiveness in the Context of South Africa's Truth and Reconciliation Process'. *Pacifica* 16 (2003): 195–215.

Stinespring, William R. 'No Daughter of Zion'. *Encounter* 26 (1965): 133–41.

Sunder Rajan, R., and Y-M. Park. 'Post Colonial Feminism/Post Colonialism and Feminism'. Pages 53–71 in *A Companion to Post Colonial Studies*. Edited by H. Schwarz and S. Ray. Oxford: Blackwell, 2000.

Thomas, Heath A. 'Feminist Interpretation(s) and Lamentations'. Pages 166–74 in *Great Is Thy Faithfulness? Reading Lamentations as Sacred Scripture*. Edited by R. A. Parry and H. A. Thomas. Eugene, OR: Pickwick, 2011.

Thomas, Heath A. 'Justice at the Crossroads: The Book of Lamentations and Feminist Discourse'. Pages 246–73 in *Tamar's Tears: Evangelical Engagements with Feminist Old Testament Hermeneutics*. Edited by A. Sloane. Eugene, OR: Pickwick, 2012.

Thomas, Heath A. 'Lamentations in Rembrandt van Rijn: "Jeremiah Lamenting the Destruction of Jerusalem"'. Pages 154–60 in *Great Is Thy Faithfulness? Reading Lamentations as Sacred Scripture*. Edited by R. A. Parry and H. A. Thomas. Eugene, OR: Pickwick, 2011.

Lena-Sofia, Tiemeyer. 'Geography and Textual Allusions: Interpreting Isaiah xl-l as Judahite Texts'. *Vetus Testamentum* 57 (2007): 367–85.

Tigay, Jeffrey, and Alan Cooper. 'Lamentations, Book of'. Pages 446–51 in *Encyclopedia Judaica*, 12. Detroit: Macmillan Reference USA, second edition with revisions, 2007.

Weinberg, Saul S. 'Post-Exilic Palestine: An Archaeological Report'. *Proceedings of the Israel Academy of Sciences and Humanities*. Jerusalem: World Union of Jewish Studies, 1969–70.

Westermann, Claus. 'The Role of the Lament in the Theology of the Old Testament'. *Interpretation* 28 (1974): 20–38.

Willey, Patricia T. 'The Servant of YHWH and Daughter Zion: Alternating Visions of YHWH'S Community'. *SBL Seminar Papers* (1995): 267–303.

Williamson, Hugh G. M. 'The Governors of Judah under the Persians'. *Tyndale Bulletin* 39 (1988): 59–82.

Williamson, Hugh G. M. 'Laments at the Destroyed Temple'. *BibRev* 4 (1990): 12–17, 44.

Williamson, Hugh G. M. 'Structure and Historiography in Nehemiah 9'. Pages 117–31 in *Proceedings of the Ninth World Congress of Jewish Studies*. Jerusalem: Magnes Press, 1985.

Zorn, Jeffrey R. 'Tell en-Nasbeh and the Problem of the Material Culture of the Sixth Century'. Pages 413–47 in *Judah and the Judeans in the Neo-Babylonian Period*. Edited by O. Lipschits and J. Blenkinsopp. Winona Lake, IN: Eisenbrauns, 2003.

INDEX OF AUTHORS

INDEX OF REFERENCES

www.ingramcontent.com/pod-product-compliance
Ingram Content Group UK Ltd.
Pitfield, Milton Keynes, MK11 3LW, UK
UKHW020703280225
455688UK00004B/228